Biblical Resistance Hermeneutics within a Caribbean Context

BibleWorld
Series Editor: Philip R. Davies and James G. Crossley, University of Sheffield

BibleWorld shares the fruits of modern (and postmodern) biblical scholarship not only among practitioners and students, but also with anyone interested in what academic study of the Bible means in the twenty-first century. It explores our ever-increasing knowledge and understanding of the social world that produced the biblical texts, but also analyses aspects of the bible's role in the history of our civilization and the many perspectives – not just religious and theological, but also cultural, political and aesthetic – which drive modern biblical scholarship.

Published:

Forthcoming:

BIBLICAL RESISTANCE HERMENEUTICS WITHIN A CARIBBEAN CONTEXT

Oral A. W. Thomas

Routledge
Taylor & Francis Group

LONDON AND NEW YORK

First published 2010 by Equinox, an imprint of Acumen

Published 2014 by Routledge
2 Park Square, Milton Park, Abingdon, Oxon OX14 4RN
711 Third Avenue, New York, NY 10017, USA

Routledge is an imprint of the Taylor & Francis Group, an informa business

Notices
Practitioners and researchers must always rely on their own experience and knowledge in evaluating and using any information, methods, compounds, or experiments described herein. In using such information or methods they should be mindful of their own safety and the safety of others, including parties for whom they have a professional responsibility.

To the fullest extent of the law, neither the Publisher nor the authors, contributors, or editors, assume any liability for any injury and/or damage to persons or property as a matter of products liability, negligence or otherwise, or from any use or operation of any methods, products, instructions, or ideas contained in the material herein.

British Library Cataloguing-in-Publication Data

A catalogue record for this book is available from the British Library.

ISBN-13 978 1 84553 656 5 (hardback)
         978 1 84553 657 2 (paperback)

Library of Congress Cataloging-in-Publication Data

Biblical resistance hermeneutics within a Caribbean context /
Oral A.W. Thomas.
    p. cm.—(BibleWorld)
    Includes bibliographical references and indexes.
    ISBN 978-1-84553-656-5 (hb)—ISBN 978-1-84553-657-2 (pb) 1. Bible—Black interpretations. 2. Bible. N.T. Philemon—Black interpretations. 3. Bible—Criticism, interpretation, etc.—West Indies, British. 4. Bible. N.T. Philemon—Criticism, interpretation, etc.—West Indies, British. I. Title.
BS521.2.T48 2010
227'.8606089969729—dc22
                                2009034224

Typeset by S.J.I. Services, New Delhi

CONTENTS

Introduction: Stating the Case

In my modest, rural and single-parent family home, attendance at the weekly Sunday worship experience in the village chapel, the Bethesda Methodist church, was a discipline. Regular attendance at weekly Sunday worship experiences reflects a Caribbean-wide tradition. Whatever the weather, whoever the preacher or liturgist, however much we demurred, with clean unfashionable clothing, at 11 o'clock on Sundays, we were present in the village chapel for worship. Given that the lyrics of the hymns sung were not born out of the crucible of Caribbean social realities; the prayers offered were read from the English Book of Common Prayer and adopted without modifications on most occasions; and the proclamation from the Bible was geared towards those who sinned and not to those who were sinned against, the worship experience was unreal and unrelated to the particularity of the sociality of existence of the society.

More precisely, while concern was expressed and prayers offered for victims of violence, injustice, the hungry, naked and ill, whatever the nature of the social ill or injustice, such concern and prayers did not result in social action or planned strategies for resistance that exposed the system and practices in the society that engendered violence, injustice and social deprivation. We go to worship, offer our prayers or have prayers offered for us, sing the hymns, listen to the proclamation from the Bible, and go home and wake up on Monday morning, go to work, school, play and shop for the rest of the week and wait for the weekly Sunday worship experience again. Thus, the worship was an escape from reality; a place more for, if not only for, personal examination rather than agency and radical social possibility.

At the heart of the worship experience, however, was, and still is, the proclamation from the Bible. For many, preaching is the most important activity of the worship experience. It is not unknown for many to attend the worship experience depending on who is preaching. The pulpit in the Caribbean is of critical importance. Apart from the open-air political meetings during the political elections season, no other event or institution in the Caribbean has such a captive audience and accepted authority, where people *en masse* present themselves, in most cases willingly, to hear "truth" proclaimed, and open themselves to change and be challenged.[1] Yet the proclamation from the pulpit in the Caribbean is one of those activities that do not give the kind of agency to social forces and struggles that would make proclamation from the Bible an effective agent of social change.

Two factors account for this lack of agency in the proclamation from the Bible. One is the disjuncture created between religious life and the particularity of the sociality of existence. William Watty points to a number of erroneous antitheses in the dialectics of perspectives in traditional Caribbean biblical theological formulations that explain this disjuncture.[2] Watty claims that, in the Bible, the real antithesis is not between belief in God and atheism but belief in God and atheism and belief in false gods; not between the spiritual and material but the spiritual and material to the carnal; not between the sacred and the secular but the sacred and secular to the profane; not between creation and salvation but creation and salvation and what it means to be human in a world wherein the environment is continually effaced and raped, and in which the gap between rich and poor gets wider.[3] Here, it is not so much a question of a duality as a complex range of unacceptable alternatives to spirituality. As such, that disjuncture between faith and the particularity of the sociality of existence is built on an understanding that cannot claim the Bible as either its source or its authority.

What is being highlighted here are two of the aspects of proclamation from the Bible in the Caribbean pulpit. First, preachers are not inclined either to lead by example in the commitment to and involvement in the struggle for social justice or second, call for the kind of social involvement that would not lead to resigned acceptance of the status quo, depreciation of material concerns and interests, co-option and complicity of religion in oppression and an otherworldly faith and compensation in the hereafter. In reality, proclamation from the pulpit stops short of "offending" the ruling class and incarnating the Gospel for fear of being criticized of involvement in "politics"; and by that reality it has remained unconvinced that involvement with the material and profane is one salvific act

The other factor, which is a fundamental failure in Caribbean hermeneutical practice, and the major concern of this study, is that less agency is given to understanding of biblical texts as products of social forces and struggles, as socio-ideological productions, but more to how the biblical text says what it says or interpreting the biblical text as it stands and the contextual relevance of biblical texts for the church and society. This fundamental failure is an unforced error of biblical hermeneutical practice within a Caribbean context.

What has happened and is happening, thus far, is that many of the literary works on Caribbean biblical theology and hermeneutics tend to focus on reading strategies that are centred in the literary-rhetorical characteristics of biblical texts or how the text says what it says, derive meaning from biblical texts mainly for spiritual truth and formation, and provide answers for existential realities.[4] The majority of the studies have focused on the meaning of the biblical texts for lived realities and thereby on the world in front of the text (Hamid 1971, 1973, 1977; Gayle and Watty 1986; Kirton 1982; *Caribbean Journal of Religious Studies* 1987, 1991, 1992, 1993, 1995; Deane 1980; Caribbean Lenten Booklet Series, Caribbean Christian Living Series, Fashion Me A People Series 1981).[5] Even where the exegetical starting point for biblical interpretation is the existential realities, the focus is still on the literary features of the text (Mulrain 1995; 1999; Persaud 2000; James 2000; Nicholas 1993; Jagessar 2002).[6]

Attention in Caribbean biblical hermeneutical practice, therefore, needs to concentrate on the interests and practices that shaped the biblical writers' version of the realities they are interpreting. In this regard, what warrants investigating is the question: To what extent have biblical texts as socio-ideological productions and products of social practice give agency to or condition or shape interpreting the Bible in the Caribbean or are doing so now?

Focusing on the meaning of biblical texts for lived realities in Caribbean biblical hermeneutics is itself a critical response to one of the legacies of colonialism to the church: failure to come to grips with the meaning of faith and challenges to faith in its context.[7] This failure of faith to know the historical realities in which God is revealed is due to the fact that Christianity was introduced to the Caribbean by conquest. A gospel of submission to authority (God and "Massa"), a spiritualized understanding of salvation, thereby ignoring the material dimension, and the teaching of an eschatology that was futuristic were proclaimed. Such proclamation and teaching were used to legitimize and perpetuate an unjust economic and political system to the benefit and advantage of the colonizing empire. Religion was in the service of empire.

The intention here, however, is not to suggest that the reading strategy geared towards contextualization is wrong or even irrelevant. Caribbean hermeneutes do contextualize faith out of their reading of biblical texts. Even so, for Caribbean biblical hermeneutics to be truly resistant to oppressive structures of spirituality and theologies, it cannot focus less on the socio-ideological interests and social practices that have influenced the theological shape of the biblical text and more on contextual realities. If it wants to be truly relevant, meaningful, effective, and resistant and claim the Bible as its authority, then Caribbean biblical hermeneutics must balance concentrating on both biblical texts as products of socio-historical practice and the particularities and peculiarities of Caribbean contextual realities.

On the contrary, the contention is to advance that biblical texts are historically and contextually conditioned. They reflect the socio-historical and ideological interests and social practices of the contexts out of which they emerged. In other words, biblical texts come from somewhere and were written from some perspective. Three phases are at work in the composition of biblical texts. First, there was the original experience, which was not written as it happened; second, collective memory of the experience; and third, ideological and theological interpretation of the experience.[8] There is an ideological and theological agenda at work in biblical texts. As such, Biblical texts are "readings" of social realities – events, structures and systems of the society, values, roles, institutions, social class, conflicts and behaviour – in which their authors lived. Biblical texts do not produce themselves. Writers produce texts. Biblical texts are written documents, a passive though by no means a neutral and disinterested process. As a result, they were subjected to some form of ideological and theological interpretation, before they are read.[9] Thus, who wrote what and why is critical.

For instance, biblical scholars have postulated that there are some four versions of Jewish history or history of Israel in the Hebrew Scriptures known as JEPD: J, the Jahwist account justified David's rule (950–922 BCE); E, the Elohist account justified Jeroboam I's revolt against Judah (South) (800–750 BCE); D, Deuteronomist history justified revival of state religion under Josiah (722 BCE); and P, Priestly account posited the right of priests to rule Judah (South) and show loyalty to Persia (586).[10] Israel's history, therefore, was written from a variety of perspectives out of a variety of contexts representing contradictory and conflicting social and political interests and social practices between different groups taking contrasting positions.[11] A case in point is the conquest tradition – settlement of the Israelite tribes in Canaan after "their" Exodus out of the Pharaoh's oppressive Egypt. After their arrival in Canaan, however, they had no regard for the human rights of those they met in the land. The once oppressed now oppress.

Moreover, in writing about the purpose of two of the Gospel accounts of the life of Jesus, R. S. Sugirtharajah contends that the Gospel of Mark uses the Kingdom of God as an alternative to all imperial kingdoms; and the Gospel of Luke is about accommodation to Roman power in which Jesus is a religious reformer who poses no threat to Roman power.[12] Writers of the one life of the same Jesus, therefore, produce two accounts to suit their particular audiences, interests, concerns and issues.

Put another way, Stuart Hall explains that where events in newscast are not presented live, such events are signified with the aural-visual form of television language.[13] In television language, subjected as it is to the "rules" of language, the event is now a story. In other words, "event becomes a 'story' before it can become a communicative event".[14] This explanation, therefore, holds the Bible as "story": the events do not come as mirror reflections of the real; they are signified practices.[15] As such, they are particular productions of historical and social events and relations that need decoding by a hermeneutical strategy that give agency to the material and ideological conditions that produced the text.

The point being made making here is that the Bible is a "produced" text.[16] The Bible reflects Israel's socio-historical praxis – an account of how the promise of salvation was lived and reflected on by successive generations. So the text maker and the text produced are not only saying something but doing something: generating a version of the reality portrayed. Biblical texts take sides. Hence, it is the socio-ideological interests and practices that influenced or shaped the production of the text and the consequent theological shape of the text that is of concern to this study.

In other words, to underline further, the major concerns are what is produced (the text itself, who wrote what and why) and the agency it is given; who is reading what and how and the agency this reading has; and how the produced text and its interpretation allow for subverting or resisting oppressive systems and structures thereby bringing about social transformation. Besides, this concern about biblical texts as products and the agency they receive foregrounds that what happens before exegesis – one's presuppositions, praxis, social location and hermeneutical suspicion – is not only valid but also critical. What happens before exegesis is yet determinative of how exegesis is actually done. Admittedly, therefore, all three aspects – what happens before, what happens during and the interpretation that comes after – are crucial to the hermeneutical process. Nevertheless, the focus still remains what agency biblical texts as products are given. Even so, a critical eye is maintained as to what is happening before and after exegesis or the agency given to the social forces and struggles that condition the culture of exegetes.

The intention here, therefore, is to locate interpreting the Bible within the context of experiences of faith and the struggle for authenticity and relatedness to the particularity of the sociality of existence. Besides, a *space* is created, an imagined counter-reality to unreality and unrelatedness by which to do biblical interpretation. It is in the worship experience, however, at least in the Caribbean, that interpreting the Bible has the greatest potential and possibility for social good. Locating the interpretation of the Bible within the context of worship is not to depreciate the Bible's use in personal and family devotional exercises and in the weekday Bible study sessions, where admittedly it is not intentionally and conscientiously engaged in for purposes of social change. Rather, in terms of sheer numbers and opportunities, it is in the weekly Sunday worship experiences that possibilities exist abundantly. Essentially, those 52 opportunities per calendar year present the greatest untapped potential for social change in the Caribbean.

However, if interpretation of biblical texts is to have agency in effecting social change, then one needs to increase understanding of biblical texts as products of social forces and struggles. In essence, if worship experiences are to be kept real and the pulpit or the proclamation from the Bible within those experiences meaningful, significant, effective and a cultural tool of resistance, then the social forces and struggles of worshippers' experiences and culture and the social forces and struggles that produced biblical texts cannot be seen as unrelated to the particularity of the sociality of existence.

What is more, if the unreality and unrelatedness of the structures of spirituality and theologies, the disjuncture between faith and the sociality of existence in the Caribbean faith experience and biblical hermeneutical practices are to become real, integrated and conjoin, then those extant oppressive structures and their causes need finding out, standing against and transforming.

As such, an understanding as to how and why resistance develops is in order. To resist means constructing a consciousness that results in challenging, exposing and conquering those social systems and practices that oppress. For Chris Mullard, there are some four movements in the conceptual framework of resistance:[17] one, protecting of interests and power by the ruling class, which of necessity requires oppression and repression; two, such protecting of interests and power result in the relative "powerlessness" of the ruled which of necessity produces a consciousness of an alternative social order; three, the ruling class responds with more oppressive and repressive measures to legitimize their supremacy; and four, camps of interest are consequently established, with the ruling class acting to protect power and interests and the ruled agitating to construct power in order to transform the unjust social system.

While Mullard's four movements are used to ascertain where resistance is occurring and what gives agency to resistance in Caribbean biblical hermeneutical practices, at the same time, an examination of the particularity and peculiarity of the Caribbean context will help to answer the question of how and why resistance develops in a way that is different from Mullard's four movements. Further, a keen awareness is maintained to determine whether the three elements in the ethic of resistance are having any influence. Those three elements are – *separating* oneself from any socio-economic and political system that is not organized with the well being of the community as its ultimate goal; *denouncing* the hidden intentions or undisguised pretensions of any social system that is organized for hegemony; and *announcing* the judgement of God on any socio-economic system that oppresses.[18]

Resistance, though, is not as unproblematic as may have been made out here. Seemingly, the understanding of resistance is confined to that which takes place outside the system. However, that which takes place from without is not exclusive of that which takes place from within (opposition).[19] Resistance and opposition are not antagonistic relatives. At times, opposition utilizes tools from outside the system for purposes of reformation. For instance, the psychosocial resistance of the uncooperative practices of strikes, malingering, insubordination, control of fertility and (h)ideology[20] by slave women in the Caribbean during slavery took place from within the system but were not injurious to the desired intention of resisting racial and socio-economic domination. Thus, there is not one form of resistance but resistances or resistance-opposition syncretism. Even so, the form of resistance that this study is concerned with is running away as a means of contesting domination or as an anti-hegemonic stance.

In sum, in Caribbean biblical hermeneutical practice less agency is given to the materiality of the context of biblical texts in interpretation and more to their literary-rhetorical features and contextual relevance, with the consequence of little resistance against oppressive systems. This imbalance in agency is illustrated in one of the works of George Mulrain, former tutor at the United Theological College of the West Indies, Jamaica. Mulrain acknowledges "when a passage of Scripture is properly expounded, one ought to be in a position of knowing more about the historical facts behind that passage and its context, *but more important still, its meaning for today"* (Emphasis mine).[21] Yet Mulrain goes on to recognize that in studying biblical texts "it is important for us to know something about those who wrote them, *and in whose interests they had been written ... bearing in mind that the Bible itself was written from a biased point of view"* (Emphasis mine).[22] In other words, the quarrel is not about the need for emphasizing the contemporary meaning and contextual relevance of biblical texts. Rather, the quarrel is that it is not the socio-ideological interests and social practices that produced biblical texts that receive agency.

The aim, therefore, is to develop a biblical resistant reading strategy within a Caribbean context that seeks to come to grips with and gives agency to both the material conditions out of which biblical writers produced texts and the particularities and peculiarities of Caribbean socio-historical realities. Fulfilling this aim addresses the current need to give agency to the material conditions out of which biblical texts emerged, absent in Caribbean biblical hermeneutical practice. Here the purpose is not an attempt to recover the original audience, message and intention of biblical texts. Neither is it to recount the actual history or artifactual evidence as against focusing on the epigraphical evidence, the confession of faith in God that portrayed the world (interpretation of reality) in which the writers lived and discovered themselves in the light of faith in God. Instead, it is to understand or to see that biblical communities lived as part of a real, inhabited world, with real people and places[23] and expose and foreground the ideology, social forces and relationships that gave shape to biblical writers' "readings" of their social realities.

The endeavour, therefore, is to make contact between the "readings" of the socio-historical realities of both the biblical writers and Caribbean readers of biblical texts. A resistant reading strategy necessitates giving self-conscious attention to the world or interests or practices in which the text was produced (behind the text), the writer's version of reality (on the text) and the influences and experiences that shape the reader's interpretation (in front of the text) or the particularities and peculiarities of the context of the interpreter. Both the production and reading of biblical texts are modes of social action. It is out of these modes of social action in which all three hermeneutical moves are involved – behind the text, on or within the text and in front of the text – that a biblically resistant hermeneutic within a Caribbean context will take shape. Essentially, the resistant reading strategy allows for identifying which biblical ideologies, struggles and social practices one is hermeneutically connecting with.[24]

A brief overview of the influences and experiences that shape the Caribbean reader of biblical texts is necessary in order to show that the mode of existence is resistance. In the interpretive process, it is not biblical texts alone that stand in a given historical context or conjuncture and are shaped by the social forces at work in that context. Interpreters also stand in a given historical and social context.

The Caribbean is a "created" community. The indigenous inhabitants of the Caribbean – Tainos, Caribs and Arawaks – were exterminated mercilessly by the marauding Colonialists of the fifteenth and sixteenth centuries. Africans, against their wills, and later Asians as indentured labourers, were brought to the Caribbean not to people the Islands but specifically for purposes of plantation labour. So from its inception, the Caribbean was to serve purposes that were extrinsic to or not in the interest of its own economic and political advancement and development.

In addition, the Caribbean has never had, neither then nor now, full control of the decision-making processes and the forces and systems of production. Where a people are deprived of the right to self-definition or to name who or what they are, and denied pursuing self-determination or decide their own future, they are powerless. Powerlessness is a cause, not merely a symptom of the deprivation of the opportunity to pursue self-definition and self-determination. The cause of this powerlessness continues to influence the reading of scripture within the Caribbean context.

What this brief historical overview of the Caribbean shows is that the structures of our spirituality and socio-political economy are so integrated within, dominated and controlled by foreign forces and influences that our mode of existence is resistance.

Given, therefore, that our mode of existence is resistance, then central to distinguishing and resisting the causes of powerlessness will be, one, isolating and examining the issues of decision and production, that is, how others see us and we see ourselves; and two, addressing what are our social relations to production and power in Caribbean societies. Consequently, advocating the case for giving agency to the socio-historical and existential realities of the Caribbean reader of biblical texts and the ideological or dominating influences on those realities, without ignoring that biblical texts are ideological productions or the products of social practice is a necessity. In fact, it is history that conditions theology and the culture of the reader that shapes or conditions exegesis.[25]

The claim being made here, therefore, is that interpreting biblical texts is also conditioned by the social, economic, cultural and religious context of the interpreter. A disinterested interpreter does not exist. I am undertaking this study as a powerless Afro-Caribbean/male/Methodist. My main concern that biblical texts are socio-ideological products is not without interest in following the agency that the social forces and struggles of Caribbean peoples are given in the interpretive process. My voice is that of a Caribbean Subaltern, one who lives in a context of and subject to geo-political and economic hegemony.

Despite the stated interest, however, in the socio-historical realities of the Caribbean, the exegetical starting point for the resistant reading strategy remains the biblical text as evidence from and for the social environment in which it was produced. To start with interpreting the ideology, social forces and relationships that shape biblical texts is markedly different from the perceived mode of reading of Caribbean biblical hermeneutical practice. As indicated earlier, in Caribbean biblical hermeneutical practice, the tendency is to start with either analysis of the literary features of the biblical text or how the biblical text says what it says and then moving on to biblical-theological reflections on social realities of readers or the meaning of the biblical text for lived realities.[26]

Even so, whatever the starting point, a focus on biblical texts as products is nonetheless crucial. The issue is what happens "there". Contextual realities need not always be the starting point for interpretation to be liberating. Pushing the biblical text all the way back to its socio-historic environment is also valid and relevant, and holds within it liberating possibilities. It is a socio-structural analysis of biblical texts that is more likely to bring about exposure of and challenge to oppressive and exploitative systems and structures in society as well as the need for social transformation. This possibility exists because it is a resistant reading strategy which concentrates on socio-structural realities and that most readily exposes, challenges and questions the nature of social relationships, systems and structures embedded within biblical texts and societies.

To fulfil the aim of developing a Caribbean biblical resistant hermeneutic, an interdisciplinary approach is necessary as no one mode of reading the Bible will suffice. As such, postconialism, associated with the reading strategy of R. S. Sugirtharajah,[27] the historical-materialist approach, in the manner of Itumeleng J. Mosala,[28] and as critiqued by Gerald O. West,[29] are the analytical concepts that will serve as the tools of analysis.

For Sugirtharajah, postcolonialism primarily concerns detecting, questioning, challenging and exposing how the dominated are represented by the dominant, the link between power and knowledge and the tracking down of ideologies in plots and characterizations in texts and their interpretations; as such, postcolonialism's interest is located in the biblical writers' version of their reality and how that reality gets re-inscribed in interpretation.[30] Since the interest is in the socio-ideological agenda and social practices that produced biblical texts, postcolonialism is a critical tool of analysis.

For Mosala, the historical-materialist approach deals with unearthing the social, gender, class, vested interests, social practices and struggles of biblical texts. In the oppressive context of the then apartheid South Africa in which Mosala crafted his biblical interpretive approach, identifying the socio-structural issues in biblical texts was a necessary first step as a way of enabling critical discourse in the struggle for liberation. There are three aspects to the historical-materialist approach that are of interest: the nature of the mode of production, that is, whether communal, tributary or capitalistic; the formation of socio-economic classes on the basis of their relation to the mode of production; and ideological manifestations arising out of the mode of production[31] and the concomitant social class structure.

Ideological manifestations, however, are not only a function of class struggle. Richard Horsley has posited that Roman imperial power relations rested not only in armies, taxes and administrative apparatus but was contained also in the imperial cult – temples, shrines, images, sacrifices and festivals.[32] In spite of this, however, interest here lies in the underlying material relationships within the Roman Empire and the socio-ideological agenda and social practices that produced those material relationships, with specific reference to the socio-historical context of Philemon. It is this interest in the ideology and social practices that produced the material relationships in Philemon, and not the imperial cult, that suit the Caribbean context.

West advances the need for no single approach to Bible "reading" to have privilege.[33] As such, West argues for all three hermeneutical moves in biblical interpretation, namely behind the text, on or within the text, in front of the text, to interact in "reading" biblical texts against a specific human condition, within the context of faith and with a commitment to personal and social transformation. This reading strategy gives agency to the materiality of the biblical text and the context of the interpreter.

Moreover, other proponents of the historical-materialist approach are drawn into the discussion. For example, the work of Norman K. Gottwald,[34] Richard A. Horsley,[35] C. L. R. James[36] and Fernando F. Segovia[37] are drawn upon, as all make critical contributions to the perspective that ideology, social forces and relationships shape and influence the "reading" of social realities.

Besides, Paul's letter to Philemon in the New Testament is the biblical text chosen because of the parallel it holds with the Caribbean's experience of slavery and thereby the possibilities it possesses to develop a resistant biblical-theological hermeneutic. Admittedly, slavery in the first century is different in nature and character from slavery as practised during the halcyon days of colonialism in the Caribbean. However, Philemon is still relevant, for the principles of justice, dignity, self-determination and self-definition do not change with changing circumstances. An oppressed person or community, whether in the first century or the twenty-first century, is still an oppressed person or community; as the Caribbean still is.

Philemon as a text case is not without significance for biblical interpretation in Caribbean social history. Like Caribbean societies with their history of colonialism and cultural imperialism, the community of faith in the household of Philemon, and by implication the wider community of faith, was challenged to find a liberating praxis in the oppressive system and structure of the Roman Empire. In addition, being similar to the Caribbean's experience of slavery, Onesimus does not have a voice or a say in his own future; he has no right to self-definition and self-determination.

This work has three parts, with each part having two chapters. In Chapters 1, 3 and 4, there is a section entitled Eisegetics and Exegetics. These sections identify and discuss issues, problems and contradictions raised in the foregoing stage. In addition, many of the hermeneutical issues that are needed to form the proposal in Chapter 5 will already have been delineated.

In Part 1, a critical assessment of the history and development of biblical hermeneutics within a Caribbean context is undertaken. In Chapter 1, a division is made of Caribbean social history into the three specific historical periods, which will form the basis for the analysis of each period:

- Colonial   1492–1838
- Post-"emancipation"   1838–1960s
- "Independence"   1960s onwards

The division into specific historical periods are for three reasons. One, to advance and identify the distinctive shifts in social relations and socio-historical realities; two, to discover the biblical "reading" strategies used in each period by the interpreters cited and the consequences of the "reading" strategies employed; and three, to ascertain the understanding of biblical texts with which Caribbean hermeneutes work. In other words, the specific periods are not just about the general sequencing of events in Caribbean social history.

Moreover, in Chapter 1, where and what gives or does not give agency to resistance are identified in the biblical interpretive strategies of the interpreters cited, whether in the socio-historic environment out of which biblical texts emerged or in the socio-historical realities of the interpreters.

Tracking the contours of Caribbean biblical hermeneutical practice in this way allows for assessment of whether agency is given to the ideological agenda and social practices that produce biblical texts and/or the socio-historical realities of the Caribbean. Moreover, it permits seeing what happens in the stages prior to exegesis – praxis, presuppositions, social location and hermeneutical suspicion – and what happens afterwards or, in other words, the social consequences of interpreting biblical texts.

In Chapter 2, biblical hermeneutical practices within the Caribbean context are analysed. These practices are gathered from the findings of the empirical study undertaken in six Caribbean countries and the reading strategies found out in biblical hermeneutical practices in Caribbean social history.

Part 2, Philemon as text case, supports the claim that biblical texts are products of dominant socio-ideological interests, theological perspectives and social systems and practices. Chapter 3 puts Philemon in its "place" by focusing on the socio-ideological and theological agenda, and the socio-economic and political practices that led to its production. The hinged issue here is verse 16 as to what do "in the Lord" and "in the flesh" mean. When the community of faith gathers *(House church)*, Philemon and Onesimus are brothers; but when it scatters to live its life in the community *(Household)*, they are Master and slave. Can Philemon be both Onesimus' Master and brother and Onesimus Philemon's slave and brother? As such, is Paul proposing manumission? If so, to understand Paul's intention from the point of view of manumission is to reduce a personal but by no means private issue to the level of Master-slave relationship and thereby ignore the communal significance and implications of this text case for the institution of slavery itself. The difficulty here is that Paul gets caught in his own dichotomies and the grip of Empire: there are no male or female yet women are to keep silence in the church; no Jew or Gentile yet Paul himself is a Pharisee of the Pharisees; and no slave or free yet Onesimus is to return to a slave master.

Before these issues are addressed, however, one needs to address verse 1 and verse 12. Verse 1 suggests that the issue of Onesimus' return to Philemon is not solely between Philemon and Onesimus but is a public matter demanding public attention and a public solution. Do we not have here, then, a model of an egalitarian system and structure of social relations independent of social distinctions, which were an alternative society to Roman rule?[38] Further, if in verse 12 "sending back" is taken as the technical term for "run away", what then does "run away" mean? Did Onesimus "run away"? Was the priority to achieve reconciliation over against social justice? Or is the issue "the sharp distinction between more or less humane treatment of individual slaves by individual masters and the inhumanity of slavery as an institution".[39] Or was "run away" an anti-hegemonic stance by Onesimus? Moreover, if the priority was neither social justice nor the inhumanity of slavery as an institution, what then accounted for Paul's complicit or pacifist or less than revolutionary position?

In the end, the objectives of Part 2 are: one, to examine the system, practices and socio-economic and political structure of imperial Rome in the light of what is happening in Philemon; and two, to discover the socio-ideological interests and social practices that produced Philemon, and the impact and nature of the resistance taking place as a consequence.

Chapter 4 examines and evaluates "readings" *of Philemon* by investigating its appropriation by pro- and anti-slavery proponents and slaves from liberal, liberationist and postcolonial perspectives. One of the deafening silences in Philemon is the absence of the voice of Onesimus. Paul's is the only voice; or is Paul's voice the voice of the budding church? If so, was the budding church guarding against being seen or taken as an alternative model of egalitarianism or a challenge to the social relations of power in the Roman Empire?

Consequently, the "readings" of Philemon are evaluated to ascertain whether Philemon was abstracted from its socio-historic environment in its appropriation and with what interpretive results; or how biblical scholarship "read" Philemon. Specifically, interest is in the socio-ideological lenses through which the interpreters cited "read" Philemon, with a view towards determining whether Philemon was used and understood as a site of struggle. And essentially, to discover, first, how the socio-ideological and theological agenda at work in Philemon influence "readings"; second, to determine whether it is the rhetorical features of the letter or the experiences of and influences surrounding their contextual realities that determine the interpreters cited reading strategies or have agency; and third, to uncover where resistance is or is not taking place

The intention in Chapter 4 is to widen the understanding of biblical hermeneutical practices beyond the Caribbean context. This widening of biblical hermeneutical practices enables me to appreciate whether, in other biblical hermeneutical practices, besides the Caribbean, agency is given to materiality in interpreting biblical texts and how the interpretation of Caribbean interpreters compares with the other interpreters cited.

Part 3 proposes and weighs up the implications of *a biblical resistant hermeneutic within a Caribbean context.* Chapter 5 develops the proposal by bringing together insights from the whole study and grounding practice and theory. In other words, the biblical resistant hermeneutic is not an intellectual exercise or about abstract analysis. Rather, it lays heavy emphasis on commitment to and involvement in social struggle as a strategy for social transformation.

Chapter 6 evidences some seven *implications of developing a biblical resistant hermeneutic within a Caribbean context* for oppressive structures of spirituality and theologies, biblical hermeneutical practice and for challenging oppressive systems and structures in Caribbean societies.

Finally, there is a *Conclusion* and *Suggestions for further research.* Already, I am seeing the need for the analytical concepts as espoused by Caribbean social scientists such as C. L. R. James, George Lamming, Walter Rodney *et al.*, in their understanding of how social forces and struggles shape and are shaped by social realities serve as sites for doing theology and devising biblical "reading" strategies.

The *Conclusion* summarizes the main findings of the work and make judgment, where necessary, on issues.

In summary, in this work, the tension between that which gives agency and that which gives conjuncture[40] are held together. On the one hand, agency has to do with those experiences of marginality and injustice of the people and the development of a critical consciousness that gives rise to praxis as well as to interpreting biblical texts as products of social forces and struggles. Where such agency is given, ideological agenda and ruling class ideas are identified and exposed. On the other hand, conjuncture involves an awareness of the significance and impact of socio-economic and political circumstances both local and international on one's community. It is the tension between agency and conjuncture that will give rise to resistance and the imagining of an alternative social world as well as providing strategies for realizing the coming into being of that alternative social world. Wherever such imagining occurs, whether in worship experiences, Bible study sessions or in communities of interests, that space is not an escape from reality but a space of reality in which to nurture strategies for social change and resistance with a view to re-engaging with the sociality of existence.

Notes

1. C. H. L. Gayle and W. W. Watty, eds, *The Caribbean Pulpit, An Anthology* (St Michael, Barbados: Cedar Press, 1983), p. v.
2. William W. Watty, *From Shore To Shore, Soundings in Caribbean Theology* (Barbados: Cedar Press, 1981), p. 35.
3. Ibid., pp. 35–39.
4. Idris Hamid ed., *In Search of New Perspectives* (San Fernando, Trinidad, 1971); *Troubling Of The Waters* (San Fernando, Trinidad, 1973); Idris Hamid, ed. *Out Of The Depths* (San Fernando, Trinidad, 1977); Kortright Davis ed., *Moving Into Freedom* (Bridgetown, Barbados, 1977); William Watty, *From Shore To Shore* (CEDAR Press, Barbados, 1981); Noel Leo Erskine, *Decolonising Theology* (Orbis Books, Maryknoll, NY, 1981); Hemchand Gossai and Nathaniel Samuel Murrell, *Religion, Culture and Tradition in the Caribbean* (Macmillan, New York, 2000).
5. The list in parentheses provides the main studies in Caribbean theological works with this approach.
6. The work of the theologians listed provides examples of this approach.
7. Allan Kirton, "Current Trends in Caribbean Theology and the Role of the Church", *Caribbean Quarterly*, 37 (1): 102.
8. Notes from class lecture by R. S. Sugirtharajah.
9. Christopher Rowland and Mark Corner, *Liberating Exegesis: The Challenge of Liberation Theology to Biblical Studies* (London: SPCK, 1991, 2nd edn), p. 191.
10. See Robert B. Coote and Mary P. Coote, *Power, Politics and the Making of the Bible* (Minneapolis, MN: Fortress Press, 1990), pp. 4–9; David Robert Ord and Robert B. Coote, *Is the Bible True? Understanding the Bible Today* (London: SCM Press, 1994).
11. Ibid.
12. R. S. Sugirtharajah, *The Postcolonial Biblical Reader* (Massachusetts, MN: Oxford, Victoria: Blackwell Publishing, 2006), p. 68.
13. Stuart Hall, "Encoding and Decoding in the Television Discourse", Paper presented to the Council of European Colloquy on "Training in the Critical Reading of Television Language", University of Leicester, September 1973, p. 2.
14. Ibid.
15. Itumeleng J. Mosala, *Biblical Hermeneutics and Black Theology in South Africa* (Grand Rapids, MI: William B. Eerdmans Publishing Company, 1989), p. 124.
16. J. Severino Croatto, *Biblical Hermeneutics: Towards a Theory of Reading as Production of Meaning* (Maryknoll, NY: Orbis Books, 1987), pp. 66–67.
17. Chris Mullard, *Race, Power and Resistance* (London, Boston, Melbourne: Routledge & Kegan Paul, 1985), pp. 38, 47–48, 172–73.
18. See Dagoberto Ramirez Fernandez "The judgment of God in the Multinationals: Revelation 18" in Leif E. Vaage ed. *Subversive Scriptures – Revolutionary Readings of the Christian Bible in Latin America* (Harrisburg, PA: Trinity Press International, 1997), pp. 96–100.
19. M. Certeau, "On The Oppositional Practices of Every Day Life" *Social Text*, 1980 3: 3–43.
20. Robert Beckford, *Dread and Pentecostalism, A Political Theology for the Black Church in Britain* (London: SPCK, 2000), p. 103.

21. George Mulrain, "Is There a Calypso Exegesis?" in R. S. Sugirtharajah ed., *Voices From the Margins – Interpreting The Bible in The Third World* (Maryknoll, NY: Orbis/SPCK, 1995), p. 37.
22. Ibid., p. 38.
23. Norman Gottwald, *The Hebrew Bible – A Socio-literary Introduction* (Philadelphia, PA: Fortress Press), pp. 35–78.
24. Mosala, *Biblical Hermeneutics*, p. 122.
25. George Mulrain "Is There A Calypso Exegesis?" in R. S. Sugirtharajah ed. *Voices From the Margin – Interpreting The Bible in the Third World* (Maryknoll, NY: Orbis/SPCK, 1995), p. 42.
26. Stephen Jennings "The Word in Context: The Essential Criterion For Doing and Reflecting Authentic Caribben Theology" in *Caribbean Journal of Religious Studies*, 8 (2) April 1988: pp. 1–10.
27. R. S. Sugirtharajah, *The Bible and the Third World – Precolonial, Colonial and Postcolonial Encounters* (Cambridge: Cambridge University Press, 2001); R. S. Sugirtharajah, *Postcolonial Criticism and Biblical Interpretation* (Oxford: Oxford University Press, 2002).
28. Itumeleng J. Mosala., *Biblical Hermeneutics and Biblical Theology in Southern Africa* (Grand Rapids, MI: Eerdmans, 1989).
29. Gerald West, *Biblical Hermeneutics of Liberation: Modes of Reading the Bible in the South African Context* (Pietermaritzberg: Cluster Publications, and Maryknoll NY: Orbis Books, 1991).
30. R. S. Sugirtharajah, *The Postcolonial Biblical Reader* (Boston, MA, Oxford, Victoria: Blackwell Publishing, 2006), p. 88.
31. Mosala, *Biblical Hermeneutics*, p. 103.
32. Richard Horsley ed., *Paul and Empire, Religion and Power in Roman Imperial Society* (Harrisburg, PA: Trinity Press International, 1997) p. 23–24 ; see also, Richard Horsley, "Submerged Biblical Histories and Imperial Biblical Studies" in R. S. Sugirtharajah, *The Postcolonial Bible* (Sheffield: Sheffield Academic Press, 1998), pp. 162–67.
33. West, *Biblical Hermeneutics of Liberation*, p. 157.
34. Norman K. Gottwald, ed. *The Bible and Liberation: Political and Social Hermeneutics* (Maryknoll, NY: Orbis Books, 1993, revised ed.); Norman K. Gottwald, ed. *The Tribes of Yaweh: A Sociology of the Religion of Liberated Israel 1250-1050 B.C.E.*, (Maryknoll, NY: Orbis Books, 1979).
35. Richard A. Horsley ed., *The Bible and Liberation: Political and Social Hermeneutics* (Maryknoll, NY: Orbis Books, 1993, revised edn).
36. C. L. R.James, *Beyond A Boundary* (London: Stanley Paul & Co., 1963).
37. Fernando F. Segovia ed., *Reading From This Place vol.1 Social Location and Biblical Interpretation in the United States* (Minneapolis, MN: Fortress Press, 1995).
38. Horsley, *Submerged Biblical Histories*, p. 165.
39. Moses I. Finley, *Ancient Slavery and Modern Ideology* (London: Chatto & Windus, 1980) p. 122.
40. Brian Meeks, *Narratives of Resistance – Jamaica, Trinidad, the Caribbean* (Jamaica: The University Press of the West Indies, 2000), p. 58.

Chapter 1

Tracking Biblical Hermeneutical Practices within the Caribbean

Introduction

In Caribbean Christianization and civilization the cross arrived before the Bible. When Columbus landed by chance on the Caribbean island of Guanahani in the Bahamas, October 1492, his first act was to plant a cross. Thereupon, he renamed the island San Salvador (Saint Saviour or liberator). Columbus performed this act of renaming islands wherever chance took him in the Caribbean on some four voyages (1492, 1493, 1498 and 1502). By doing so, however, he usurped the right of Caribbean inhabitants to self-definition and self-determination in the name of the Spanish crown. Thereafter, for some five centuries, Britain, France and Holland followed in the footsteps of Spain to conquer, rule and dominate through massacre, cultural genocide, slavery and indentureship. Imperial and commercial interests were the driving forces for their involvement in the Caribbean. Consequently, the order – cross first, "civilization" second – meant that Christianization was subordinated to "civilization" with the Bible faithfully in the service of domination.

When Columbus made his second voyage to the Caribbean in 1493, accompanied by the Benedictine, Friar Boyl, and other missionaries to the indigenous Arawaks and Caribs Indians, he landed at Hispaniola. On 6 January 1494, a worship service to mark their safe arrival, inclusive of scripture and song, was held in Hispaniola.[1] The Bible's arrival was celebrated. By year's end, however, Boyl and others returned to Spain disturbed and perturbed by the unjust and cruel treatment meted out to the indigenes in the name of Christianity. The cause of their unscheduled return was but an early omen of the sanction the Bible was expected to give to such cruelties.

Throughout the centuries, the story and song of Caribbean history has been the struggle of a particular people to emancipate themselves from these imposed foreign values, customs and control. These struggles against domination and oppression as well as the struggle for emancipation provided the context of and for the interpretive approaches in Caribbean Biblical hermeneutical practice.

In what follows, the use of the Bible is explored in the social history of those countries that fell mainly to British conquest and colonialism. Here the social history of these countries is divided into three overlapping periods.

The periods are as follows:

- Colonial   1492–1838
- Post-"emancipation"   1838–1959
- "Independence"   1960s onwards

Dividing Caribbean social history into these distinctive periods serves three purposes. One, they provide a picture of the context of interpretation or the socio-historical realities (material conditions) of each period. Two, they indicate what agency these realities are given in the appropriations of the biblical story. Three, they help identify the various interpretive approaches employed. Each new historical period brought with it a different theological stance and accordingly a different interpretive approach or practice.

This approach to the task is not an attempt to examine the whole history of the Caribbean. Such is beyond the scope of this study. However, the principal areas of British conquest and colonialism will form the main focus of biblical hermeneutics, mainly Jamaica, Barbados, Guyana and the Leeward Islands. The interest in these periods lies in highlighting the material conditions of the Caribbean context and their agency in biblical hermeneutical practices as they pertain to the readers of the biblical texts, their social location, reading strategies, choice of texts, location of meaning, understanding of the Bible, where resistance occurs, and the social consequences or effects of the hermeneutics.

Moreover, dividing Caribbean social history into these three periods – Colonial, Post-"emancipation" and Post-"independence" – places both the Caribbean readers of biblical texts as well the foreign missionaries, who read biblical texts in a Caribbean context, within their socio-historical context. In addition, the reading strategies are contextualized within the prevailing biblical criticism of each period and highlights how those reading strategies cited reflected or pushed boundaries of the dominant biblical thinking of their time.

In the colonial period, the readers engaged in a hermeneutical practice that concentrated on the original audience, message and intention such that what counted was what the text meant and what it does mean. In biblical criticism, this hermeneutical practice is known as *historical criticism*. In historical criticism, the social location, presupposition, culture and experience of readers did not matter, as only the text mattered.[2] The readers' task was to read *out* of the text, not *into* the text. A notable exception to this reading strategy, despite the fact that it was the era when the indigenous voice was suppressed,[3] was that of Sam Sharpe who "read" the oppressive socio-economic circumstances into the biblical texts with revolutionary consequences.

The post-"emancipation" period was the era in which biblical criticism was experiencing a paradigm shift from text-dominant approaches to reader-dominant reading strategies or *literary criticism*. In literary criticism attention is focused on the artistic or rhetorical features of the text, that is, who wrote what and how and for whom meaning is derived from the interaction between the reader and text. What this means is that the social location, presupposition, culture and experience of the reader matters little and less emphasis is placed on the socio-economic, political and ideological aspects of the text.[4] Even so, the reading strategies of the readers cited in this period showed the influence of their socio-economic, political and cultural context illustrating thereby that "every reader is historically and socially conditioned".[5] Additionally, these reading strategies mark the onset and prevalence of liberation hermeneutics within Caribbean biblical hermeneutical practice with its emphasis on the theological reading and implication of socio-economic, political and cultural realities in the light of faith based on the Bible.

Against this background of interest in the social realities of readers, in the post-"independence" period, "readers 'read' biblical texts from within specific locations and with specific interests in mind".[6] Interest, therefore, in this post-"independence" period is not limited to the different reading strategies that different readers employed but why different readers "read" in different ways. What the tables on pages 34, 47 and 58 show is that the different ways of reading resulted from the positionality of readers – race, gender, religion, class, ethnicity, ideology – or the mixed status and marginalized subject or dominant positions[7] the readers embodied and to which they belonged.[8] In biblical criticism, this reading strategy where attention is given to the socio-economic, political and cultural circumstances of the context of biblical text and readers as well as the ideological commitment and stance of readers[9] is known as *cultural criticism*.

Absent from the tracking of Caribbean biblical hermeneutical practice and hence from the tables below, but not without significant influence on this study, is *postcolonial criticism* to biblical studies. The father of postcolonial criticism to biblical studies is R. S. Sugirtharajah who first introduced postcolonial biblical criticism in 1996.[10] Whereas in historical, literary and cultural criticism the focus is either on the biblical texts or the readers or both, postcolonialism "perceives its task as critiquing, problematizing, and exposing contradictions and inadequacies in both the text and its interpretation".[11] For Sugirtharajah, this task is both historical and hermeneutical. It is historical in that it takes genuine and deep interest in colonial domination and suppression of the voice of the "other" exposing thereby "the imperial assumptions and intentions of biblical interpretation, as those who opposed them;[12] and hermeneutical in that it re-reads biblical texts from the perspective of postcolonial concerns of creolization, "home" as a different reality in the Diaspora and multiculturalism.[13] In Caribbean biblical hermeneutical practice, the reading strategies of Sam Sharpe, Paul Bogle, Marcus Garvey and Rastafarianism fall within this postcolonial criticism to biblical studies trope with their challenge to hegemony and discriminatory colonial representations.

Colonial Era: 1492–1838

Socio-historical and Political Realities and Forces
Natal Alienation.[14] The period 1492–1838 marks the beginning and "legal end" of slave trading in the Caribbean. It was the era of genocide, slavery and indentureship. Against their wills, Africans were brought to the Caribbean to labour on the sugar plantations as slaves in the Caribbean. In Africa, they had professions, belonged to and had families of their own and had dignity and worth. Thus, in their homeland of Africa, they were socialized and civilized. But when forcibly brought by the slave traders in Africa and bought by European Planters to the West Indies, they immediately became merchandise or the sole property of the Plantation Owners. All rights and sense of human worth and dignity were taken away forcibly. For instance, the baptismal records of the Anglican churches of St Dorothy's, Old Harbour and the cathedral in Spanish Town, both in Jamaica, showed that only the name of the plantation and the race factor that were of importance to the white European curate, and not the full identity of the slave.

Table 1.1: Identification of slaves
Example: St Dorothy's Anglican Church, Old Harbour, Jamaica

Condition	Estate (1811–1879)
Sambo	Old Yarmouth
Mustee	Sutton's Estate
Negro	Colbeck's Estate
Mullet	Bushy Park
Mulatto	Windsor Estate
Black Boy	McKenzie Estate

Source: Cited in *Caribbean Journal of Religious Studies*, April 1996, 17 (1): 28.

Commodification and Exploitation of Black Humanity

To the insults of dehumanization and demoralization was added the further injury of commodification or thingification as slaves were listed in Estate inventories with cattles, horses, shovels, hoes, forks, picks. Richard Pares, British historian, noted that "in all the inventories which are to be found among the West Indian archives, it was very unusual for the mill, cauldron, still and buildings to account for more than one-sixth of the total capital; in most plantations one-tenth would be the mark. By far the greatest capital items were the value of the slaves and the acreages planted in canes by their previous labour".[15] During this era, black humanity had value only in the framework of slavery. Black humanity, however, existed outside of slavery and before slavery and achieved great accomplishments and civilization.

Furthermore, besides denying the enslaved Africans their humanity and suppressing their capacity for realizing their full human potential, the system was further consolidated by the fact that this inhuman condition was written into the laws of the lands. The Barbados *Act for the better ordering and governing of Negro slaves of April 1668* regarded Africans as belonging to the animal kingdom and thereby not worthy to occupy the same socio-geographic space as the Whites.[16] The Act states in its preamble:

> Whereas a very considerable part of the wealth of this Island consist of Negro slaves ... It is hereby ordained and enacted ... that ... all Negro slaves in all courts of judicature, and other places within this Island shall be held, taken and adjudged to to be Estate Real, and not chattel, and shall descend unto the heir and widow of any person dying intestate according to the manner and custom of lands of inheritance held in fee-simple.[17]

Women and children were not spared these indignities. The principle – *partus sequitur ventrem* (the child follows the condition of the mother regardless of the race of the father) – was mercilessly applied. Essentially, the principle ensured stockbreeding and sexual exploitation. A woman's worth and dignity were reduced to and measured by her reproductive ability to produce a "herd of subhuman labour units".[18]

Both in fact and on the statute books, Africans were considered property with the slave master having absolute control and power over the slave. Indignity was further heaped upon indignity as this was accompanied by the slave owner's perception of slaves as extensions of their will and themselves as gods since they recognized no other power but their own over the slaves.[19] Not only were the slaves denied their humanity but they suffered the loss of self-determination or freedom, the right to govern and order their own lives.

Furthermore, in the economic system of plantation slavery, the enslaved Africans were organized into gangs along lines of ethnic divisions. The policy was not to keep too large a number of any single ethnic group together on a single plantation who spoke the same language and were from the same family, kinship, folklore, religious, economic and political systems.[20] The logic was that if ethnic groups were left to form economic and social power bases they would have been a direct challenge to the strength, effectiveness and viability of the Plantocracy and a security danger. In reality, this was a policy of divide to rule. Through this schema, however, the slaves lost touch with aspects of their identity through language and cultural practices.

Complicity and Duplicity of the Church

For the slaves, a bad situation got worse. The church, the salt of the earth, was also in the embrace and influence of the Plantocracy. There was none in the earth to call on beside Thee. On a visit to Barbados, Richard Ligon, a British colonial historian of the 1900s, recounted how a slave by the name of Sambo expressed his desire to him to be made a Christian.[21] Ligon reported this request to Sambo's slave owner who replied thus:

> that the people of the Iland were governed by the laues of England, and by those laues we could not make a Christian a slave.[22]

Ligon retorted that Sambo's request was different in that he was not asking for a Christian to be made a slave but for a slave to be made a Christian. The slave owner responded thus:

> that it was true that there was a great difference in that: But being once a Christian, he could no more account him a slave, and so lose the hold they

had on them as slaves, by making them Christian; and by that means should open such a gap, as all Planters in the Iland would curse him.[23]

It is to be noted here that Ligon took Sambo to the slave owner, not to the church or the pastor for a matter that was inherently religious. This was an unpretentious indication of the totality of the control of slave owners as well as the self-consciously complicit role of the church within the status quo. This self-consciously complicit role of the church was due in large measure to the fact "that the missionaries regarded slavery as a political, rather than a moral institution, and based their work in the West Indies upon an acceptance of its legality".[24] As one steeped in his British history, Ligon should have known that the missionaries were on a mission decided.

Relations to Production: Role of Slaves, Plantocracy and Missionaries
Despite, the observation that slaves were regarded as property, which explains the concomitant inhumane treatment, that view was unbalanced and biased. Richard Pares, a British historian and scholar of the seventeenth century, contended that the slaves were no idiots. In his work, *Planters and Merchants*, he advanced that the slaves had such technological capabilities that they actually ran the Plantations' productive systems. Pares gave the following assessment of the economic value of the slaves:

> Yet, when we look closely, we find that the industrial capital was much greater than a sixth of the total value. With the mill, the boiling houses and the still went an army of specialists – almost all of them slaves, but nonetheless specialists for that.[25]

In other words, the slaves ran the plantations. It is no stretch of the imagination to submit that the "specialists", slaves, in the colonies, produced the wealth of the British society during the industrial revolution of the seventeenth and eighteenth centuries. For all the justification found to disregard slaves as humans, they were not idiots.

Nevertheless, the socio-historical context of the era 1492–1838 was, on the one hand, for the slaves, one of alienation, oppression and exploitation and the consequent lost of humanity, roots or identity and freedom. And, on the other, for the Plantocracy, it was one of dictatorial control of the economic, political and religious decision-making machinery of the society. It was out of and because of this context that the shape of the Biblical interpretive approach adopted by some Planters and the missionaries was pre-determined. Before the missionaries set foot on Caribbean soil they were instructed as to what to say and do. For instance, the instructions given to missionaries by the Baptist Missionary Society can be taken as the model for all missionaries:

> You are quite aware that the state of society in Jamaica is very different from that under which it is our privilege to live in this country, and that the great majority of its inhabitants are dependent upon their superiors in a degree altogether unknown here. The evidence of the fact will probably especially at first, be painful and trying to your feelings; but you must ever bear in mind that, as a resident in Jamaica, you have nothing whatever to do with its civil and political affairs; and with these you must never interfere ... the Gospel of Christ you well know, so far from producing or countenancing a spirit of rebellion or insubordination, has a directly opposite tendency ... let your instructions, both to young and old, be conceived in the spirit and corresponds with the directions and example of our Divine Teacher, as laid down in the New Testament at large; and then, whatever disposition may be felt to obstruct or misrepresent you, none will justly be able to lay anything to your charge.[26]

So, the missionaries arrived in the Caribbean, not primarily on a mission, but decidedly with a mission: to ensure that moral education and their religious work neither challenged nor disaffected the institution of slavery.[27] The missionaries were willing accomplices, genuflecting to economic power as they chose not to see anything conflicting between Christianity and slavery.[28] The missionaries saw no evil, heard no evil, and more to the point, spoke not against the evil of slavery. Never was it truer that there is none so blind as s/he who would not see.

Biblical Interpretive Approaches

Below, some five hermeneutes of the colonial era are cited. Their social status is especially noted as interpreters of biblical texts are always socially positioned and interested:[29] Count Zinzendorf, a Moravian missionary to the Caribbean from Germany; William Hart Coleridge, Anglican bishop of Barbados sent out from England, a member of the Parish Council and thereby a member of the establishment; George Liele, a former slave turned Baptist missionary from the state of Virginia, in the United States of America; Sam Sharpe, a domestic slave and Baptist preacher; and William Knibb, a Baptist missionary from England, a trained school teacher and an untrained academic theologian, who arrived in Jamaica in 1825. Though these examples are few, they are representative of the general biblical interpretive approach of the era and will bear out the conclusions drawn.

Uncritical Retelling of the Biblical Story

With Gen. 1–2:4a and 9:18–27, Ephesians 5 and 6 and the moral and social responsibility of the church in the interpretive frame, Count Zinzendorf counselled slave converts in 1739 this way:

> Be true to your husbands and wives, and obedient to your masters and
> bombas. The Lord has made all ranks – kings, masters, servants and slaves.
> God has punished the first Negroes by making them slaves, and your
> conversion will make you free, not from the control of your masters, but
> simply from your wicked habits and thoughts, and all that makes you
> dissatisfied with your lot.[30]

In one stroke, the Count over-looked Eph. 2:14 in which the super-structure of superiority and inferiority was destroyed by the death of Jesus and thus formed the interpretive key to and the basis of the other relationships between parents and children, husbands and wives, masters and slaves which the Epistle went on to describe. He conveniently misrepresented God's purposes as Creator and in the Creation, invoked his racist hermeneutic with his undisguised reference to the "curse"[31] of Ham in Genesis and espoused an understanding of salvation that was highly individualistic and other-worldly. Here there was no analysis of the context of the biblical text but a rather hasty move to point to the significance of the biblical text for the contemporary situation. The failure to analyse the context of the biblical text highlights the issue that there can never be effective application of text to context without first examining the socio-historical environment out of which biblical writers composed and shaped their version of the reality in which they lived. Where the intention is to reinforce the status quo, critical analysis is not necessary, is even dangerous, for the ends justify the means.

William Hart Coleridge, in a sermon to newly confirmed slaves, exhorted them to be obedient and submissive by drawing upon Eph. 5:15–33; 1 Pet. 2:11–25; 3:1; Tit. 2:1–15; 3:1,2; Rom. 12:6–21. Coleridge proclaimed:

> In all things and in every station, strive to approve yourself the chosen of
> God ... being diligent as rulers, loyal as subjects; just and equal as masters,
> obedient as servants; as parents kind, as children dutiful, faithful in marriage
> ... liberal in wealth, contented in poverty, if bond, with good will doing service,
> if free, not using your liberty as a cloak of maliciousness, but as servants of
> the Lord.[32]

One is left to consider the bishop's intention as damning, if not ambiguous, with his reference here to slaves as "rulers", "masters", "wealthy" and "free" as nothing was further from the reality. Bishop Coleridge's choice of Biblical text is of significance here. The Ephesians, Peter and Titus texts all come from a time when the church was accommodating to the patriarchal and hierarchical imperial Graeco-Roman society around it. The liberating tendencies of egalitarianism and inclusivity of the earlier Jesus Movement were practised less and less. In addition, the Roman text has to do with submissiveness. Coleridge's Biblical interpretive approach was consistent with and a reinforcement of the colonial strategy to engender submission to authority. What one can say here is that biblical hermeneutics as shaped by the social realities of the day is not only a hermeneutic of "convenience" but of "necessity". However, though Bishop Coleridge's hermeneutic of "necessity" was questionable in the circumstances, it was genuine.

In a document published on Christmas Day 1795,[33] the reading strategy of George Liele (1783) was made obvious. The articles in the document concluded with the phrase "according to the word of God" or "agreeable to the word of God" followed by a proof-text. *Article 1* cited Matt. 3:1–3 and 2 Cor. 6:14–18 as support for the Baptist's theological position being the same as that of the Anabaptists.[34] But was the use of these texts a veiled way of dealing with the ideology of racism in the slave society of his day? *Article 11* had to do with public worship and preaching as to whether Sunday was a "legal" day of rest or worship.[35] Mark 16:2–6 and Col. 3:16 were used as proof-texts. This interpretation was in conflict with the official dictate of using Sunday as a market day for the slaves. *Article XV* considered the conditions for church membership with 1 Pet. 2:13–16 and 1 Thess. 3:13 as proof-texts.[36] Here these texts encouraged that deference be shown to rulers. But were the scriptures being used here to assist in regulating the behaviour of congregants in order to ease the tension between the plantation owners and the slaves? And *Article XVII* discussed punishment for slaves' misconduct with 1 Tim. 1:6, Eph. 6:5 and 1 Pet. 2:13–21 as proof-texts.[37] Where Liele's reading strategy does not isolate Biblical texts from their contexts, it puts them in opposition.

A Resistant Reading[38] of the Biblical Text
Sam Sharpe was born in Montego Bay, Jamaica, in 1801 and, therefore, not an uprooted African slave.[39] Though he was given the name of his owner, Samuel Sharp Esq., Sharpe was given the aliases "School master Sharpe", "Daddy" and "Ruler" for his ability to read and write and the way he was revered in the plantation society by his peers. Despite the fact or more precisely because of the fact that Sharpe was treated well and kindly as a domestic slave, Sharpe's location within the social system as a slave and his

consciousness of the oppression and indignity of his class as slaves located him in a different place socially and ideologically from his owner.

Sharpe's relatively humane domestic obligations and treatment did not dull his sense and passion for justice for his oppressed and exploited class. For Sharpe, it was not so much how he or any other individual was treated but how the whole socio-economic and political machinery was built to dominate and exploit blacks and grant social privilege and rank to whites. Edward Kamau Brathwaite, Caribbean poet and historian, captures the dilemma of the house slave and field slave, in which Sharpe was forced to live, imaginatively in the contemporary era this way:

> Kind people treat their dogs, cats and horses kindly; but kind treatment for slaves is like putting expensive and beautiful clothes on the back of leper. The beautiful clothes do not change the condition of the leper. Kind treatment does not change the condition of a slave ... slavery is the greatest violation of the human spirit; kindness does not correct the violation. Only freedom can.[40]

Sharpe was a deacon in the Baptist church, but a black Baptist. Black here does not refer to the colour of Sharpe's skin but to socio-political status of marginalization, domination, exploitation and alienation within plantation society and economy over against the privilege and rank of whites. In the Baptist church, Sharpe was exposed to the Bible teachings of the missionaries and their works of secular freedom through literacy campaigns and the building of schools. In their evangelizing work, the missionaries had a philosophical dilemma: slaves could be spiritually free but temporarily enslaved, that is, free soul but slave body.[41] Sharpe solved and broke through this dilemma or dichotomy between soul and body and presented the missionaries with a "new" hermeneutical key: spiritual freedom equals physical freedom, as no man can serve two masters.

What Sharpe did was to organize a two-pronged attack on the plantation system of slavery. First, Sharpe centred his interpretive approach in his praxis, his daily struggle for freedom and equality in an oppressive and unjust society. Sharpe placed the struggle for freedom within the Biblical tradition of emancipation. The Exodus story, Luke 4:16–18, the Matthean teaching of Jesus that no man can serve two masters (Matt. 6:24) and Col. 3:11 *(in that renewal there is no longer Greek and Jew, circumcized and uncircumcized, barbarian, scythian, slave and free; but Christ is all and in all, NRSV)* were the ideological basis for what was called the Baptist War of 1831.[42] As such, he saw and had reasons to demonstrate discontent with the oppressive political circumstances. Sharpe inverted the concept of religious freedom into civil freedom. Unlike the Maroons, Sharpe and his followers did not want freedom as rebels but as lawful human beings, as a right of law.[43]

Integral to Sharpe's praxis was the practice of "religion". Within the context of plantation society and economy, "religion" for Sharpe and his followers was not confined to the received and accepted doctrinal practices and beliefs and as such "a dispassionate system of God-talk and a code of behaviour".[44] On the contrary, "religion" had to do with a nevertheless faith expression in God and the gods born out of the experience of suffering and struggle that celebrates and advocates dignity, freedom and self-identity. The use of the body in religious rituals, dreams and visions, river, spirit was (re)-introduced in black Baptists' church practice. Such an understanding, which divided the Baptists into "white" Baptists and black Baptists, went deeper than a colour divide, white as opposed to black. It was rather the distinction of lived realities and world-view. Black was a condition of oppression and the lens through which to view emancipation.

Second, Sharpe politicized and radicalized the attempted disinterested reading of the Bible and "religion" by the missionaries. Sharpe contrasted what he was hearing from the missionaries and what he and they were reading from the Bible – *if the Son therefore shall make you free, you shall be free indeed* (John 8:36); *you are bought with a price, be not ye the servants of men* (1 Cor. 7:23); *there is neither Greek nor Jew, there is neither bond nor free* (Gal. 3:28), *no man can serve two masters* (Matt. 6:24) – with the social life of material ease and privilege of the plantocracy and the lives of degradation, alienation, inauthenticity which he and his fellow slaves were forced to live. Amidst such lived realities not only were the political implications of exclusion and discrimination clear to him but also the political imperative and consequence of rebellion. For Sharpe and his followers, politicizing biblical interpretation and "religion" was a precondition for revolt and for religion as an instrument of social change.

Furthermore, for Sharpe and his followers, the rewards in heaven after death for obeying the ideals of the Christian faith proved unsatisfactory rewards for enduring chattel and wage slavery of their day. Slaves wanted freedom and rewards on earth, in this present life. Sharpe read the Bible from the slave's perspective of the struggle between the powerful and the poor and hence his different interpretation and course of action. It is possible for both the oppressed and the oppressor to read the same Scriptures but come to different conclusions, as each begins from a different "place" or epistemology.

Thus, based on the understanding that before God and in Christ, all persons were created equal in freedom and no social distinctions existed and that natural equality meant that the White man had no authority to hold the Black man in slavery, a rebellion of "passive resistance" was hatched. After the Christmas holidays of 1831, slaves were to down tools and refuse to work until freedom was acknowledged or granted and a decision reached to pay slaves for their labour, after due negotiations. His intention was not revolution or the violent overthrow of the system of slavery. Sharpe's vision was to transform the socio-economic system of exploiting labour, wherein slaves had no say in determining the cost of their labour, to that of wage labour, wherein slaves had bargaining power over their labour cost. This plan of "passive resistance" showed that Sharpe understood the effects of industrial strike action upon an industrial system at a time when the critical and central role of labour for productivity and profitability in a plantation economy was not given due recognition as labour, but as chattel.[45] The rebellion led by Sharpe challenged the idea that slaves were mindless property. Slaves as mindless property were the tinder to which Sharpe and his followers literally scratched match.

This vision of wage labourers, however, pitted Sharpe against his trusted comrades – Dover and Gardner – who wanted not just bargaining power over labour for slaves but also to become freeholders of estates or to control the productive forces of the plantation economy.[46] With no plan for a post-emancipation society in place, the plan of "passive resistance" escalated into a full blown armed rebellion in which some twenty thousand slaves became embroiled.

The rebellion was sparked, too, by the rumour, which had reached the colonies, that the authorities in Britain had already abolished slavery and that colonialists were simply denying the slaves their freedom, which was theirs by Divine right. Slaves felt that they were no longer bound by the dictates of plantation owners. It was estimated that some £1.5 million of damage was caused to property. Needless to say this rebellion was mercilessly crushed and the innocent and guilty made to pay the ultimate price for their troubles, death by hanging in the public square.[47] Though the colonists crushed the rebellion mercilessly, the conviction that the Bible stood in opposition to slavery was not subdued. Hope for a better life in the world to come became hope for a better life in this world after abolition.[48] The natural equality of human beings and bondage as unlawful and unbiblical (freedom and self-respect) were the biblical ideology of the rebellion.

Scriptural Allusions and Quotations

William Knibb arrived in Jamaica at a time when revolts against slavery by the slaves in the colonies were getting more bold and more frequent and abolitionists' sentiments against slavery were getting stronger in Britain. This knowledge of these events shaped his interpretative approach as can be observed in his use of scriptural allusions and quotations in his letters to his mother and sister as well as in his contribution to the anti-slavery debates in England.[49] For example, with Isa. 61:1–4 and Luke 4:16–18 in the interpretive frame, in a letter to his mother, he exclaimed that it "cheers the heart of your son which would otherwise sink to proclaim liberty to the captives and the opening of prisons to them that are bound, is a delightful employment, and I will dwell that I may be thus employed".[50] Though Knibb's interpretive approach was limited to the use of scriptural allusions and quotations, the locus for interpretation and meaning was not the biblical text in its original context per se but the prevailing material realities. Thus, the consequence was a challenge to the status quo and solidarity with the victims of injustice and inhumanity.

Outcome: Social Control and Stability Versus Social Reconstruction

The consequences of these interpretive strategies is summed up rather aptly by Benjamin La Trobe, a leader of the Moravian church in Britain in 1768 and a promoter of foreign missions, in a letter to a friend in 1770: "these Negroes are alfo a proof that a genuine reformation in principle and practice is always infeperable from true conversion … the magiftrates themfelves have more than once declared, the baptised Negroes are a greater fesucurity to them than their forts".[51] The colonies were safer with slaves who were Christians than with battalion stations and fortresses. Indeed, one of the chief roles of missionaries was to complete the act of enslavement by enslaving people in mind so they believed slavery was their lot. Fundamentally, social security was of a higher value than social justice as taming the enemy within was deemed to be more necessary and profitable than defeating the enemy without. In other words, the ideology of security and stability shapes hermeneutics.

Stability, though, depended upon who did the interpreting and whose interests were being served by the interpretation. While the missionaries focused on law and order and emphasized conformity and obedience, acceptance of the status quo, submission to authority, passivity and docility, the slaves, as led by Sharpe, wanted equity in the system and structures of the society. Theirs was not a millenarian movement with a prophetic figure announcing the will of God and an anticipated new world to be brought about in time by "divine intervention". Sharpe and other slaves did not want to establish a new world but freedom from chattel slavery and the unconditional right to sell their labour for wages. So their aims were tangible and thereby geared towards specific economic and social reconstruction.

Eisegetics and Exegetics

In the reading strategies of the foreign missionaries and slaves highlighted above, the crucial factors were who did the interpreting and the choice of biblical texts. Here the Bible was in the service of both oppressive and liberatory purposes.[52] There is quite often a huge difference between the "readings" of social reality by biblical writers and the interpretation of those realities by biblical interpreters.[53] What actually happens, especially when those in positions of power interpreted scripture, is that their interpretations were rendered true and normative as they are turned into societal norms. During slavery, the Planters and Missionaries who had power read their biases, prejudices and interests into their interpretations, to the total neglect of the fact that biblical texts are products of socio-ideological interests and social practices. Thus, they created and supported social structures that sanctioned and legitimized the inferiority and subjugation of the slaves.

Consequently, what is observed in the reading strategies of foreign missionaries – the uncritical retelling of the biblical story, scriptural allusions and quotations – is that socio-historical realities are not given agency in the interpretive process. As a result, the interpretation focuses on the literal meaning of the biblical text, without any serious intention of applying its significance or message to the context. Interpretation is open to what Itumeleng Mosala calls "the escapist option of textual selectivity".[54] the deliberate choice of texts to support one's class and ideological interests.

However, when the oppressed, those without power – in this case the slaves – did the interpreting, the materiality of both biblical texts and contexts were given agency and thereby formed and informed the interpretive process. This resistant reading strategy by the victims of the system resulted in the challenging of the status quo, brought about solidarity among the victims and was geared towards achieving tangible goals.

Another aspect of the reading strategies has to do with the difference between literalism – taking texts to mean literally what they say – as against literary criticism – biblical texts as message. With literalism, the reader's task is read out of the text, not into the text. Here the meaning of the text is fixed; it is for all times and for all places. What it means in Britain, it means in the Caribbean. With literary criticism, because the emphasis is on how the text says what it says (the rhetorical features), the reader has a role in producing meaning. Thus, this inference highlights the hermeneutical moves in the reading strategy of the missionaries and Sharpe. The missionaries went from text, without analysis of the ideological interest and social practices of the world inhabited by the biblical writers, to social reality; while Sharpe went from praxis or social struggle to interpretation of the text for lived realities. Whereas the missionaries' reading strategy reinforced the status quo, Sharpe's led to the economic and social reconstruction of the status quo, the attempted overthrow of the oppressive system, albeit an unintended consequence for Sharpe and his fellow rebels.

In sum, resistance resulted from Sharpe's or the slaves' interpretive reading strategy, but did not come about from the foreign missionaries' literal readings. The foreign missionaries' interpretive strategy was not centred on the material concerns of alienation and the brutal exercise of power, which it legitimized, resulting in complicit support for the status quo. However, Sharpe and the slaves came to the biblical texts through the interpretive lens of alienation and brutal domination. Their agitation for an alternative social order was derived from the Bible – the Exodus story, Luke 14:16–18 and the creation story where all have equality before God. Thus, in the resistant hermeneutic of Sharpe and the slaves, there were four movements. First, there was the protecting of socio-economic and political interests and power by plantocracy by oppressive and repressive means, with the tacit support of the church; second, agitating for an alternative social order of justice and equality by the oppressed (Sharpe/slaves) based on the Bible; third, added oppressive measures to deny self-determination and self-identity by the plantocracy to legitimize power and thereby create camps of interests; and four, camps of interest in conflict. Hence for Sharpe and the slaves both the materiality of biblical texts and context mattered; the result was neither justifying nor legitimizing the status quo.

Thus, we may conclude that both the interpreter and the choice of biblical text matter, indeed neither biblical text nor the interpreter is innocent.[55] In the end, no interpretation is derived apart from who we are (identity), where we are (social location) and what we know (experience). Identity, social location and experience become embedded within what we say about God and understand about God and the world.

Table 1.2: Biblical reading strategies during the colonial period 1492–1838

Reader/Interpreter	Social location	Biblical Texts	Socio-historical realities	Reading strategy	Location of meaning	Understanding of Bible	Consequences
Count Zinzendorf	Male, Missionary	Gen. 1–2:4a, Ephesians 5 and 6					Acceptance of the status quo, pietism, escapism
Bishop William Hart Coleridge	Male, Missionary	Ephesians 5 and 6, 1 Pet. 2:11–25, Tit. 2:1–13, 3:1–2, Rom. 12:6–21					Submission to authority
George Liele	Male, former Slave	Matt. 3:1–3, 2 Cor. 6:14–18, Mk 16:2–6, Col. 3:16, 1 Pet. 2:11–25, 1 Thess. 3:13, 1 Tim. 1:6, Eph. 5 and 6	(cultural) genocide, slavery, indentureship	Uncritical retelling of the Biblical story	In the text	Authoritative	Passivity and docility
Sam Sharpe	Male, Slave	Matt. 6:24, Luke 4:16–18, Col. 3:11		A resistant reading of the Biblical text	Interaction between text and reader		Economic and social reconstruction
William Knibb	Male, Missionary	Luke 4:16–18		Scriptural allusions and quotations	Biblical texts	Formative	Solidarity with victims

Post-"Emancipation" Era: 1840–1959

Socio-historical and Political Realities and Forces
The Economics of Dispossession. The abolition of slavery was essentially a change in the basis of exploiting labour.[56] The race-based ideology of slavery days functioned to ensure the large supply of a domesticated and unskilled labour force. Moreover, freedom was hollow, as those "freed" had no economic (land ownership) and political (say in the decision-making process) power. There was as a triangular hierarchy of domination[57] and pyramidic wealth system based on social stratification which was directly related to a system of property relations: the "Backra" group (White minority at the top) – had economic and political power; these were the Governors, Planters, Attorneys, Government officials, Book-keepers, Artisans and Poor Whites who made up less than 5 per cent of societies; the "Malata" group (Brown, in the middle, included free Blacks) – enjoyed caste privileges, owned property and refused to form any social organization to challenge the status quo given their social position of privilege as well as material and status interests. They made up less than 10 per cent of Caribbean societies; the "Nayga" (Black majority at the bottom) – had no rights and no power; these were overseers, skilled and unskilled labourers, peasants and African and Indian agro-proletarians; and made up over 80 per cent of the population. Emancipation was no more than an intensification of exploitation characterized by the economics of dispossession.

Racially Stratified Society. Slavery, therefore, produced a racially stratified society with wealth concentrated in the hands of the White minority at the top of the pyramid. In this stratified society, to be a person of consequence or worth was to be white or of fair complexion. In addition, throughout the British colonies, with the exception of the Baptists in Jamaica, ecclesiastical affairs and leadership were confined to white expatriates.

Inculcation of British Values. The British being in control was able to transmit their values and interpretation of the Bible and Christianity. Given this position of influence, it was inevitably English values that were inculcated in Africans: education in English, adherence to the Christian religion, which is not inherently English, correctness of speech in English, being known by the company you keep, church membership in an established church community, being of fair complexion and abhorrence of manual or agricultural labour.[58] In other words, in this racially stratified society, to be a person of consequence and worth was to be white or of fair complexion and professedly Christian. And to be black was to be socially inferior.

Furthermore, the British who now constituted a minority ruling class consolidated its hold on power by taking the middle class under its wings. Members of the middle class filled many of the positions in the Civil Service and related organizations. A grateful and pacified middle class, allowed themselves to be anglicized in exchange for the few opportunities for upward social mobility through the attainment of the status symbols of a secondary education, church affiliation and employment, were subjected to a thoroughgoing programme of enculturation into an alien culture: the absorption of the language, customs and worldview of the British. However, while the middle class lacked direct and hard contact with the struggles of the masses, they were unable "to attain the freedoms and economic and political power of the ruling or leisured class".[59] Essentially, the minority British ruling class took on the role of the "father who produced children and had to guard against being supplanted by them".[60]

As such, the context was one of, on the one hand, privilege and power, for the "Backra" minority group, and on the other, powerlessness and inferiority, for the "Nayga" majority group. In the middle, the "Malata" group, who despised association with the "Nayga" majority as such may jeopardize their opportunities for upward social mobility, was itself denied control of the decision-making processes and the forces of production of the society by the "Backra" ruling minority. The guardians were the guards, as the Backra minority group was the guardian and gatekeeper to the Malata and Nayga groups.

The Quest for Political and Economic Self-determination
The post-emancipation era was also one in which the Caribbean peoples and their various governments sought to address their right to name themselves and to determine their own future and way of life. This was an undertaking that was easier said than done. The attempt to galvanize the region into one economic and political bloc, with the formation of the West Indian federation in the 1950s, failed with the withdrawal of Jamaica. Prime Minister of Trinidad and Tobago, Eric Williams' now famous mathematical dictum of, one from ten leaves nought, captured that failure. Never was a more serious blow dealt to regional unity. The Puerto Rican model of industrialization by invitation did not eliminate poverty and unemployment, and so came to nothing. With the US invasion of the

Dominican Republic in 1965, the region was given another lesson in who controlled its right to self-determination.

But all was not gloom and doom. There was a challenge to the neo-colonial order with the Cuban revolution in 1959 that forced other Caribbean countries to search for a development model other than by revolution. If the Haitian revolution marked the awareness that Caribbean peoples were capable of self-determination, then the Cuban revolution ushered in the quest for self-definition.[61] The rise of the Black Power movement in the Caribbean pointed to the fact that poverty could not be dealt with without addressing the issues of race and class in the society. And the formation of CADEC in 1969 (Christian Action for Development in the Eastern Caribbean) sought to wrestle with the question of the causes of underdevelopment and poverty rather than merely offering relief.

Thus, the post-emancipation era was one in which Caribbean peoples were struggling to recover from the trauma of slavery, find themselves and be themselves, and their way forward.

Biblical Interpretive Approaches

In this section, reference is made to the work of Paul Bogle, Marcus Garvey, Rastafarianism and Philip Potter. The social locations of these interpreters are of particular interest, as interpreters read text from within specific social location that conditions interpretation.[62] The reading strategy shared by all four interpreters was primarily one of a critical re-interpretation of the biblical text wherein the reader contributes much to the meaning of the text through social engagement. What is of crucial importance here is the reader's ideological stance and commitment.

Resistant Reading Strategies
Paul Bogle. Paul Bogle, a Baptist deacon and National Hero of Jamaica, and his followers, focused his biblical interpretive strategy on the oppressive material conditions the souls lived in rather than on the need for soul salvation. The base for his ministry operations was the village chapel in Stony Gut in St Thomas-in-the East. For Bogle, the chapel was the seat of the God of justice and the chapel had the responsibility to judge the Courthouse, the dispenser of justice for the people of God. Consequently, the failure of the courthouse to guarantee justice was seen as a symbol of injustice and oppression. The Courthouse, therefore, became the focus for protests in 1865. In Bogle's context and mind, the Courthouse had run afoul of the chapel.

Bogle's religious convictions were shaped by his love of the Psalms and the hymns composed by Isaac Watts, especially those hymns based on the Psalms.[63] It was known that he carried around with him the Psalms of David with supplementary hymns by Isaac Watts.

Bogle's hermeneutical key was the Last Judgement, based on Psalms 11, 50 and 143.[64] Judgement though was not suspended to some far off, future time. In the protest and advocacy of the people, God was dispensing judgement against the present ruling class. Bogle and the people's struggles were against flesh and blood and the Rulers of this Age. Bogle stood in that tradition of the Psalms that held that God wills justice and righteousness (Psalms 96–99). It is the earthly authorities that are responsible to administer justice and righteousness (Psalm 72:1–7), which means precisely the crushing of oppression. Where the lives of the poor and needy are especially threatened and vulnerable, God singles them out for special attention (Psalm 72:12–14; 82). Bogle's praxis, his daily struggle for justice for the poor and his presupposition that God is on the side of the poor, fuelled his advocacy and protests for social justice, and marked his exegetical strategy. In other words, Bogle comes to the biblical text through involvement in and out of a real life context.

Marcus Garvey. Marcus Garvey was born in August 1887 in St. Ann's Bay, Jamaica, some 60 years removed from the "emancipation" of slavery in the Caribbean, and died in 1940. As one of Jamaica's national heroes, Garvey was known more for his political activisms than for his theology. Yet, his politics was never divorced from his religious praxis.

In Garvey's interpretive approach, the focus and the starting point of biblical interpretation was his involvement in the socio-cultural and political realities of the community. The reason for this approach was experiential. The experience of racism that came first in his pre-teen years and later in professional life was of profound effect. His white girl friend was instructed not to communicate with him, on her arrival in Scotland from Jamaica to attend school, because he was black. Likewise, in his sojourns in Latin America as a migrant worker, he became sickened by the subjugation and abuse of Black Workers in the fields, mines and cities on the basis of skin colour. And in the United States of America he saw that the same race-based theory held true as Blacks had to bear the burden of economic and political discrimination, racial violence and the violation of constitutional rights following the Second World War. Principally, Garvey's Biblical reading strategy emerged from his experiences of seeing Blacks regarded and treated as inferior and chattels.

Out of these experiences of racial discrimination, political and economic exploitation, the biblical creation narrative of Genesis and Psalm 68:31 shaped Garvey's understanding of human origin, purpose and emancipation. In time, the Creation narrative, Africa and people of African descent became the organizing principle of his biblical interpretative approach. The fundamental issue for Garvey was that denigration, racial discrimination and political and economic exploitation of Blacks despoiled God's purposes as Creator in the created order.

Garvey posited that human identities have their origin in God. Consequently, this excluded any exclusive claims on God by any race. In the *Universal Negro Catechism* of the African Orthodox church, it was claimed that any race could identify with God. The catechism gave the following responses to the questions posed pertaining to the being and perception of God:

Q. *What is the colour of God?*
A. A spirit has neither colour, nor other natural parts, nor qualities.

Q. *But do we not speak of His hands, His eyes, His arms, and other parts?*
A. Yes; it is because we are able to think and speak of Him only in human figurative terms.

Q. *If, then, you had to speak or think of the colour of God, how would you describe it?*
A. As black; since we are created in his image and likeness.

Q. *On what would you base your assumption that God is black?*
A. On the same basis as that taken by white people when they assume that God is of their colour.[65]

Though it was affirmed here that God was black, this was not to make any exclusive claim. God identifying with humanity did not depend upon race. And even more to Garvey's contention, Blacks were co-equal with all other races. However, while the colour of God was "non-specific", God has a colour when it comes to the perception and the articulation of human realities.

In his *Dissertation on Man*, Garvey claimed that "when God breathed into the nostrils of man the breath of life, made him a living soul, and bestowed upon him the authority of 'Lord of Creation', God never intended that that individual should descend to the level of peon, a serf, or a slave. But rather he should be always man [*sic*] in the fullest possession of his senses and with the truest knowledge of himself ...".[66] In other words, wherever in human relationships ranks were found and potential stifled, these were human inventions and thereby contrary to the creative purposes of God. Thus, the place of Blacks in the world could never be a subordinate one.

Garvey was so consumed by his understanding of God's creative purpose for human beings that this knowledge found its way even into the passion narrative. In an Easter sermon delivered at Liberty Hall, New York City, 16 April 1922, Garvey proclaimed:

> The work of the UNIA for the past four and a half years has been that of guiding us to realise that there should be a resurrection in us, and if at no other time I trust that at this Easter-tide we will realise that there is great need for a resurrection – a resurrection from the lethargy of the past – from that feeling that made us accept the idea and opinion that God intended that we should occupy an inferior place in the world.[67]

Here it can be seen that Garvey's religion had concrete political goals. Garvey founded the UNIA (Universal Negro Improvement Association) in Kingston, Jamaica, 20 July 1914, "as a benevolent or fraternal reform association dedicated to racial uplift and the establishment of educational and industrial opportunities for Blacks".[68] The commitment to racial uplift meant that the work of the UNIA was concerned with both the welfare and well being of the total person. Through its activities and programmes, it was intended that Blacks would have seen themselves as the equal of any race and capable of defining themselves and determining their own future.

Furthermore, self-determination was not the prerogative of one particular race, in this case the White race. For Garvey, the authority that God gave to human beings to regulate human affairs and society and for enjoyment was not given to one particular race. In his *Dissertation on Man*, Garvey wrote:

> After the creation and after man [*sic*] was given possession of the world, the Creator relinquished all authority to his Lord, except that which was spiritual. All that authority which meant the regulation of human affairs, human society, and human happiness was given to man [*sic*] by the Creator, and man [*sic*], therefore, became master of his own destiny and architect of his own fate ... In the process of time we find that only a certain type of man [*sic*] has been able to make good in God's creation.[69]

Consequently, Garvey challenged Blacks to take responsibility for their own liberation and reject the notion that God had ordered their estate. For Garvey, Blacks had a responsibility to themselves for themselves.

Moreover, the key biblical text for Garvey's vision of God's fulfilment of history was Psalm 68:31 *(Princes shall come out of Egypt, Ethiopia shall soon stretch out her hands unto God)*. In the editorial of his Blackman newspaper of 1929, Garvey noted that Ethiopia represented God's special concern for Africa itself and for people of African descent. He observed further that *"stretch out her hands"* had to do with the redemption of Africa from foreign domination as well as the emancipation of all descendants of Africa from structural and systemic bondage that kept them from realizing their full potential as human beings. Garvey spelt out his vision of the future thus:

> The redemption of Africa is a great commission, not only to recover Africa for Africans, but to rescue the souls of Africa's sons and daughters from social, political, economic and spiritual bondage, and place them on a ground of vantage to secure the true uplift of the race, and the general good of the human family. ... Where they (Negroes) find themselves, they can be absolutely loyal citizens and at the same time absolutely loyal to the cause of Africa redeemed. They may build up the nation and government just where they are with great success. They may build up their social, intellectual, political and economic dependence, a common consciousness and a great confraternity of all Negroes all over the world.[70]

In other words, God's fulfilment of history had concrete goals. The hope of Blacks for self-definition and self-determination was not consigned to the not-yet but also to the here-and-now. Hope was essentially a reality within history. Even so, Garvey failed to hold in tension the understanding of the kingdom of God as already being realized in Jesus Christ but not-yet realized in its final or ultimate consummation at the end of time. In addition, while Garvey made effective reference to and use of the ideological interest and social practices of his society, he all but ignored the socio-historic environment of the biblical text.

Intercultural Hermeneutics

Philip Potter

Philip Potter's particular interest and most engaging work is in a universal dialogue of cultures. The promotion and incarnation of a dialogue of cultures is Potter's signal contribution to the ecumenical movement through the World Council of Churches (WCC)[71] that he served from 1967–83. Potter's idea of a dialogue of cultures develops out of his mixed cultural heritage, his international involvement, the call to the unity of the churches worldwide and his vision of the oikoumene (whole inhabited earth), a vision rooted in his interpretation of the biblical story of the Tower of Babel (Genesis 11) and the New Jerusalem (Revelation 21). The interpretive perspective that emerges out of Potter's development of the idea of a universal dialogue of cultures is an *intercultural hermeneutic.*

Potter is a native of the Creole and English speaking Caribbean island of Dominica, which was colonized by both France and Britain. As such, Potter originates from a region that experienced the earliest intensive and violent meeting of cultures.[72] This destructive meeting of cultures was the era of European exploration and domination of the New World in which culture was identified with civilization and thereby led to the shaping of the peoples of the New World and their cultures in the image of Europeans.

As a consequence of his origins, Potter admits that he contains within himself many cultures – Carib, African, Irish, French, and hence oppressed and oppressors, white, black and yellow. Such a mixed cultural heritage means that Potter embodies this dialogue of cultures as part of his inner and outer experience.[73] In other words, the dialogue of cultures is not an abstract idea but a lived reality.

From 1948 to 1990, Potter encountered many different cultures of the world through his international involvement.[74] But for Potter, while "encounters with people from other cultures entail shocks, mistakes, making a fool of oneself, and incomprehension",[75] these experiences did not present a threat. Rather, they afforded opportunities for full potential for human understanding and enrichment. Through his international involvement, Potter's was a voice from the "two thirds world" giving shape and direction to ecumenical thinking and work.

Furthermore, the dialogue of cultures emerges out of the ecumenical endeavour to call the divided churches of the world to covenant together in response to Jesus' high priestly prayer that "They all may be One" (John 17). What Potter found out from this call was that we cannot speak of the unity of the church without at the same time speaking of God's oikonomia (God's economy) or God's design for the unity of humanity. The unity and mission of the church are indivisible. What became critical for Potter in the quest to concretize the oikonomia was a dialogue between the cultures of the world, and hence the need to clarify the meaning of dialogue and culture.

The person who had most influence on Potter's understanding of dialogue was Martin Buber.[76] Potter sums up Buber's ideas this way:

> Real life is meeting. The history of the world is the dialogue between human beings and God. The fundamental fact of human existence is person-with-person dialogue. Where there is no dialogue, no sharing, there is no reality. The basic movement of dialogue is the turning toward the other. The limit of the possibility of dialogue is the limit of our awareness.[77]

Besides, Potter also takes his understanding of dialogue from the Latin word *conversari* (conversation), which means "to turn to another in the sense of to live with, have intercourse with, and keep company with someone".[78] Conversation is a relationship and as such dialogue is not a meaningless and unrelated discourse but a conversation with the environment, culture and other human beings.[79] In this context, culture, for Potter, is "the multiform ways in which people relate to nature and to one another and express these relationships".[80] Here culture is political as it involves decisions and judgement as to how life is lived and organized to ensure quality of life.[81] Fundamentally, therefore, dialogue is relational, a mode of existence (interpersonal), and culture is the inter-relatedness of life in community (interdependence).

Potter envisions this dialogue of cultures as a city. A city is a place of a plurality of cultures experienced as threat, violence and promise whose viability depends on its ability to maintain and open a dialogue of cultures.[82] What Potter does is to root this understanding of city in the biblical story of the Tower of Babel, Genesis 11, and the vision of the New Jerusalem, Revelation 21. Potter sees the Tower of Babel story as that of Empires doing their utmost to homogenize life, which carries with it the idea of expansionism and domination.[83] But failed efforts at homogeneity by Empires are not the last word. The story continues with the call of Abraham and thereby turns from punishment to the promise of blessing (Genesis 12: 1–3). Potter takes "to bless" in Hebrew (*barak*) to mean "to share one's strength, one's being with another, to be with the other".[84] What this means is that "all families of the earth will, by their faith in Abraham's God, be enabled to share their cultures, languages, identities with one another in all their rich variety".[85] So, over against imperial intentions to expand and dominate, in the call of Abraham, there is vulnerability and powerlessness as the way to share life with others.[86] The dialogue of cultures is not about alienating and dominating the other but rather about empowerment, freedom and self-identity.

In Revelation 21, the vision for the New Jerusalem arises as counter-point to the Roman Empire, the very embodiment of alienation and domination, and speaks of not only a new creation but also a new city[87] or the totality of cultures. In the New Jerusalem, the gates, unlike the gate of God in the Tower of Babel story, are never closed. Babel is not so much confusion as a gate or fortress of involuntary submission. In the New Jerusalem, access is free and open to the full variety of all peoples and thus it embodies the place of the universal dialogue of cultures.

This universal dialogue of cultures serves at least two purposes. One, it is the most effective means to recover the dimensions of the human element in all the cultures of the world.[88] Two, it avoids totalizing tendencies of any particular culture and renders irrelevant binary distinctions or moulds of exploiter/exploited, oppressor/oppressed, subject/object, identity/non-identity and in contradistinction promotes community and respect in which human life is appreciated in all its variousness.[89]

In sum, Potter's multicultural Caribbean origins, the fact that he was not limited by the securities and privileges of conventional and institutional structures of the church,[90] his encounters with world cultures and his understanding and vision of city brought about his intercultural hermeneutics. In Potter's intercultural hermeneutics there are at least two movements. One, the consciousness and exposure of the issues that dehumanize and violate life in both the context of biblical texts and the contexts of interpreters. Two, a dialogue concerning the judgements and decision that needs making to ensure full life for All.

Outcome: Quest for Self-identity and Self-determination

Hermeneutic of Authentic Self-affirmation

One of the concrete consequences of the post-emancipation era, which typified the struggle for self-definition and self-determination, was the emergence of *Rastafarianism* in the Caribbean. Rastafarianism emerged and flourished out of a complex of circumstances. One, the harsh economic circumstances in Jamaica in the 1930s that widened the economic gap between the upper and middle and peasant classes;[91] two, the prophecy and call of Marcus Garvey that Black people should look to Africa where a black king shall arise and such will be the day of their deliverance;[92] three, the colonial legacy of colour prejudice where light skin tone was determinative of value and a guarantee to be spared the humiliations and hopelessness of those of a darker hue;[93] four, the foreign control of the decision-making processes and the productive forces of Caribbean territories; and five, the economic and racial stratification that were in sharp relief to the flourishing tourist industry with American tourists flocking to the English-speaking countries in the wake of the Cuban revolution. With the economic and racial landscape dominated and controlled by Whites, Rastafarians reasoned that the roots of Caribbean oppression, exploitation and alienation were in the system of white supremacy,[94] or what Rasta call Babylon. Babylon was an aged and oppressive socio-economic and political system that needed to be dismantled, not simply surmounted.

Thus race and class-consciousness, pan-Africanism, and foreign domination provide not only the complex origins of Rastafarianism but also its epistemological lens in its struggle for identity, cultural freedom, and dignity and in the efforts to make sense of life and of biblical faith. Through these epistemological lenses, Rastafarians rejected as unreal and unrelated the understanding of God as transcendent and as such removed from the harsh experiences of their lived realities. God as immanent, which is a God who is in, rather than above, the fray, of the circumstances of their existential realities, was far more meaningful. God as immanent maintains distance yet relatedness and relationship. Experience, therefore, was definitive of truth about God for Rasta.

In addition, Rastafarians connect their struggle to the biblical existential metaphor of Babylon and Exodus. Babylon stems from a life of alienation and symbolizes all that tends to denigrate African origins and tame the desire for freedom. In effect, Babylon is cultural slavery. The way to liberation from cultural slavery is through Exodus, that is, the search for free cultural identity, dignity and freedom.

Furthermore, for Rasta, salvation is not in 'another world' but in Ethiopia, a specific earthly location of the Promised Land. Ethiopia is important not only for its significance in the biblical world as fulfilment of Psalm 68:31 – "Princes shall come out of Egypt, Ethiopia stretches forth her hands unto God" – but for its revolutionary implications. In 1896 at Andowa, the Abyssinians or the Ethiopians defeated the Italians, a white Western and foreign power. A black king defeating a white army was taken to represent what was possible socially and politically not only of the whole of Africa but of the black race. Religiously, this victory led to a new deification. Not only was a foreign ruler and system overthrown but with it their God. In place now were a black king and a God experience through their lived realities. As such historical knowledge was a weapon of struggle against cultural aspects of the imposition of white foreign values and customs.[95]

Consequently, what we have here is the bold outline of Rasta hermeneutics of authentic self-affirmation, which begins with those existential realities that degrade, denigrate, alienate and disempower humans and then moves to the biblical texts. In turning to the biblical texts, however, Rastafarians do not confine themselves to any sustained interpretation of any one passage or book. Rastafarians "cite up" or proofread biblical passages to suit their warrants.[96] In Rasta hermeneutics of authentic self-affirmation, therefore, what has agency are experience, immanence and historical knowledge, not the biblical texts.

Eisegetics and Exegetics

Biblical interpretation throughout the nineteenth and up to the mid-twentieth centuries concentrated, in the main, on the analysis of a biblical text in its context and the origins of the biblical text in history and culture. The concerns were with such questions as: What did the text mean? And what does it mean? How did the text say what it says? Bogle, Garvey, Potter and Rastafarianism raised questions that were different. Their questions reflected more a concern with applying biblical faith than with exegeting biblical text. In other words, they were far more concerned with addressing the question: what sense and meaning did the material realities of inferiority and political and economic exploitation have in and for a biblical faith which held that there was a just and impartial God? Their interest, therefore, was not only historical but also addressed how biblical faith promoted emancipation from enslaving conditions.

Furthermore, by starting with the human condition, Bogle, Garvey, Potter and Rastafarianism were able to penetrate and expose the inherent contradictions in the constructed opinions or interpretations of the dominant culture. By so doing, they were able to develop a theological stance in which the conception of God was not foreign to one's socio-geographic space. Conversely, a radically different understanding and vision of God's purposes for the well-being of the whole of God's created order also emerged.

Moreover, Bogle, Garvey, Potter and Rastafarianism gave a formative role as opposed to a normative role to the Bible in their method of biblical interpretation. In their interpretive approach, biblical revelation was not for all time, places and people, and thereby confined only to the Bible itself. While it was true that God spoke, it is also true that God speaks still. In addition, one is challenged to re-envision one's world in the light of the analysis of the Biblical text and thereby to make sense of and find meaning in and for their daily existence. The interpretive approach was, therefore, perspectival, as the biblical text is read in a manner allowing existential realities to inform and shape the interpretation of the text. In this way, the meaning of texts is seen to reside in the lived experiences. Thereby one is enabled to envision and develop alternative forms of existence, especially if the prevailing experiences of the social systems and practices are oppressive.

Table 1.3: Biblical reading strategies during the post-"emancipation" Period 1838–1959

Reader/ Interpreter	Social location	Biblical Texts	Socio-historical Realities	Reading strategy	Location of meaning	Understanding of Bible	Consequences
Paul Bogle	Male, Black slave, Baptist Deacon	The Psalms, Ephesians 2:14	Economic exploitation, racially stratified society,	A resistant reading strategy			Rebellion against oppression, frontal attack on the system
Marcus Garvey	Male, Black, social and political activist	The biblical Creation story, the Passion Narrative	inculcation of English values, formation and failure of West Indian Federation, industrialization	A resistant reading strategy	Interaction between biblical texts and reader	Formative	Concrete socio-economic transformation, emergence of Rastafarianism
Rastafarianism	Middle class, proletariat	Liberation: full life for all/life in all its fullness	invitation, invasion of the Dominican Republic by USA, Cuba revolution 1959, formation of CADEC 1973	Hermeneutic of authentic self-affirmation by	Relation between faith and active engagement with the Biblical texts		Challenging the status quo
Philip Potter	Male, middle class, trained theologian Serving the church outside conventional institutional structures			Intercultural hermeneutics			Advocacy for the liberation of all oppressed people

However, the above also make clear that for Bogle, Garvey and Potter the identification of socio-ideological interest and social practices was focused more in the material context of, and less so in the biblical text. This is not to gainsay the effectiveness of the work of Bogle, Garvey, Potter and Rastafarianism. History will show otherwise. Rather, it is to support my claim that to push back biblical texts to their socio-historic environment is but to expose the socio-ideological interests and social practices that produced them as well as the conflict and tension among social forces in that inhabited world.

Even so, the elements of how and why resistance in biblical hermeneutics develops are evident in the biblical interpretive strategies of Bogle, Garvey and Potter. First, their way of knowing, which penetrated into the biblical texts, was through the materiality of their contexts, which were oppressive; second, through religious symbol – the chapel for Bogle, biblical story of creation in the case of Garvey and cultural heritage for Potter, they articulated an alternative social order; and third, camps of interests in conflict were formed. Besides, Bogle, Garvey and Potter came to the biblical texts out of concrete commitment to the struggle for social justice.

Post-"Independence" Era: 1959 Onwards

Socio-historical and Political Realities and Forces
Dependency Syndrome. The post-"independence" era was one of political and economic self-determination in which Caribbean governments and peoples were seeking to build their communities by and for themselves. The efforts fell on hard times. Political self-determination was not matched by economic independence or regional unity. A dependency process was set in train that did more to enforce political and economic dependence for Caribbean countries than it did to foster the ability to determine their own future. The Puerto Rican model of industrialization by invitation during the 1960s was colonialism warmed all over again. With this model, the Caribbean countries' economies were shaped to meet the needs of the industrialized countries, low-wage labour and cheap raw materials were demanded, profits were repatriated to imperial metropolis and expatriates performed all the technically skilled jobs. With an emphasis on creating the right environment for foreign investment (road networks, holiday resorts, the construction of air and sea ports that met international standards, repression of workers' rights), agriculture and agro-based industries were virtually ignored or undeveloped.

Models of Economic Development. Moreover, the alternative models of development, with the exception of the Cuban revolution, tried in the revolutions in Nicaragua and Grenada of 1979 and the democratic socialism of the Michael Manley led PNP (People's National Party) in Jamaica, failed or self-destructed, and not entirely without foreign geo-political influence. The failure of these models of development was accelerated and aggravated by the flight of capital to foreign banks, withdrawal of foreign investments and the bitter medicine of the IMF (International Monetary Fund) with its demands to cut public expenditure and employment. The net result was a weakening of the economies of the territories as they lacked the socio-economic and political power to realize the expectations of full human development and liberation, or self-definition and self-determination, arising out of emancipation in 1838 and the liberation movements of the 1960s through to the late 1970s. The times were despairing.

Right-wing Evangelical Religion. Added to these despairing times was the explosion in the region of the American-inspired right-wing evangelical religion with its emphasis on personal salvation and triumph over earthly struggles and injustices in the hereafter.

Natural and Man-made Disasters. Despairing times got even more despairing with the experiences of natural and "human-made" disasters. Hurricanes became more frequent, powerful and destructive, and volcanoes that were dormant for hundreds of years suddenly became active. On the human front, political tribalism, nepotism and the lucrative drug trade became ways to survive.

The post-"independence" era, then, is one of economic dependence on foreign investments, stagnation and powerlessness. It was also characterized by the search for alternative models of development and the Caribbean peoples' search deep within themselves for freedom, wholeness and authenticity. The character of the times has led one Caribbean theologian, Kortright Davis, to conclude that "emancipation still comin'".[97]

Biblical Interpretive Approaches
In these changing and despairing times, the Caribbean Conference of Churches got involved in the process for self-determination and self-definition by advocating a development model for human liberation and social transformation. In 1971, an historic ecumenical consultation took place in Chaguaramas, Trinidad, culminating two years later in the formation of the CCC (Caribbean Conference of Churches) in 1973. The Caribbean

Conference of Churches declared its intention "to promote the human liberation of our people, and commitment to the achievement of social justice and the dignity of man in our society".[98] Primarily, Biblical events, motifs/tradition and personalities were used to challenge and critique the social order as well as providing the basis and impetus for a model of human development and social transformation.

Critical Re-reading of the Biblical Texts

The Exodus event was employed by Idris Hamid, one of the primary advocates for the decolonization of theology in the Caribbean, William Watty, the most astute of Caribbean theologians, and Bishop Clive Abdullah, a bishop of the Catholic Church in Trinidad. In their interpretation of the Exodus event both Hamid and Watty came away with the understanding that God liberates the oppressed and salvation is liberation. Hamid charged that the churches were captive to the ethos of colonialism – domination and subjugation, unreality and unrelatedness – and thereby could not employ the Exodus motif with its implications for deliverance without calling into question that ethos[99] or condemning itself. For Hamid, the God of the Biblical tradition, from the Exodus to the Resurrection, is a God who leads out from all sorts of bondage, external and internal, even from the bondage of death. This God is unknown in the religious imagination, the every-day-ness of our life as Caribbean peoples; God is experienced as an outsider.[100]

For his part, Watty challenged the notion that Divine sovereignty had to do with power, dominance and privilege. For Watty, the God who liberated from the power of Egypt "was on the side of the weak and oppressed and against the power and the dominance and the privileges which oppressed and dehumanised men".[101] Watty, however, was keen to point out that "a liberation theology comes not out of situation of oppression but out of a community under God".[102] In fact, for Watty, the Exodus story was revisited "*only after* they had been welded into a community under God … in terms which affected their relationships – how they reap their harvests, how they collect their dues and write off their debts, how they care for the weak, the vulnerable and stranger".[103] Thus, a theology of liberation is built on God's purposes as Creator and in the creation,[104] not based solely on the Exodus event.

In his interpretation of the said Exodus event but with an emphasis on the role of Moses, Bishop Abdullah saw that the church in the Caribbean must agitate for the transformation of unjust and inhumane societal structures. He saw the demand that God gave Moses to deliver to Pharaoh

"Let my people go" as the same self-authenticating requirement that was demanded of the Caribbean church to all oppressive powers.[105]

Robert Cuthbert, one of the founders of CADEC (Christian Action for Development in the Eastern Caribbean) in 1969, employed the prophetic tradition (Isa. 65:20–22; Amos 8:4–6; Mic. 4:3–4; Luke 4:16–18). He developed the understanding that development is liberation out of his understanding of the prophetic tradition.[106] For Cuthbert, it is the church that must agitate and set about establishing the conditions for full human development.

Also utilizing the prophetic tradition were Allan Kirton, a former General Secretary of the CCC and Leslie Lett, an Anglican priest and a key figure in the work of the CCC. Kirton turned to the prophet Jeremiah (Jeremiah 33),[107] drawing on the image of disaster to encourage making "an investment in hope"[108] despite the despairing times in the Caribbean. The senses provided the way into the text, in this case seeing. Hope, for Kirton is an act of faith, the substance of things not seen.

Critical Reflection on Praxis
While utilizing both the Exodus and prophet tradition, Leslie Lett, one of the Regional officers of the Caribbean Conference of Churches, advocated a different hermeneutical approach. Lett began the interpretive process with a critical reflection on praxis. Analysis of the socio-political realities and commitment to and involvement in the struggle for social justice came first, as providing the context for interpretation and meaning; and then the move to the analysis of the biblical text armed with an understanding of the social realities.[109] This meant that a process of conscientization of existential realities was introduced into the interpretive process.

This reading strategy – critical reflection on praxis and then analysis of Biblical texts – is identified in the work of a number of Caribbean hermeneutes throughout and beyond the 1970s: Ashley Smith, Burchell Taylor, Noel Erskine, John Holder, Joyce Bailey, Leslie James, Marjorie Lewis Cooper, Nathaniel Samuel Murrell *et al.*[110] For example, John Holder, former principal of the Codrington Theological College, Barbados, pointed out that the hermeneutical approach of Caribbean theologues in the 1970s and 1980s was one in which the Bible was used to speak to and illuminate the experiences of Caribbean people.[111] As such, in his hermeneutical approach, in dealing with the issues of land, identity and leadership, Holder first placed these issues in a Deuteronomical context and then analysed and applied their relevance to the Caribbean.[112]

For their part, the American-inspired right-wing evangelicals engage an interpretive approach that focuses primarily on the literal meaning of biblical texts. Biblical texts are mined for their value in personal salvation and piety, spiritual formation and an otherworldly hope, thereby avoiding addressing socio-political concerns. For these fundamentalists, humanity is basically evil, the present world is beyond redemption and hope lies in the reward of salvation in the after life. This means that that there is a disconnect between engagement with the material realities of the people, the context of the reader, and the biblical text.

What the foregoing shows is that whatever the reading strategy engaged – text to context, context to text – it is the ideological interest and social practice of the reader that dominate, not that of the text, with the possible exception of Watty.

Reading into the Biblical Texts
A markedly different hermeneutical approach is observed in the work of George Mulrain, a distinguished Caribbean theologian and former tutor of the UTCWI (United Theological College of the West Indies), Winston Persaud, a Caribbean Diaspora (USA) theologian, and Joseph Nicholas, a former tutor of the UTCWI, Michael Jagessar, a Caribbean Diaspora theologian, J. Michael Middleton, another Caribbean Diaspora theologian and Althea Spencer Miller, a female Caribbean Diaspora theologian. All six theologians used aspects of Caribbean culture as "texts" for their context of interpretation and meaning in biblical hermeneutics. Mulrain used calypso, Nicholas and Gossai cricket, Jagessar literature and Middleton reggae music.

For Mulrain, a calypso is a narrative folk song.[113] At once, a calypso has to do with methodology (how it says what it says), culture (the way of life of a particular people) and communication (use of the voice as a medium of expression which covers, in this case, the whole spectrum of human experience). The starting point for Mulrain's interpretive approach was belief in the existence of spirits and demons or Jumbie stories, as we called them in some Caribbean countries, and laughter. As an example, for belief in communication between the living and the dead, Mulrain cites the occasion, reflected in a calypso, when two lovers went into a cemetery, for private reasons, and were frightened by a voice, which claimed they were courageous to be consorting on his "abode". After beating a hasty retreat in record time back to civilization, in relief, they recounted the incident to the first man they met in the street. His reply did very little to still their beating hearts:

He said: 'I can understan'
You're a wild young man
But you are not to be blame
When I was alive I was jus' de same.[114]

Mulrain then made the hermeneutical move to Colossians 2:9 and Eph. 6:11–13. As such, without denying the possibility that issues of the living communicating with the dead are judged as cases for psychologists and psychiatrists, calypso exegesis made it possible for text to be interpreted without being demythologized.

Another example alluded to by Mulrain is laughter. One of the characteristics of Caribbean people is their ability to laugh even when the chips are down or to pick up the pieces, smile and move on. Mulrain claimed that the ability to laugh in situations of dread is indicative of a theological concept: in spite of what happens, all things will work for good.[115] In addition, laughing is in itself liberating[116] as one refuses to give in or give up when the going gets rough.

In setting the parameters for his interpretive approach, Persaud's starting point was a socio-cultural analysis of cricket as "text", referring to Rohan Kanhai, an Indo-Guyanese cricketer, as example, and then moving to an exegesis of the biblical book of Ruth.[117] Essentially, Persaud is focusing on the issue of identity in the book of Ruth. In so doing, Persaud ascribes to cricket the religious or sacred designation of "text" that informs and interprets the life of the people in the English speaking Caribbean, even while the Bible remains as the primary religious text. Of the 11 players in a cricket team who took the field, it was important to note who fielded where and who was captain as these "were primary indicators of power and authority, subservience and deference".[118]

Persaud made the claim that a cricket match itself is more than a game or a pastime and instanced Frank Birbalsingh, a writer on "West Indian" cricket, who holds that cricket is "a spectacle that can galvanize a people's spiritual resources, stimulate their national self-esteem, remind them of their place in the world … it recognizes West Indian resistance to an oppressive colonial legacy; for it acknowledges test cricket as the first opportunity that West Indians had of demonstrating their abilities on the international scene".[119] For Caribbean people, cricket is more than a game; it is a reflection of who we are and how we live our lives. Persaud's ascription of cricket as "text", therefore, debunked the stereotypes to demonstrate that the people of the Caribbean, with their history of slavery, are not as marginalized, powerless and essentially inferior as that experience might have implied.[120]

With Rohan Kanhai, an Indo-Guyanese cricketer, his inclusion in the team to tour India in 1958–59 meant that more than cricket was at stake. Kanhai's inclusion in the team was loaded with symbolic meaning because it was an allegorical journey back 'home' for all Indo-Guyanese. In Kanhai, there was a communal identity. The test match to be played at Calcutta was awaited with feigned interest. Calcutta was the port from which Indians were transported to the West Indies, between 1838 and 1917, to work on the sugar plantations. As such, Calcutta was evocative, a metaphor for dislocation, separation, and the loss of traditional certainties.[121] Kanhai did not disappoint, eventually. His 256 in the third test match at Calcutta was hailed as a "gift of newfound identity to a people who were not disgraced in returning 'home'".[122]

Kanhai, though, did not carry in himself significance for Indo-Guyanese only but for all Caribbean peoples. Notwithstanding ethnicity, all the people of the Caribbean share in the history of slavery or subjugation and exploitation. His further success in Australia during 1960–61 series and the unbridled and favourable comments on Kanhai's batting skills and dominance made all Caribbean people felt that they were somebody and mattered.[123]

Persaud's next hermeneutical move was to consider the question: how does cricket as "text" help in reading and interpreting the book of Ruth? In other words, how will his socio-cultural analysis of cricket inform and shape his exegesis of the book of Ruth? In this regard, for Persaud, "Ruth the 'foreigner' *(Rohan Kanhai)* became a symbol of courage and inclusiveness, even to the 'exiled' people *(Indo-Guyanese)* of Israel who had to come to grips with their new 'home' *(Guyana)*"[124] (Emphasis mine).

Unlike Persaud, Nicholas in his work[125] made three hermeneutical moves. He began with an historical critical analysis of the invincibility of Zion in its ancient context. Then he drew comparison between the historical circumstances between West Indies cricket and Zion to show that their invincibility was not due mainly to the strength of their batting defences or superior skills but to their faith in God. And then lastly, an analysis of the socio-cultural significance of West Indies cricket in the light of the theological insights gained from the exegesis of the text.

Both Jagessar and Middleton have observed that some Caribbean cultural artists work from a decidedly biblical theological perspective. Christianity is so interwoven in the life and institutions of Caribbean societies and people that reflection on matters biblical and theological has not been without influence on their work, entirely outside their sphere of interest or beyond their competence. Thus, both Jagessar and Middleton have been able to show how Caribbean cultural artists have made use of biblical theological allusions, concepts and constructs and activated biblical texts as part of their system of meaning and tools of analysis and critique.

For example, one of the ways Jagessar enters the biblical text is through Caribbean literature. Jagessar[126] has acutely observed the use Derek Walcott, a St Lucian and Nobel Peace laureate, made of the Exodus tradition in his work. In his work *What the Twilight Says – Essays* and in a chapter on "The Muse of History" Walcott makes this comment about the Middle Passage: "the passage over our Red Sea was not from bondage to freedom but its opposite (from freedom to bondage) so the tribes arrived at their new Canaan chained".[127] Jagessar uses this inversion of the Exodus as a way of interpreting the Caribbean historical experience of bondage. He goes on to suggest how in doing this, Walcott is in fact opening new vistas for the Caribbean hermeneutes to re-read the biblical narrative in a critical and authentic way rather than buying into liberation theologians' use of the Exodus paradigm.

Even more tellingly, however, Jagessar uses Anansi, an elusive, trickster and anti-establishment figure in Afro-Caribbean folklore, as cultural and discursive partner in deconstructing totalizing tendencies and practices in perspectives on Christianity and the Bible within a Caribbean context. For Jagessar, in a diverse and socio-religious, ethnic and cultural context such as the Caribbean, Anansi is an effective conversation partner "by which to engage biblical texts from a multiplicity of views and not a view".[128] Anansi moves across and between cultures, flouting categories and embodying the "manifoldness of what is".[129] As such, there is a multiversity of ways, through the Anansi optic, by which to understand and interpret social realities.

Consequently, in Jagessar's multiverse hermeneutics, Anansi is the sub-type of the underdog and trickster who functions to unsettle and subvert the status quo and elude to counter hegemony, oppression and pride. For Jagessar, in multiverse hermeneutics, there are some four movements:

1. Alternative God-talk within the context of "space" as opposed to place. The concern here is not about physical dimensions and conditions but the freeing of the mind, the mental faculties, daring to dream, to envision a preferred future.[130]
2. Reflecting the preferred future in arts of resistance praxis. Such resistance praxis involves the dramatic use of jokes, speech, calypso, carnival, and gossiping as acts of retelling and re-envisioning lived realities towards creating a new reality that cannot be easily domesticated,[131] and

3. A search and inquiry into the context of biblical texts, from the perspective of the underdog and trickster, to release and extend biblical texts in lived realities.[132]

4. Indeterminacy of texts and interpretation, that is, puncturing any tendency to lock texts and their interpretation into exactitude. The task of the hermeneute is to unend the interpretation as no interpretation is fixed.[133] Interpretation is dynamic. In other words, all conclusions are challenged and questioned.

Middleton's point of entry into the Biblical texts, especially biblical creation theology built around Gen. 1:26–27, is the lyrics of the reggae music of Bob Marley and the Wailers. Middleton's reading strategy appeals to historical memory and God's intent from the creation of the world as an alternative to the status quo.[134] Middleton's reading strategy perceives how Bob Marley and the Wailers contemporize and extend the biblical story to include Black struggle against dehumanization and degradation. As such, the biblical story of redemption stretches from the Exodus to Marcus Garvey and beyond:

> I'll never forget, no way
> They crucified Jess-us Christ
> I'll never forget, no way
> They stole Marcus for rights
> I'll never forget, no way
> They turned their backs on Paul Bogle
> So don't you forget, no youth
> Who you are
> And where you stand in the struggle.[135]

The appeal to God's purposes as Creator and in the creation challenges the oppressive social relations in the world with a view to reconciliation before the Eschaton. So, in the song "One Love" Marley and the Wailers make a call

> Let's get together to fight this Holy Armagiddyon (One Love)
> So when the Man comes there will be no, no doom (One Song)
> Have pity on those whose chances grow thinner
> There ain't no hiding place from the Father of Creation.[136]

Thus, through this reading strategy, Middleton understands Gen. 1:26–27 as gift of human dignity and a call to responsible action for justice and blessing in a world that belongs to Jah.[137] The function of Gen. 1: 26–27 is, therefore, to "resist the system", that is, to affirm human identity and dignity as the *Imago Dei* in the face of degradation, oppression and domination.

Spencer Miller engages in an act of prophetic imagination by conscripting Lucy Bailey to recognize the trajectory of struggle, survival, creativity and resourcefulness of Caribbean peoples.[138] For Spencer Miller, Lucy Bailey is an icon of Caribbean peoples and their religion.[139] What Spencer goes on to do, by way of example, is to represent Lucy Bailey in a popular Jamaican aphorism – likkle but Tallawah – in her appropriation of Luke 21:1–4. "Likkle but Tallawah" means "small but strong, effective and great" or "we bigger than our size".[140] Though Lucy Bailey was "likkle", small of stature and despite the violent neighbourhood in which she lives, residents and gangsters respect her. So, Lucy Bailey is "tallawah" in mi(gh)et.[141] In comparison, the Widow's mite was her uncomplicated faithful living which unveils the complexities of the insincerity and guile" of the Scribes and Temple system.[142] And the widow's mite was her allegiance to the system that exploited her.[143] Spencer Miller's interest here is to identify and analyse power relationships at work in the text. This she accomplishes by centring her reading strategy in a socio-structural analysis of the text.

Outcome: Economic Dependency Versus Human Liberation and Social Transformation

For the post-independence period, natives undertook the interpretive process. Even with heavy dependence upon the euro-centric historical critical method, because the starting point was existential realities, the interpretive approaches were mainly perspectival and illuminating. The consequence was one of critique and challenge of the social order with the aim of bringing about the social transformation of that order for purposes of social justice, notwithstanding the American-inspired evangelicals with their emphasis on "verticalism" or futuristic and triumphal Christianity.

Eisegetics and Exegetics
Some three reading strategies are discernible from the foregoing:
- Analysis of the biblical text in its contexts and then analysis of the context of the reader in light of biblical texts;
- Critical reflection on praxis or/and analysis of the context of the reader and then analysis of biblical text in its context;
- Culture as "text" then analysis of the biblical text in its context in light of "text" or the culture.

One of the commendable aspects of these reading strategies is the sustained emphasis that is placed on the material dimensions of both text

Table 1:4: Biblical hermeneutics during the post-"Independence" period: 1959 onwards

Reader/Interpreter	Social location	Biblical Texts	Socio-historical Realities	Reading strategy	Location of meaning	Understanding of Bible	Consequences
Idris Hamid, William Watty, Bishop Clive Abdullah	Male, Indian, Black, middle class, trained theologian	Exodus tradition		Critical re-reading of Biblical texts			
Robert Cuthbert, Allan Kirton	Male, Brown, black, middle class, trained theologian	Prophetic tradition	Enforced economic and political dependence, undeveloped	Critical re-reading of Biblical texts			
Leslie Lett, Ashley Smith, Burchell Taylor, Noel Erskine, John Holder, Joyce Bailey, Leslie James, Marjorie Lewis-Cooper, Nathaniel Samuel Murrell	Male, female, black, middle class, trained theologian	Liberation tradition	agriculture and agro-based industries, Nicaragua and Grenada revolutions 1979, withdrawal of foreign investments, IMF demands cut public expenditure and	Critical reflection on praxis	In existential realities/in the text	Formative	Advocacy for human liberation and social transformation
George Mulrain, Winston Persaud, Michael Jagessar, J. Michael Middleton, Althea Spencer Miller	Male, female, black, middle class, trained theologian	Culture as "text"	employment, democratic socialism, American-inspired evangelicalism, formation of CCC	A reading into the Biblical texts	In socio-cultural realities		
Oral Thomas	Male, black, middle class, trained theologian			Cultural Historical-materialist	In socio-historic environment of both text and context		

and context. However, it is observable that the exposure of the nature of social relationships, systems and structures is taking place increasingly in the context and culture, and less so in the biblical text.

Interestingly, as in the case of Sam Sharpe and the slaves, Bogle and Garvey discussed above, resistance is not taking place with the same social effects as a result of the interpretive strategies of those cited in the post-independence period. And this is not due to the fact that they do not give agency to both the materiality of the biblical texts and their contexts. Rather, it is due to the fact that they are doing their interpretive work from within an institutionalized system, not from without and therefore their praxis is more oppositional than resistant. It is a praxis of resistance conjoined with an interpretive strategy that gives agency to the materiality of both biblical texts and the context of the interpreter that result in resistance. Such a praxis will lead to a critique and exposure of and challenge to oppressive systems and practices in society.

Conclusion

As we have seen above, the biblical resistant reading strategy of Sharpe, Bogle and Garvey resulted in concrete socio-economic transformation of oppressive social systems and practices. The critical constitutive elements of this reading strategy were the reading of biblical texts out of a concrete commitment to and involvement in the struggle social justice and the particularity of the socio-economic and historical realities of the context. Where the other reading strategies did not end up in complicity with the status quo (uncritical retelling of the biblical story, scriptural allusions and quotations), they resulted in advocacy for liberation and social change (citing biblical texts, dialogue of cultures, critical re-reading of biblical texts, critical reflection on praxis, a reading into biblical texts). The critical difference between the resistant strategy and the others is praxis. And at the same time, what is missing from all the reading strategies is that agency is not given to the socio-ideological interests and social practices that produced biblical texts. In effect, what we have here in biblical hermeneutical practice within a Caribbean context is a fluid reading strategy that moves from the universal (Bible as the word of God) to the particular (socio-economic and historical realities of the context) and vice versa.

Analysis of hermeneutics within a Caribbean context by Mulrain reflects the fluidity between the universal and the particular. Situating Caribbean biblical hermeneutics within Black theology, Mulrain asserts that in hermeneutics it is the readers' context that is crucial.[144] The readers' context as epistemological lens allows for particular slants to the interpretation of biblical texts and likely results in radical opposition to and confrontation with, though not resistance to, political and economic powers.[145] Here is a biblical reading strategy that moves from the particular to the universal. In the foregoing analysis, the reading strategy from the particular to the universal is characteristic of critical re-reading of biblical texts, critical reflection on praxis and a reading into biblical texts.

However, Mulrain holds "we must not assume that the authors of biblical books were pure and unbiased. They had their points of view and understood God in ways that were unique to them.[146] As biblical texts are subject to bias and written from particular perspectives and out of particular contexts, is it not then essential to deduce that bias, perspective and context in the hermeneutical process? This is a biblical reading strategy that moves from the universal to the particular but which gives agency to the material conditions that produced biblical texts in the hermeneutical process. It is this reading strategy that holds the fluidity in Caribbean biblical hermeneutical practice together. The point is, that whatever the hermeneutical process, or whichever side of the divide the process begins, one must interpret biblical texts such that the material conditions that produced the text are analysed. It matters little where in the hermeneutical process or on which side of the divide this analysis is undertaken, so long as it is done.

Therefore, the fluidity of reading strategy is not the critical issue in biblical hermeneutical practice within a Caribbean context. How the Bible is understood and "read" are the decisive issues. This is not to say that one's social location or epistemology is redundant. On the contrary, the cultural meaning of one's social location is a key in the biblical hermeneutical process. Instead, it is to say that the preference of this study is for a movement from the particular (context) to the universal (biblical text). Even so, wherever the biblical text comes in the hermeneutical process, exegesis of that biblical text for its ideological interests and consequent socio-structural formation and practices cannot be a missing step. Failure to include this dimension may result in the interpreter siding unwittingly with oppressive systems and practices.

In the Caribbean today, self-definition is still unclear and self-determination is still manipulated and controlled by foreign influences and forces. Resisting those foreign influences and forces is still the primary challenge. The challenge is to develop a biblical hermeneutic as a weapon of struggle to resist, not just to oppose, and eventually overthrow those influences and forces.

It is, however, necessary first of all to demonstrate that biblical texts are produced, that there is a socio-ideological and theological agenda as well as social practices at work in their composition. The letter to Philemon provides ample evidence to support this perspective. A further task arising from this process of analysis is to examine whether that agenda and those practices influence hermeneutical practice other than that of the Caribbean. By so doing, the particularities of biblical hermeneutics within a Caribbean context are placed in sharp relief within the wider context of hermeneutics. Fulfilling the tasks of illustrating that biblical texts are products and situating biblical hermeneutical practice within a Caribbean context in a wider context positions one to make proposals for biblical hermeneutics within a Caribbean context and draw implications therefrom.

Notes

1. Brian Gates (ed.), *Afro-Caribbean Religion*, (London: Ward Lock Education, 1980), p. 38.
2. Fernando F. Segovia and Mary Ann Tolbert, *Reading From This Place – Social Location and Biblical Interpretation in the United States Volume 1* (Minneapolis, MN: Fortress Press, 1995), p. 13.
3. Fernando F. Segovia, *Decolonizing Biblical Studies – A View From the Margins* (Maryknoll, NY: Orbis Books, 2000), pp. 147–50.
4. Segovia and Tolbert, *Reading From This Place*, pp. 19–20.
5. Fernando F. Segovia and Mary Ann Tolbert, *Teaching the Bible – The Discourses and Politics of Biblical Pedagogy* (Maryknoll, NY: Orbis Books, 1998), p. 123.
6. Segovia, *Decolonizing Biblical Studies*, p. 43.
7. Mary Ann Tolbert, "Reading For Liberation" in Segovia and Tolbert, *Reading From This Place*, p. 266.
8. Segovia and Tolbert, *Reading From This Place*, pp. 28–31.
9. Ibid., p. 28.
10. R. S. Sugirtharajah, "From Orientalist to Post-Colonial: Notes on Reading Practices" *Asia Journal of Theology*, 10(1) 1996: 20–27.
11. R. S. Sugirtharajah, *Voices From the Margins, Interpreting the Bible in the Third World*, revised and expanded third edition (Maryknoll, NY: Orbis Books, 2006), p. 5.
12. Ibid., p. 72.
13. Ibid.
14. The term comes from Orlando Patterson who holds "slaves were not allowed to integrate the experience of their ancestors into their lives; to inform their understanding of social reality with inherited meanings of their natural forbears; or to anchor the living present in any conscious community of memory" see in *Slavery and Social Death* (Cambridge, MA: Harvard University Press, 1982), p. 5.
15. Richard Peres, *Planters and Merchants* (Cambridge [England], published for the economic history review at the Cambridge University Press, 1960), p. 24; See also

Douglas Hall, "Incalculability as a Feature of Sugar Production During the Eighteenth Century", *Journal of Caribbean History*, 35(1) 2001: 82–83.

16. Hillary Beckles, *Black Rebellion in Barbados, The Struggle Against Slavery, 1627–1838* (Bridgetown: Caribbean Research and Publication Inc., 1987), p. 24.

17. Ibid., p. 24.

18. Angela Davis, *Women, Race and Class* (Reading, UK: Cox & Wyman Ltd., 1981), p. 15; but see also pp. 3–29, "The Legacy of Slavery: Standards for a New Womanhood", where Davis shows that oppression of women is not only a consequence of economic determinism but has multiple causes such as class, race and gender.

19. Noel Leo Erskine, *Decolonising Theology, A Caribbean Perspective*, (Maryknoll, NY: Orbis Books, 1981), p. 39.

20. Don Robotham, "The Development of a Black Ethnicity in Jamaica", in Rupert Lewis and Patrick Bryan, eds., *Garvey: His Work and Impact* (Trenton, NJ: 1994), p. 26.

21. Alfred Caldecott, *The Church in the West Indies, West Indian Studies No. 14*, (London: Frank Cass & Co. Ltd., first published 1898, Reprinted 1970), p. 65.

22. Caldecott, *The Church in the West Indies*, p. 65.

23. Caldecott, *The Church in the West Indies*, p. 65.

24. Elsa Goveia, *Slavery in the British Leeward Islands at the End of the Eighteenth Century* (New Haven, CT, London: Yale University Press, 1965), p. 270.

25. Richard Pares, *Merchants and Planters*, p. 24.

26. E. A. Payne, *The Baptists in Jamaica*, pp. 20–1, quoted in Francis Osborne, S. J. *Coastlands and Islands, First Thoughts on Caribbean Church History*, United Theological College of the West Indies, 1972.

27. Dale Bisnauth, *History of Religions in the Caribbean*, (Kingston: 1989), p. 129.

28. See S. Jakobsoson, *Am I Not a Man and a Brother? British Missions and the Abolition of the Slave Trade and Slavery in West Africa and the West Indies 1786–1838* (Uppsala, 1972), pp. 287, 301–02, 561–62; *Baptist Missionary Society (BMS) Periodical Account V (1813)*, pp. 292–293; J. H. Hinton, *Memoir of William Knibb, Missionary in Jamaica* (London: 1897), pp. 149–150; M. Turner, *Slaves and Missionaries, The Disintegration of the Jamaican Slave Society 1787–1834* (Urbana: 1982), pp. 8–10, 25, 76–77.

29. Fernando F. Segovia and Mary Ann Tolbert, *Teaching the Bible – The Discourses and Politics of Biblical Pedagogy* (Maryknoll, NY: Orbis Books, 1998), p. 123.

30. J. E. Hutton, *A History of Moravian Missions* (London: Moravian Publications Office, 1922), p. 44.

31. Cain Hope Felder, "Racial Motifs in the Biblical Narratives", in R. S. Sugirtharajah, *Voices From The Margins, Interpreting the Bible in the Third World* (Maryknoll, NY: Orbis Books, 1995), pp. 195–8; Here Felder posits that the curse was pronounced on Canaan, Ham's son, and not Ham.

32. William Coleridge, *Charges Delivered to the Clergy of the Diocese of Barbados and the Leeward Islands*, (London: J. G. & F. Rivington, 1835), pp. 263–64.

33. "An Account of the Jamaican Baptists, with memoirs of George Liele", *General Baptist Repository vol. 1 Supplement 1802* (London: printed for the editor by J. Skirven, Ratcliff Highway), pp. 229–40.

34. Ibid., p. 234.

35. Ibid.

36. Ibid., p. 235.
37. Ibid., p. 236.
38. See R. S. Sugirtharajah, *Postcolonial Criticism and Biblical Interpretation* (Oxford: Oxford University Press, 2002) pp. 52–55, who has pointed out that resistant interpreters do not advocate the revolutionary overthrow of oppressive systems and structures. Rather, through and based upon a re-interpretation of the Bible, they seek to establish selfhood and dignity.
39. Edward Kamau Brathwaite, *Wars of Respect, Nanny and Sam Sharpe*, Agency for Public Information, Kingston, Jamaica, 1977, p. 28.
40. Transcript from a Jamaica Broadcasting Corporation TV play entitled *Sam Sharpe* in 1973 written by Edward Kamau Brathwaite.
41. Ibid., p. 30.
42. See Philip Sherlock, *Shout For Freedom: A Tribute to Sam Sharpe* (London: Macmillan Education Limited, 1976), p. x.
43. Mary Turner, *Slaves and Missionaries – The Disintegration of Jamaican Society, 1787–1834* (Barbados, Jamaica, Trinidad & Tobago: University of the West Indies Press, 1998), p. 163.
44. Gayraud S. Gilmore, *Black Religion and Black Radicalism* 3rd edn (Maryknoll, NY: Orbis Books, 1998), p. 29.
45. Edward Kamau Brathwaite, *Wars of Respect*, p. 25.
46. Don Robotham "The Development of a Black Ethnicity in Jamaica" in *Garvey: His Work and Impact*, eds. Rupert Lewis and Patrick Bryan (Lawrenceville, NJ: Africa World Press, Inc., 1991), p. 37.
47. The square in Montego Bay where the rebelling slaves were publicly hanged is named Sam Sharpe Square in their honour.
48. Mary Reckford, "The Slave Rebellion of 1831", *Jamaica Journal* 3 June 1969: 27.
49. Hinton, *Memoir of William Knibb*, pp. 49, 66, 288–9.
50. Ibid., p. 49.
51. Benjamin La Trobe, *A Succinct View of the Missions Established Among the Heathens by the Church of the Brethren or Unitas Fratum, In a Letter to a Friend* (London: M. Lewis, 1771). Letter dated 26 November 1770.
52. R. S. Sugitharajah, *Postcolonial Criticism and Biblical Interpretation*, New York: Oxford University Press, pp. 117–22; see also Gerald O. West, *Contextual Bible Study*, Pietermaritzburg: Cluster Publications, 1993, p. 53.
53. Miguel A. De La Torre, *Reading the Bible From the Margins* (Maryknoll, NY: Orbis Books 2003), p. 4.
54. Itumeleng Mosala, *Biblical Hermeneutics and Black Theology in South Africa* (Grand Rapids, MI: William B. Eerdmans Publishing Co. 1990) p. 11.
55. Pamela J. Milne, "What shall we do with Judith: A Feminist Reassessment of a Biblical Heroine" *Semeia* 62 (1993) Textual Determinacy, Part One, p. 41.
56. Girvan, *Garvey: His Work and Impact*, pp. 15–16.
57. B. W. Higman, *Writing West Indian Histories* (London: Macmillan, 1999), pp. 194–95.
58. Bisnauth, *History of Religions*, p. 202.
59. C. L. R. James, *Beyond A Boundary* (London: Stanley Paul & Co., 1963), p. 52.
60. C. L. R. James "From *Toussaint L'Ouverture* to Fidel Castro" , in *The Black Jacobins* (London: Penguin Books, 1980 3rd edition), p. 317.
61. Anna Grimshaw ed. *The C. L. R. James Reader* (Oxford UK and Cambridge MA: Blackwell, 1992), p. 296.

62. Fernando F. Segovia, *Decolonising Biblical Studies: A View From the Margins* (Maryknoll, NY: Orbis Books, 2000), pp. 5, 9–32.

63. Devon Dick. Masters Thesis unpublished written to advocate that Paul Bogle was a Christian Hero; see also Clinton Hutton, PhD Thesis *Colour for Colour: Skin for Skin* (1992).

64. Ibid., p. 36.

65. Robert A. Hill, (ed.), *The Marcus Garvey and UNIA Papers,* Berkeley, CA: University of California Press, 1983–85, Vol. 111. pp. 302–03.

66. Amy Jacques-Garvey (ed.), *Philosophy and Opinions of Marcus Garvey,* Vols. 1 and 11, p. 24.

67. Jacques-Garvey (ed.), *Philosophy and Opinions: Easter Sunday Sermon*, Liberty Hall, New York City, 16 April 1922, p. 67.

68. Hill (ed.), *Garvey and UNIA Papers,* p. 435.

69. Jacques-Garvey (ed.), *Philosophy and Opinions,* p. 24.

70. Ibid., p. 140.

71. *Cultures in Dialogue,* Documents From a Symposium in Honour of Philip A. Potter, Cartigny, Switzerland, October 3–7, 1984, p. vi.

72. *Cultures in Dialogue,* p. 86.

73. Philip Potter, *Life in All Its Fullness,* Geneva, World Council of Churches, 1981, p. 142.

74. Mission secretary of the British Student Christian Movement (SCM), 1948–50; 1950–54 missionary/Methodist minister in Haiti; 1954–60 secretary of the Youth Department of the WCC; 1960–66 overseas secretary for West Africa and the Caribbean with the Methodist Missionary Society (MMS); 1967–72 director of Commission on World Mission and Evangelism WCC; 1972–83 General Secretary of WCC; 1984–90 lecturer and chaplain at the United Theological College of the West Indies (UTCWI) and University of the West Indies (UWI), Mona Campus, Jamaica. See Michael Jagessar who wrote a book on the life, work and theology of Philip Potter, *Full Life For All*, Uitgeverij Boekencentrum, Zoetermeer, 1997.

75. *Cultures in Dialogue,* p. 86.

76. Potter, *Life in All Its Fullness,* p. 162.

77. Ibid, p. 162

78. Philip Potter, "Towards a Universal Dialogue of Cultures" in *A Vision For Man, Essays on Faith, Theology and Society in Honour of Joshua Russell Chandran*, ed. Samuel Amirtham (Madras: Christian Literature Society, 1978, p. 323.

79. Ibid.

80. Philip Potter, "Culture and the City", *Whither Ecumenism?* ed. Thomas Wieser (Geneva: World Council of Churches, 1986), p. 9.

81. Philip Potter, *Towards a Universal Dialogue of Cultures,* p. 325.

82. *Cultures in Dialogue,* pp. 68–69.

83. Ibid., p. 70.

84. Philip Potter, *Towards a Universal Dialogue of Cultures,* p. 318.

85. Ibid.

86. *Cultures in Dialogue,* p. 71.

87. *Cultures in Dialogue,* p. 71.

88. Philip Potter, *Towards a Universal Dialogue of Cultures,* p. 316; see also Potter, *Life in All Its Fullness,* p. 154f.

89. cf. Jagessar, Michael N., *Full Life For All: The Work and Theology of Philip A. Potter – A Historical Survey and Systematic Analysis of Major Themes* (Zoetermeer: Uitgeverij Boekencentrum, 1997), pp. 227–47.

90. Konrad Raiser "Celebrating and ecumenical pilgrimage: and address to honour Philip Potter on the occasion of his 80th birthday", *Ecumenical Review*, October 2001, p. 523.

91. Leonard E. Barrett, *Soul Force* (New York: Anchor Press, 1974), pp. 182–83.

92. Horace Campbell, *Rasta and Resistance From Marcus Garvey to Walter Rodney* (London: Hansib Publishing Limited, 1985), p. 48.

93. Noel Erskine "Biblical Hermeneutics in Modern Caribbean Experience: Paradigms and Prospects" in Gossai and Murrell, *Religion, Culture and Tradition in the Caribbean*, p. 223.

94. Catherine A. Sunshine, *The Caribbean: Survival, Struggle and Sovereignty* (Washington, DC: EPICA Publications, 1985), p. 53.

95. Robert Beckford, *Dread and Pentecostal* (London: SPCK, 2000), pp. 114–15.

96. Noel Erskine "Biblical Hermeneutics in Modern Caribbean Experience: Paradigms and Prospects", pp. 221–24, and Nathaniel Samuel Murrell "Dangerous Memories, Underdevelopment, and the Bible in Colonial Caribbean Experience", pp. 28–32 in Gossai and Murrell, *Religion, Culture and Tradition in the Caribbean.*

97. "Emancipation still comin" is also the title of Kortright Davis' book *Emancipation still comin': Explorations in Caribbean Emancipatory Theology* (Maryknoll, NY: Orbis Books, 1990).

98. *Called To Be*, pp. 23–24, 33–34.

99. David I. Mitchell ed., *With Eyes Wide Open* (Kingston, Jamaica: 1973), pp. 123–26.

100. Ibid., p. 122.

101. Idris Hamid ed., *Troubling of the Waters* (San Fernando, Trinidad: Conference on Creative Theological Reflection, 1973), pp. 70–71.

102. William Watty, *From Shore to Shore: Soundings in Caribbean Theology* (Barbados: CEDAR Press, 1981) p. 45.

103. Ibid., pp. 44–45.

104. Ibid., p. 45.

105. Ibid., p. 17.

106. Mitchell, *With Eyes Wide Open*, p. 111.

107. Allan Kirton and William Watty eds., *Consultation for Ministry in a New Decade* (Barbados: CADEC, 1985), p. 5.

108. Kirton and Watty, *Consultation for Ministry*, p. 6.

109. Leslie Lett, "Working for Peace in the Caribbean" in *Peace: A Challenge to the Caribbean*, ed. Allan Kirton (Barbados: CADEC, 1982), p. 27.

110. See Hemchand Gossai and Nathaniel Samuel Murrell, *Religion, Culture and Tradition in the Caribbean* (New York: St Martin's Press, 2000).

111. John Holder, "Is This the Word of the Lord?" in Hemchand Gossai and Nathaniel Samuel Murrell eds. *Religion, Culture and Tradition in the Caribbean* (London: Macmillan, 2000), p. 136.

112. Ibid., p. 136.

113. See George M. Mulrain "Is There a Calypso Exegesis?" in R. S. Sugirtharajah ed. *Voices From The Margin, Interpreting the Bible in the Third World* (Maryknoll, NY: 1995), p. 39.

114. Ibid., p. 43.

115. Ibid., p. 42.

116. Ibid., p. 44.

117. See Winston Persaud, "Hermeneutics of the Bible and 'Cricket as Text': Reading as an Exile" in Fernando F. Segovia, *Interpreting Beyond Borders* (Sheffield: Sheffield Academic Press, 2000), p. 175–88.

118. Ibid., p. 176.

119. Ibid., p. 177.

120. Ibid., p. 178.

121. Ibid., p. 181.

122. Ibid., p. 180.

123. Ibid., p. 182.

124. Ibid., p. 183.

125. See Joseph Nicholas, "West Indies Cricket and Biblical Faith" *Caribbean Journal of Religious Studies*, 13 (2), September 1992–April 1993: 23–30.

126. Unpublished Master's Thesis entitled "A Theological Evaluation of Wilson Harris' Understanding of Community as reflected in the 'Guiana Quartet', An Interdisciplinary Study of Theology and Caribbean Literature" (Jamaica: University of the West Indies, 1992).

127. Derek Walcott, *What the Twilight Says – Essays* (London: Faber & Faber, 1998), pp. 36–64.

128. Michael Jagessar and Anthony Reddie, *Postcolonial Black British Theology – New Textures and Themes* (Peterborough: Epworth, 2007), p. 126.

129. Ibid., p. 129.

130. Ibid., p. 177.

131. Ibid., pp. 136–38.

132. Ibid., pp. 137–38.

133. Michael Jagessar, "Unending the Bible: The Book of Revelation Through the Optics of Anancy and Rastafari"; unpublished paper presented at the Black Theology Annual Conference on Reading and Re-reading the Bible, 27 July 2006, Queens College, Birmingham, p. 12.

134. Gossai and Murrell, *Religion, Culture and Tradition* p. 182.

135. From the *Exodus* album by Bob Marley and the Wailers (Island Records, 1977).

136. Ibid.

137. Gossai and Murrell, p. 183.

138. Kathleen O'Brien Wicker, Althea Spencer Miller and Musa W. Dube eds. *Feminist New Testament Studies, Global and Future Perspectives* (New York: Palgrave Macmillan, 2005), pp. 211–14.

139. Ibid., p. 213.

140. Ibid., p. 214.

141. Ibid., p. 234.

142. Ibid., p. 234.

143. Ibid., p. 234.

144. George Mulrain "Hermeneutics within a Caribbean Context" in R. S. Sugirtharajah ed. *Vernacular Hermeneutics* (Sheffield: Sheffield Academic Press, 1999), p. 122.

145. Ibid., p. 122.

146. Ibid., p. 127.

Chapter 2

ANALYSING BIBLICAL HERMENEUTICAL PRACTICES WITHIN
THE CARIBBEAN

Introduction

"On the ground", that is, in weekday Bible study sessions, Sunday school classes, roadside preaching and devotions in homes, biblical hermeneutics within a Caribbean context, in the main, is a leader-centred activity. Though reading the Bible receives much purchase in the privacy of homes devotionally, it is principally in the worship experiences, weekday Bible study sessions and Sunday school classes that the Bible gets interpreted. In these experiences and sessions, the purpose for reading and interpreting is for the nurturing of faith and having "a faith that is relevant to what people face every day of their lives".[1] As such, "on the ground", in a Caribbean context, biblical hermeneutics is undertaken to satisfy both ecclesiological and personal functions.

What happens, therefore, is that in biblical hermeneutics, in large measure, the Bible is not read and interpreted by a community of interests or from the point of view of community interests. Mulrain recognizes the necessity, relevance and consequences of reading biblical texts as a community by pointing out that:

> Maybe it is "safer" to apply the Bible to individual situations. In so doing, you address individual sins and shortcomings and point to the need for individuals to be saved. Once you read it through the eyes of the community or society or nation, then you find yourself radically opposed to and confronting political and economic powers.[2]

The point is that reading biblical texts from the interests of the community and as a community of interest rather than as a leader-centred activity carries with it the possibility of societal and systemic transformation, not just nurturing faith and having a relevant faith. In addition, merely reading the Bible to nurture faith and for having relevant faith whilst not seeking to critique, transform and challenge oppressive societal realities blunts the Bible as a cultural weapon of struggle for social change.

The contention here is not to assert that the Bible is not read within a Caribbean context. It is read. Rather, the argument concerns how it is read. In other words, what are the beliefs, assumptions and practices that are brought to bear on the reading process? What part do social location, gender, ethnicity, hybridity, lived realities and history play in the act of reading and making sense of biblical texts? Is there awareness in the reading or listening strategies that biblical texts are mixed with the voice of dominant interests and the silencing of the voice of the oppressed? Which voice do Caribbean people listen to and act upon? The fact is "the strategies one employs in reading a text will depend in large part upon what one's overall disposition is towards the act of reading itself ... texts are read not only within contexts; a text's meaning is also dependent upon the pretext(s) of its readers".[3] Contextual realities condition reading and they are just as critical as those social realities out of which biblical texts emerged.

Biblical Hermeneutical Practices "On the Ground"

In order to develop a clearer picture of biblical hermeneutical practices "on the ground", or prevalent within a Caribbean context, the results of exercises carried out in some six Caribbean islands – Antigua, Dominica, St Lucia, Barbados and St Thomas (United States Virgin Islands) are shared. The results of these exercises are discussed in light of the issues arising from the reading strategies and their consequences from the three periods of Caribbean social history discussed above.

Three reading strategies surfaced from the exercises in response to the question, how would you go about interpreting Philemon? What reading strategy would you use to interpret this letter? The reading strategies which emerged are on the text, the text as it stands and interest in universalities. I will discuss each in turn.

On the Text

First, *on the text*, the meaning of the text for lived realities was the predominant reading strategy identified. Participants mined verses within a paragraph for insights into how the text says what it says. This approach of exploring mainly grammatical structure, key words, meaning of words and characterization meant that participants focused more on the rhetorical features of the letter and less on the material circumstances that gave rise to the writing of the letter. Below is a flavour of the hermeneutical practices, by way of example, from the transcript of an ecumenical study group of some 25 persons in Antigua, giving their reading strategies, insights and comments on the verses:

vv.1–3   Paul states that he is a prisoner of Christ;
           the church meets in Philemon's house;
           nature of prison life in Rome;
           letter is written to Philemon and not the house meeting in his house;

vv. 4–7   thanksgiving

vv. 8–16   humility of Paul; appeal on the basis of love;

           Onesimus as Paul's convert.

           Onesimus went to prison to seek Paul's help (Divine purpose); Onesimus ran away because he wanted freedom; no one wants to be a slave.

           In that time, it was natural for persons to have slaves; and run-aways are put to death or other consequences; Paul was appealing to Philemon's Christian beliefs and practices in pardoning Onesimus. Paul was using his influence being a close friend to Philemon to accept his former slave as friend and a Christian because he was converted in prison and a great help to Paul in preaching the good news. He wanted Philemon to soften his heart and forgive.

           These passages speak of forgiveness, accepting each other, breaking the social barriers of status; self-acceptance. They speak of faith and the quality of Christian faith.

           Seemingly Paul was presumptuous without compelling Philemon.

           Philemon must forgive Onesimus on the basis that Onesimus was a converted man and now a brother in Christ.

           Onesimus is to return not a slave but a mission partner; what has changed is his role, not his status.

           Slavery is unacceptable yet the means of freedom must be the proclamation of the Gospel, not the killing of the slave master or the overthrow of the system indirectly;

           Onesimus' freedom was physical, not spiritual; and the change of ownership was not physical but spiritual.

           Did Onesimus' changed life have anything to do with him running away? Was his life changed before he ran away? Who has the power when one runs away? Did Onesimus conversion come about in prison? There is a freedom that binds and a bondage that liberates.

           The right belongs to Philemon to free Onesimus.

v. 17-25   Paul's willingness to take responsibility;
radical Paul: due to their debt to Paul they should accept Onesimus.

Paul's plea for a new relationship of love;

Making it possible for there to be spiritual fellowship, this is what
it means for Philemon and Onesimus to be brothers.

As may be observed from this reading strategy, where interpretation
does not wrestle with the material circumstances out of which biblical
texts emerged, it permits the spiritualizing of insights. For example, some
participants acknowledged that slavery was unacceptable and that where
there was genuine repentance social activism is inevitable. Yet the same
participants advanced the idea that the means of freedom must be the
proclamation of the Gospel, rather than challenging the exploitative and
oppressive system of slavery based on their understanding of the Gospel.
As such, freedom is spiritualized as deliverance from oppressive habits,
not oppressive structures and systems.

Text as it Stands

Moreover, seldom was an in front of the text approach used. With all the
participants having a slave history, one would be forgiven for taking for
granted that slavery might be employed as the epistemological lens. Instead
participants interpreted the *text as it stands*. When slavery was referenced
as a lens, there was general agreement that such would have served to
contextualize interpretation. Here is the commentary on the letter by one
group that gives an appreciation of reading the text as it stands:

> Paul wrote to specific individuals while he was imprisoned. Paul was asking
> for forgiveness for Onesimus for running away from his master. Paul
> converted Onesimus to Christianity and Paul considered him as his son and
> sent him back to his master as a brother in Christ. Paul used strong arguments
> to appeal for love and acceptance for Onesimus. Once a person has accepted
> Christ, forgiveness is very important in that person's life. Sin enslaves; we
> can become slaves to sin by continuing with things that are wrong. Christ
> died to free us from this kind of slavery. Even though Paul was in prison, he
> still showed love and compassion for Onesimus. We, too, should show love
> and compassion to our fallen brothers and sisters through our prayers and
> actions.

This commentary shows no interest in dealing with the social structures,
practices and systems that defined the nature of the relationship between
Philemon and Onesimus and the society in which they lived. Instead, it
sees the personal and emotional aspects of the relationship between
Philemon and Onesimus as the significant issues, with its concentration

on forgiveness, love and compassion. Even so, a material understanding of love and compassion as the willingness to take risks or to care for the other in a way that causes the other's fate to affect one's own or to give to the other at the real cost of oneself[4] gives significance to the material nature and conditions of the relationship and society. As a consequence, the commentary does not demonstrate the understanding that slavery is caused by bondage to oppressive structures and systems and thereby limits the understanding of slavery to binding personal habits or sin. Further, the understanding of salvation derived from this understanding of slavery is limited, too, to liberation from guilt and sin, not from unjust social structures and systems that destroy people's lives.

Interest in Universalities
Further, more *interest was shown in universalities than in casual particularities*. In other words, participants were less inclined to deal with the social implications of their exegetical results. One would have thought so with participants since this letter to Philemon bespeaks a context of social inequality and distinction. This disinclination, however, was in answer to the issue of *what the letter to Philemon is about*. For participants, the letter to Philemon is about reconciliation, understood as the forgiveness of wrongs committed against another in the past. Besides, participants identified a number of socio-historic, economic and theological issues that do have social implications but they did not see these as the main focus of the letter:
  • What makes a brother a brother?
  • If Onesimus were not converted, would he still be a brother?
  • Philemon and Onesimus are brothers in Christ in that there is a change in being, doing away with social distinctions, not material circumstances; and
  • How is freedom in and through Christ to be understood?

Possible Reasons for Reading Strategies

Not Seeing Texts as Products
One reason for the reading strategies highlighted in the findings of the empirical study is not seeing texts as products. Where biblical texts are not pushed back to their socio-historic foundations, it is difficult for consequent interpretation to examine those issues arising from the biblical text for their social implications. As Norman Gottwald notes "an unstructural understanding of the Bible, that is, the history of social forms and ideas

from biblical times to the present, leads to or reinforces or confirms an unstructural understanding of the present".[5]

This approach of not seeing biblical texts as products allows for a spiritualized interpretation. Such spiritualized interpretation is void of working out the social implications of its interpretation and thereby leaves the offending or offensive system unaffected. For instance, some participants took the purpose of the letter to Philemon as an appeal for reconciliation between Philemon and Onesimus. So, Onesimus returns to his master Philemon as a brother in Christ, which means that social distinctions are removed while social inequality remains entrenched. Again, the system remains unaffected. For biblical hermeneutics to be meaningful and used as a weapon in the struggle for social justice, it must have social transformation, not personal morality only, as its purpose.

Reading Out of the Text

Even more significant were the issues that were not raised and questions that were never asked, since all the participants had a slave history and since on the text was the predominant reading strategy. Little attention was paid either to the issues of the denial of Onesimus' personhood, silence of Onesimus in the letter or to the questions: was running away an act of resistance and hope? What kind of value or belief system did the letter promote? How did the social relations of power affect the livelihood of the members of the house church and household in the letter? This disinterest poses a question: why a people who have had a history of subjugation and exploitation and live in an underdeveloped society did not come to Paul's letter to Philemon through the epistemological lens of marginalization, domination, resistance, ideology and power? One response is that participants focused more on the location of meaning (text as text) rather than on social location (text as means). In other words, participants sought to *read out of the text* rather than into the text.

Tradition

Another reason is *tradition*. By tradition one means the accepted way for many a year in which confessional bodies teach and study the Bible. In fact, for some 15 years as a Christian minister in the Methodist church, and I am not singular in this, I conducted Bible study by what Paulo Freire, a former professor of philosophy of education in Brazil and best known for his works on literacy as a weapon of social change,[6] calls the banking system of education. The banking system of education takes for granted that learners are empty vessels to be filled.[7] The traditional approach requires me standing before some ten or 15 persons and expounding to them from the chosen book or passage verse-by-verse or by paragraphs of a chapter or chapter-by-chapter, with occasional questions or comments from the group. In other words, it is the minister or leader who is the fount of knowledge, or the "expert" from whom participants must learn. This traditional way of teaching and studying the Bible, that remains unchanged to date, is but the offer of a ready-made interpretation that can only lead to application of that which is "taught". In effect, what the traditional reading strategy takes as method is really content. What is needed is for the "expert" to facilitate learning rather than impart knowledge.

What is little observed and questioned is that the social location of the "expert" is often more privileged and elitist that the members he or she teaches. After the Bible study session, the pastor leader in many cases drives to the suburbs and those who attended the session go off to their rural abodes. Such a contrast in social location holds out slim possibilities for any examination and exploration of biblical texts for socio-structural analysis, beginning with a socio-structural analysis of social realities. Such a hermeneutical undertaking is a threat to privilege and undermines it. By the same token it is complicit implicitly with the status quo, however oppressive.

Trust Invested in the Trained Interprets the Bible

This banking method of studying and teaching the Bible has bearing on the fact that so much authority and trust is invested in those who are trained to interpret the Bible, and entrusted to lead congregations.[8] But this leads to the issue of where those in whom authority is placed get their authority to interpret the Bible. In other words, who decides the meaning of biblical texts, as biblical texts cannot interpret themselves? So, who generates meaning? Who has the authority – text or "expert"? And as such what then becomes the role of the reader or the interpretive community?

Hermeneutical Presupposition

Furthermore, the *presupposition* with which participants came to the letter to Philemon is another crucial factor. The willingness to spiritualize interpretive results is indicative of the view that justice and grace, politics and religion, in interplay with social relations of power, must stay separate. Thus, for the participants, reconciliation does not have socio-economic dimensions.

In spite of this, even if where you stand is compromised or penetrated, that is where you stand. And that social location still determines what you see. Whilst they may not have to come to the letter to Philemon – their epistemology, way of knowing into the text – through the lens of their social history but that does not remove them from where they are standing. For all one knows they may be standing at a place where they have been brainwashed, colonized, suffering from mental slavery, but that is still a place. What you see does depend on where you stand. The challenge is to have them "stand" in a place or places where they can "see".

Cultural Illiteracy
The failure to come to grips with the socio-ideological dimensions of biblical texts and lack of political awareness observed in the reading strategies of participants may reflect the fact that the participants were not sufficiently attuned to hermeneutical suspicion or sufficiently conscious of the critical value of social location in biblical hermeneutics. Even so, there is no disinterested reader of biblical text. A hermeneutical suspicion in questioning what factors gave rise or cause to master and slave in the society and the consciousness that who we are, what we believe, where we are from are all genuine aspects of the interpretive process might have yielded a different understanding and interpretation of Philemon. This failure to be so attuned and conscious is reflective of what happens when one's social location is compromised culturally, suffers from cultural imperialism or penetration, that is, where there is buy-in to foreign values, customs, language and ideology. An excuse albeit but reality nonetheless as it exposes one of the lasting legacies of slavery and the way Christianity has been used to enslave people mentally.

Reflective Summary

In sum, what the research experience in full points to is the need for biblical hermeneutics within a Caribbean context to give deliberate attention to the reader, who is reading what, and how; in other words, for analysis of the Caribbean reader of biblical text, which includes not only the psychosocial dimensions but the socio-geographic space. Ralph Gonsalves, a Caribbean social commentator and critic, has charged: "Our geographic space has been more influential in determining our being than our history ... our geography and history jostle".[9] Caribbean biblical hermeneutes need to bring that whole issue of the cultural meaning of being, the socially and historically conditioned situated reader[10] – sexuality, ethnicity, gender, class, ideology and religion – into the hermeneutical experience. No one comes to the text *tabula rasa*. All readers come to the biblical text positioned and interested.[11] Every interpreter has an address and falls within a class in society.

Moreover, what the research experience shows is that participants are far more interested in deepening their knowledge of the biblical texts rather than in biblical texts as cultural weapons in the struggle for social change and transformation. Seemingly, the purpose of Bible study is to "indwell" the insights of the biblical text over against "embodying" its lessons. Where "indwelling" takes priority over "embodying" in the study of the Bible, biblical texts are neutered and there is no need either to take action or sides.

Reading Strategies from Caribbean Social History

Furthermore, from the reading strategies extrapolated from Caribbean biblical hermeneutical practices, one sees no homogeneity of reading strategy. Below, is outlined reading strategies for the different periods of Caribbean social history and conclusions drawn there from.

Reading out of the text was the reading strategy utilized mainly by the missionaries, namely Zinzendorf, Bishop Coleridge and Liele. Though Knibbs, too, was a missionary, he sided with the natives to read text against the colonizer, the class to which he belonged. Nibbs, therefore, was a dissident and as such engaged in a dissident reading strategy, which resulted in solidarity with the victims of the system.

Table 2.1: Reading strategies the missionaries during the colonial period

Period	Reading strategy		
Colonial	reader (missionaries) male, middle class privileged slavery as natural to socio-economic and political order	text as text a reading out of the text proof-texting	context
	Consequence: Uncritical support for the establishment.		

Conclusions:
- Who the reader is and how the biblical text is read matter.
- Whatever the social location, the reader is always positioned and interested.

- An uncritical retelling of the biblical text leads to escapism, passivity and docility and thereby a reinforcing of the status quo.

Hence, where no agency is given to the materiality of biblical texts and the context of the interpreter and biblical texts are not read with any critical consciousness of social location and from concrete commitment and involvement to social struggle, there is no resistance to oppressive systems and structures. Besides, there was no separating of oneself and the church from the oppressive plantocracy system and denouncing that system as contrary to God's just creational purposes.

Table 2.2: Reading strategy of the slaves during the colonial period

Period	Reading strategy			
Colonial	reader	praxis/experience	context	text as message
	(enslaved Africans) male, oppressed, discriminated against fighting for freedom, justice and a vindication of rights	a reading into the text a resistant reading		
	Consequence: Socio-economic and political reconstruction.			

The reading strategy of enslaved Africans was markedly different from the missionaries, though it took place in the same era and they were reading from the same Bible.

Conclusions:
- A resistant reading comes from those whom the system deprivileges.
- A resistant reading leads to a reconfiguring of the social system.
- A resistant reading leans hard towards being revolutionary but not necessarily to a revolution. According to Chris Mullard, resistance has a negative and a positive dimension. On the negative side, for Mullard, resistance targets the ruling class and justifies its actions, its alternative and utopian beliefs and values.[12] Positively, resistance aims to construct and acquire power and replace ruling class ideology and systems with that of its own based on its alternative and utopian beliefs and values.[13] As such, resistance is about the quality of the change it effects (revolutionary), not the manner of that change (revolution).
- Where your socio-economic status is not determined by birth or participation in the commanding heights of the economy, your access

to power and privilege or human dignity is blocked. Thus, your social location is subordinate. However, at whatever point or stage such blockage occurs, it results in outrage, rage and alienation,[14] all of which brings about a vision for a different reality. A change of social system, which allows for partnership and participation, will give access to power and privilege to the marginalized and engender human dignity.

Accordingly, resistance became both probable and unavoidable with the protecting of privilege and socio-economic and political power by the ruling elite by exploitative and oppressive means and the failure of the church to protect the vulnerable and exploited. The fact that biblical texts

Table 2.3: Reading strategies during the post-"emancipation" period

Period	*Reading strategy*			
Post-"emancipation"	reader	praxis	context	text as message
Bogle	hope: a reality within history questioned the status quo oppressed/deprivileged	conflict between courthouse (justice) and chapel (grace)	a reading into the text a resistant reading	
	Consequence: rebellion against and a frontal attack on the system			
Garvey	racism, struggle against Despoils God's purposes as Creator and in the creation		a reading into the text (a resistant reading)	
	Consequence: organizational attack on the system			
Rastafarianism	Oppressed/ Deprivileged and for self-determination and self-definition	struggle against downpression	a reading into the text (a resistant reading)	
	Consequence: challenge to reconstruct the system			
Potter	middle class Questioned the establishment within a system (church & academy)	struggle against domination and for fullness of life but from	an intercultural reading	
	Consequence: advocacy for the transformation of unjust systems			

were read from a concrete commitment to and involvement in social justice issues provided the vision of and hope for an alternative social order. Also, the slaves separated themselves from the oppressive social system, denounced the social system as unjust and set about to usher in God's rule on earth as it is in Heaven.

Conclusions:

- Those whom the system deprivileges develop a resistant reading of biblical texts, which leads to an attack on or challenge to oppressive social systems and practices; whereas those privileged by the social system and structure and thereby struggle from within the system, lead to advocacy.

- A resistant reading of biblical texts exposes the socio-ideological agenda and practices at work in the social system and structure.

- With a resistant reading strategy to take biblical text as products mean that the class, economic, cultural, political, theological and ideological interests, values, beliefs, ideas in the biblical text are conjoined with the class, economic, cultural, political, theological and ideological interests, values, beliefs, ideas of the reader. That conjoining of the biblical text and the context of the interpreter enables critique and exposure of the social system of both text and context with the avowed intention to bring about both a new person and a transformed socio-economic order.

- Further, resistant reading ensures that the reader not only recovers the voice of the oppressed buried in the biblical text but is not aligned with ruling class ideas and interests.

- Biblical texts were read out of a concrete commitment and involvement or struggle and from the perspective of the marginalized, dispossessed and underdeveloped or in contexts of underdeveloped societies. For Bogle, it was the courthouse and chapel; Garvey emphasized racism and humanity as created in the image of God; Potter stressed domination and selfhood; and Rastafarianism highlighted downpression and self-definition and self-determination.

Inevitably, since oppression was perceived as caused by the social system, the dominant voice embedded in biblical texts identified, biblical texts read from concrete social commitment and involvement and biblical texts served as the ground and impetus for an alternative social order, resistance was the result. Moreover, resistance occurred as the exegetes stood outside the social system and condemned it as inimical to the well being of the community and in conflict with the rule of God.

Table 2.4: Reading strategies during the post-"independence period

Period	Reading strategy			
Post- **"emancipation"**	reader	praxis	context	text as means
Idris Hamid *et al.*	middle class Female	struggle for development And self-deter	a contextual reading	
	questioned the status quo	mination but from within a system (church and academy)		
	Consequence: advocacy for the transformation of unjust systems			

Conclusions:

- A contextual reading of biblical text leads to advocacy, not revolutionary change of the social system.
- Those in institutions are caught between ideological commitment and stance and struggle to remain faithful to specific or certain traditions, while at the same time wanting to break down hegemonic and oppressive systems and structures of that tradition.

As a consequence, the interpreter may have a suspect praxis and thereby not entirely free from co-option by and complicity with the status quo. Equally the social system is being challenged from within and not from without and resistance therefore loses its revolutionary edge. In other words, though proclaiming the rule of God was heralded, its authenticity and integrity were questionable as the separation from the social system and declaring it as deplorable by those complicit with the status quo was not entirely convincing.

Table 2.5: Reading strategy by the Fundamentalists

(Fundamentalists)	reader	text as text	life (eternal)
	middle class proletariat divorce between religion and politics	a reading out of the text	
	Consequence: an otherworldly orientation		

Conclusions:

- Social location, hermeneutical suspicion and contextual realities, seemingly, neither influence nor condition the hermeneutical process. Social experiences do not inform the reading of biblical texts. And this is in view of the fact that the movement fundamentally concerns survival in the midst of the marginality of life. Such has led Garnet Roper, a Pentecostal pastor, to charge "while Pentecostalism and Evangelicalism are *in touch* with the masses, at the same time, it is not *for* the poor ... they speak *from* the position of the underclass without speaking *for* them".[15] So, conceptually, the Bible is the infallible word of God and source of irrefutable truths. It is the Spirit that provides agency, not social circumstances.
- Justice is postponed in favour of a crude Adventism;[16] individuals are so driven by the satisfaction of their charismatic experience and personal possession of the Holy Spirit and confidence in the outcome of all history as to be disinterested in this-worldly concerns.
- Meaning resides in the biblical text and is, therefore, determinate.

Consequently, with no interest in identifying the dominant voice embedded in biblical texts, or in systemic inequities and inequalities and a disjuncture between faith and praxis, resistance does not happen and the ethic of resistance is turned on its head. However, the separation from oppressive social system that takes place here is not to demonstrate a different ideological stance and commitment. Rather, it is to publicly and harshly critique an oppressive social system, as a consequence of heralding God's justice.

Table 2.6: Reading strategies during the post-"independence period

Mulrain, Persaud, Jagessar	reader	praxis	culture as "text" context	text as product
Spencer Miller, Middleton	middle class male,	struggle for identity, hybridity,	a reading into the text	
	question the status quo	multi-logues, inclusiveness, embrace of indigenous culture but from within a system (church and academy)	a cultural reading	
Consequence: advocacy for cultural relevance				

Conclusions:
- Meaning takes place in the interaction between "worlds".
- Whatever the analysis of the reader, however the text is taken and in whatever manner the text is approached, where the praxis is within a system, the consequence is advocacy, not revolutionary change of the socio-economic structure.

Here, the intention is not so much to resist as being relevant in culturally diverse and changing contexts. Even so, to be relevant demands aligning oneself with those social systems and practices that promote well-being for all and decrying those that are unjust.

Conclusion

In sum, it can be argued that both "on the ground" and within Caribbean social history biblical hermeneutical practices within a Caribbean context are influenced more by the need to contextualize biblical texts than by examining them as socio-ideological productions and products of social practice. Besides, it is noticeable that it is the resistant reading strategy that effects resistance or brings about challenges to and affects oppressive systems and practices. The resistant reading strategy of Sharpe, Bogle, Garvey and Rastafarianism are not attempts simply to surmount the system. On the contrary, what unfolded are thoroughgoing attempts to transform the system into an order of liberation.

Transforming socio-economic systems into an order of liberation is simply the historic mission of enslaved Africans and their descendants in the Caribbean: *to acquire and reconstruct power so that Caribbean people own and control the socio-political and cultural economy.* This historic mission is but the reversal of the biblical liberation/Exodus tradition as identified by Derek Walcott. Walcott divined that, in the Bible, the emancipatory movement is *from bondage in Pharaoh's Egypt* **to** *freedom in the land of promise,* **via** *the Sea of Reeds*; for Africans who were captured and brought against their wills to the Caribbean and the Americas, the movement, which is not emancipatory, was *from freedom and civilization* **to** *bondage and Christianization,* **via** *the Atlantic sea.*[17] Emancipation is still the Caribbean historic mission and social project. A resistant biblical hermeneutic within a Caribbean context is a cultural weapon of struggle in that mission and project.

Notes

1. George Mulrain "Hermeneutics Within a Caribbean Context" in R. S. Sugirtharajah ed., *Vernacular Hermeneutics* (Sheffield: Sheffield Academic Press, 1999), p. 119.
2. Ibid., p. 122.
3. Renita J. Weems "Reading Her Way through the struggle: African American Women and the Bible" in Norman K. Gottwald and Richard A. Horsley eds. *The Bible and Liberation, Political and Social hermeneutics*, rev. ed. (London: SPCK; Maryknoll, NY: Orbis Books, 1993), p. 35.
4. William C. Placher, *Narratives of A Vulnerable God* (Philadelphia, PA: Westminster John Knox Press, 1994), p. 73
5. Norman K. Gottwald, "Socio-historical Precision in the Biblical Grounding of Liberation Theologies", address to the Catholic Biblical Association of America at its annual meeting, San Francisco, August 1985.
6. See *Education for Critical Consciousness, Pedagogy in Process (The Letters to Guinea-Bissau)*, and *Pedagogy of Hope*.
7. Paulo Freire *Pedagogy of the Oppressed* (Middlesex: Penguin Books, 1972), pp. 45–59.
8. Kathleen C. Boone, *The Bible Tells Them So – The Discourse of Protestant Fundamentalism* (London: SCM Press, 1990), p. 19.
9. Ralph E. Gonsalves, "Our Caribbean civilisation: Retrospect and Prospect", *Caribbean Quarterly* 44 (3 & 4) (September–December, 1998): 132.
10. Fernando F. Segovia and Mary Ann Tolbert, *Teaching The Bible – The Discourses and Politics of Biblical Pedagogy* (Maryknoll, NY: Orbis Books, 1998), p. 123; see also Fernando Segovia, *Decolonizing Biblical Studies, A View From the Margins* (Maryknoll, NY: Orbis Books, 2000); Fernando F. Segovia and Mary Ann Tolbert, *Reading From This Place Vol. 1 Social Location and Biblical Interpretation in the United States* (Minneapolis, MN: Fortress Press, 1995), p. 31.
11. Ibid.
12. Chris Mullard, *Race, Power and Resistance* (London, Boston, Melbourne: Routledge & Kegan Paul, 1985), p. 35.
13. Ibid., p. 35.
14. Segovia and Tolbert eds., *Reading From This Place*, pp. 312–13.
15. Garnet Roper, "The Impact of Evangelical and Pentecostal Religion", *Caribbean Quarterly* 37 (1) (March 1991), p. 43.
16. Ibid., p. 39.
17. Derek Walcott, *What The Twilight Says, Essays* (London: Faber & Faber, 1998), pp. 44–48.

Chapter 3

PUTTING PHILEMON IN ITS PLACE

Introduction

The task here is not merely to draw a possible picture of Imperial Graeco-Roman society but to discover the socio-ideological agenda and social practices at work in Philemon that are over-determined by its imperial context. In fact, the socio-historical context of Philemon is the colonial occupation of Palestine by Imperial Rome. Effectively, my purpose here is to ascertain the role of (the shadow of) empire in the production of biblical texts. Dube warns "failure to keep the empire in view as a central player unwittingly maintains the structures of oppression in the past and the present".[1] To keep the Roman Empire in view, the discussion will not be limited to a concentration on the supposed internal conflict between Onesimus, Philemon and Paul. Such a limited discussion would only serve to shelter the exploitation and oppressiveness of the Roman Empire contained within Philemon. It is by reconstructing the material condition of Philemon (the historical-materialist reading strategy) that the ideological influence of empire (the postcolonial reading strategy) is exposed.

Since the express aim of this work is to push biblical texts back to their socio-historic environment as a valid aspect of the historical-materialist hermeneutical process, it is necessary to perform three tasks here. One, identify the structural elements or signified forms of the mode of production out of which Philemon emerged, and thus to highlight the forces of production of first century Palestine. Two, distinguish the social relations of production within the letter to Philemon and hence of first century Palestine. Three, connect the class structure formation of Philemon or the social structure formation/social division in labour of Palestine (and the consequent tension between the social forces within social relationships in the structures and systems or the opposed social relations of production, exchange and distribution[2]) with the mode of production and social relations to production.

The interest here, therefore, is not so much those socio-historical issues – recovering the original audience, message and intention of the author – as in the kind of situation, social struggle, social experience, socio-ideological and theological interest and social practices that shape the letter to Philemon. In other words, what is the social class perspective from which Philemon is written and interpreted? What is the (social) ideology that influenced the production of Philemon? How are the power relationships constituted? How is the social system developed and maintained?

Mode of Production

In first century Palestine, the forces of production were mainly the land and waterways – lakes, seas, and rivers.[3] Land ownership was characterized by the "land by the spear" principle.[4] By this principle, private ownership of land was replaced by latifundia whereby large holdings of land belonged to the royal house.[5] These latifundia or large estates were under the supervision of the ruling class appointed managers who were responsible for collecting rents and taxes from those living on the land or estates.[6] In effect, latifundia were household economies. Philemon was a member of the ruling class and functioned in the interest of that class. It is the house church that met in Philemon's house, and thereby constitutive of the household economy, that is of interest in this study.

However, it was the war industry that fuelled the productive and technological bases of the economy and benefited the interests and needs of the ruling class more than the populace.[7] Finance for the war industry came from exacting tributes from the populace in the form of land taxes, animal taxes and tithes from resident alien armies and the populace.[8]

The mode of production was, therefore, tributary, structured principally to supply the Roman imperial administration with tributes. Even so, whatever the raw materials of a country, raw materials by themselves cannot produce wealth. Human labour is needed in addition to raw materials to produce wealth. Human involvement and input brings the issue of social relations to means of production into play.

Social Relations to Production

Roman tributary social formation was a cul-de-sac for the populace. None of the tribute raised was re-invested into projects for the benefit of the populace. In effect, they were paying to support the habits and interests of the ruling class. The tributary social formation had a number of characteristics.

Hierarchical Social Structure and System

Pre-industrial advanced agrarian societies such as Imperial Graeco-Rome had a *hierarchical social structure and system*.[9] At the top were the politically powerful urban elites or the imperial upper classes of Senators and Knights. At the bottom were the peasant class or the Plebs who were tenants, the rootless day labourers and artisans "far removed from the huge possessions and power of the Imperial upper classes".[10] There was no middle class. Income was derived from taxation and the productive output of the peasant class. As such, the wealth and power of the urban elites were derivative of their relations to the process of production of basic goods in the society.[11] It was relations to the mode of production that fundamentally shaped or gave rise to the hierarchical social structure and system.[12]

Pyramid Economic Structure

A direct consequence of this hierarchical social structure and system was a *pyramid economic structure*. The status and livelihood of the few, urban elites, came directly from the many. One was born into privilege, wealth and status as well as into poverty. This meant that birth, not income and lifestyles, was a determinant of livelihood.[13]

Structure of Households

Similarly, the *structure of households* also evidenced the hierarchy in the social structure and system. A typical household, for example, was constituted of members of the family, workers within the household and the subordinates. All were bonded together under the authority of a male superior.[14] This male-headed household was called a Paterfamilias. Several Paterfamilias together formed a Village; and several villages formed the Politea. This typical household economy was involved in a common agrarian or trade business. The subordinates in the households were slaves. Slaves were responsible for the administrative and practical aspects of the household; and the male head provided their material and social needs. Within the household economy emphasis was placed on collectivist values such as obligation, duty, obedience to authority, subordination and acquiescence, dependency and respect for tradition.[15] As such, households were reflective of *dominant-subordinate relationships*, which necessitated a servile culture.

Common Religion

Further, households were bonded together by a *common religion*. In effect, the household and the house church were constituted of the same persons. Religion was embedded in the economics of the household and the economics of the house church.[16] The dilemma here was that whereas in the house church there was social equality in terms of status and dignity in the household social inequality existed, in terms of material resources and power. However, co-equality in the house church did little to hide the fact that it is *only before God* that there is social equality.[17]

Agrarian Based

Moreover, Imperial Graeco-Roman society was *agrarian based*. If the imperial classes were going to derive maximum economic benefit from the system, they needed labour that was not only manual but also free of cost. Here the problem, if not the challenge, was the Free person's understanding that they were neither obligated to honour the dictates of imperial classes nor to work to their economic advantage. This refusal by the Free person was a source of tension and strain in the society. The situation was further aggravated by the fact that the wealth of free people exceeded their power and their power exceeded their status such that it caused further strain and tension in the social system.[18]

Slave as Property

In Roman law, whether one was a captive turned slave or already a slave in a household, *a slave was property*.[19] Interestingly, it was not the labour of the slave that became commodity but the slave himself or herself.[20] The law gave slave owners total control over their slave property, a "right" that extended to the slave's person and personality.[21] As Patterson puts it "a slave was a slave not because he was the object of property but because he was the subject of property".[22] Thus, the relationship between master and slave was one in which the master had absolute power over the slave as property.

Consequently, as property and unlike free person, slaves were at the behest, if not at the mercy, of their "owners". As the society was agrarian in nature, it required free manual labour to give adequate returns. However, the labour was only free if it was coerced and whipped into submission. So slaves were ruled by fear, a consequence of which was *servile fidelity*. Slavery begun in violence and was maintained by domination and exploitation.

The climate of fear was rooted in the fact that those taken into slavery lost all formal, legal and enforceable ties of blood.[23] Not only were they uprooted but also families could be separated at the pleasure of and in the manner determined by the slave "owner". It was this power to separate from native origins that gave peculiar status to slave-masters in the relation of domination-submission.[24] Essentially, the slave was the quintessential human commodity and was *socially dead*,[25] having no relations with their native origins.

Nevertheless, in whatever way the slave was perceived and thereby treated, it was undeniable that the slave was a human being. To do violence to and to humiliate the slave was to violate and degrade the slave's humanity. In spite of this, the intention was to so "undermine and degrade the slave's humanity as to distinguish the slave from human beings who are not property".[26] Corporal punishment, physical torture, sexual exploitation, branding, beatings and demeaning grown male slaves by referring to them as boys were some of the procedures used to achieve this end. The whip became the symbol of degradation and humiliation.[27]

Though few managed it, the system did make some allowances for slaves to regain their "freedom". Manumission and the use of the peculium were among those allowances.

Manumission

In theory, manumission was an attempt to redeem the humanity of the slave, either through the owner's grace or the slave paying a fee. Either way manumission was never a guarantee of freedom. So as to maintain the balance between supply and demand, the granting of manumission depended on how many persons were brought into the system and the number of enslaved depended on how many persons were gifted their "freedom".[28] Whenever manumission was eventually granted, the slave was no longer considered property or commodity and thereby was allowed to reclaim kinship ties, own property and claim citizenship. However, because the slave could not by law own property, the fee paid for manumission was considered a gift to the slave owner. The slave could never adequately compensate for the master's right to and over his slave-property "as whatever the slave gives already belongs to the master".[29] The amount paid for manumission was fixed at an amount that permitted the slave owner to purchase the bondage of another slave. So in effect, manumission was a commercial transaction that reinforced the institution of slavery or kept the system going.[30] Thus, manumission was an incentive to obedient servitude and a recapitalization of the slave's value.

As an act of redeeming the slave's humanity, Orlando Patterson, a Jamaican historical sociologist and professor at Harvard University, notes that in manumission, a double negation is taking place. Patterson is well placed to express opinions on the institution of slavery as he maintains a lifetime academic interest in slavery, freedom and ethnic inequality worldwide primarily among people of African descent. Patterson's interest is in the sociology of slave societies as a system of total domination. He likens enslavement to taking life and release at manumission to life giving or life-creating. So, in manumission, there is the negation of the negation of social death whereby the slave was separated from his or her native origins and had no independent social life at enslavement.[31] As a "freedman" the slave now rejoined all formal ties of "blood" and could live in localities where he or she chose.

However, in Roman law, manumission was only allowed *at* age 30, not *before*.[32] This allowance meant that the law was effective only in its helplessness to the slave. In those days, one was not expected to live beyond 30 years of age. So at age 30, one would have spent his/her most productive years. As such, "freedom", so grudgingly given in the twilight of one's years, was no occasion for celebration or re-engaging with ambition.

Consequently, in theory, "freedom" was gifted. In practice, "freedom" was never experienced. Liberty came at a price. Even after manumission was granted, the *obsequium*, paying obeisance to masters, and the *operae*, obligation to work specific times for masters,[33] were very much the practice and rule. In fact, "freed slaves" were recognized always as "freed" rather than freeborn; and always owed their benefactor loyalty.[34]

Peculium

The peculium was another way in which "freedom" was gifted to slaves. The peculium was basically a system of "perks" placed at the disposal of slaves. Slaves were allowed to possess and enjoy a given range of goods – cash, food, livestock, other slaves and grazing rights – at the pleasure of the master. But the fact that in and by law, a slave could not own property meant that the slave could never dispose of or transact any of the peculium without the authority of the master. In fact, it was the peculium that the slave used to pay for his or her manumission. In this way, the peculium was used as a motivating device. The master had no obligation to enter into any arrangements with the slave. However, carrots work better than sticks in the circumstances.[35] Nevertheless, in effect, like manumission, it was nothing but a capital investment by the master as the money was used to purchase the bondage of another slave. It was the prospect of self-redemption that actually made the system work and thereby reinforced the institution of slavery.

Altogether, neither manumission nor the peculium resulted in any effective change in the oppressive social systems and structures of imperial Graeco-Roman societies. The system always fated the enslaved to bondage, oppression and exploitation such that the masters or the oppressors remained firmly in control of the reins of power. Manumission was nothing more than a recapitalization scheme for slave owners and an incentive for obedient servitude for slaves. And although the peculium seemed to be a motivating device, the fact that slave owners had no binding commitment to honour obligations meant it de-energized more than motivated. Worse still, at the age which manumission was gifted, one no longer had the physical strength and youthful ambition to pursue goals. It effectively allowed old, worn-out slaves to pay for the freedom of new ones.

Even so, slaves did not always work within the system, a mission impossible, or leave it to the system to gift their freedom. Slaves, for whom manumission was long in coming, took the desperate but subversive act of running away.[36] By running away, slaves were resisting domination and alienation and subverting the system, struggling for their inalienable rights and claims of birth. Where the situation was humanly intolerable, outside the bounds of civility, running away should never be seen as escape but as an attempt to overthrow the system.[37]

One aspect of subverting the system is seen in the fact that running away is economically disadvantageous to slave owners.[38] Running away was like removing a cog in the wheel of the productive forces. On a mass scale, running away had huge social and revolutionary implications such that it could cause production to grind to a halt, destroy the socio-economic base of the society and dismantle the power structure. Hence, the draconian measures to limit or discourage its occurrence.

Formation of Social Class Structure

While institution of slavery existed already, slavery, 'in the form of labour for others',[39] was a new development. People to provide free labour had to come from somewhere. Captives as slaves from war were one remedy. Where the existing supply of slaves was inadequate, this led to new wars to secure captives as slaves for free labour. Whichever way the argument is turned, the origin of slavery lay in commercial interests: private ownership of land that required free manual labour. Commercial interests transformed captives into slaves or were the conditions that brought about slavery. Thus, the economic system of imperial Graeco-Roman society was rooted in domination and exploitation.

Socially Stratified Society of Two Classes
Essentially, the socio-economic structure and system of imperial Graeco-Roman society reflected a *socially stratified society of two classes, the dominant and the dominated.* In fact, for Richard Horsley, Roman society was divided between the rulers and ruled.[40] The fact that each estate was in effect an economy meant that the societies were agglomerates,[41] ruled and exploited by a yet more resourced estate. This division, though, has several social implications. First, there was no "social ladder"[42] or middle class and thereby no hope either for upward social mobility or for participation in the decision-making process for the ruled. Second, people were defined not by the accident of birth but by who got what and how much. Third, a great gulf was fixed between religion and economics. In theory, in the house church, there was co-equality between the ruler and the ruled, but in practice social inequality prevailed in the household. Lastly, the Peasant class or Slaves had no control of their own lives; they were mainly of utility value.

For Mosala, this Peasant or slave class was the underclass, a third class; a class that was exploitable politically, economically and ideologically.[43] With supporting evidence from New Testament texts, Mosala points out that this underclass was vulnerable politically, economically and ideologically – politically, as they were used to fight in mercenary activities that were not in their own interests (Mark 14: 10–11); economically, as they were conned into fighting against each other over wages (Matt. 20:1–16); ideologically, the objects of moral and religious double standards (John 8: 1–11).[44]

Mosala's identification of this underclass finds support, though not from the same ideological position, calculated malicious intent and hermeneutical purpose, in the disparaging characterization of Onesimus by J. B. Lightfoot, a biblical scholar of some renown. Lightfoot states:

> Onesimus represents the least respectable type of the least respectable class in the social scale. He was regarded by philosophers as a "live chattel", a "live implement"; ... He was treated by the law as having no rights; and he had carried the principles of the law to their logical consequences. He had declined to entertain any responsibilities. There was absolutely nothing to recommend him. He was a slave, and what was worse, a Phrygian slave; and he had confirmed the popular estimate of his class and nation by his own conduct.

He was a thief and runaway. His offence did not differ in any way, so far as we know, from the vulgar type of slavish offences. He seems to have done just what the representative slave in Roman comedy threatens to do, when he gets in trouble. He had "packed up some goods and taken to his heels". Rome was the natural cesspool for those offscourings of humanity. In the thronging crowd of the metropolis was his best hope of secrecy. In the dregs of the city rabble he would find the society of congenial spirits.[45]

Such a characterization of Onesimus is outlandish and held as taken from and grounded in ruling class ideology. Also, it reflects the era in which it was written. When Philemon is read from the perspective of Onesimus or the underclass, completely contradistinct conclusions are reached. Nevertheless, this representation of Onesimus concurs with the conclusion that out of the socio-economic and political domination of Palestine by Imperial Rome, some three social classes resulted: ruling, dominated and underclass.

In sum, it was economic interests that determined how the slave's humanity was defined and treated. The slave was commandeered, violated and degraded, however indiscriminately or brutally, without prick of conscience, as profit seemingly meant more than morality. Essentially, the ideology was one of the commodification of humanity. For Philemon's household, at once house church and household, this priority of economic profit over respect for the humanity of others caused Onesimus to be a witness to the contradiction between faith and practice, and the antithesis between the sacred and the secular.

What, then, did this socio-economic structure mean for Philemon's household? In Philemon's household, on the one hand, Onesimus led a marginalized existence as slave; his personhood defined by his utility value, rather than the content of his character; and he was a living witness to the contradiction between faith and practice. On the other hand, Philemon, as head of the household and owner of the estate, was in a position where he had to ensure the economic viability and profitability of his estate and at the same time practise the Christian faith. Thus, the letter to Philemon came out of a context of the working out of the socio-religious implications of master–slave relationship within the context of the house church in a household economy, which by its very being was a model of an egalitarian system and structure.

The foregoing demonstrates that the social forces and struggles in imperial Graeco-Roman society between the dominant and dominated were in conflict owing to their vested interests in the system; and that social inequality has its roots in casual relationships. While the dominant wanted to maximize economic profit and benefit at the expense and service of the dominated, the dominated desired to define themselves and control their destiny. In other words, social inequality produces social conflict. As such, there is a causal relationship between the means of production and the quality of life in a society.[46] With reference to Onesimus' action of running away, it raises the issue as to whether Paul is giving priority to reconciliation over against social justice.

We now need to turn our attention to how religion interacted with social inequality and conflict and the socio-ideological interests and social practices in the imperial Graeco-Roman society. That is, how empire or the political economy limited, influenced and shaped the theology, the thinking or the version of reality selected by the writer of the biblical text, in this case, Paul.

Pauline Theopolitics and Slavery

Brothers but Master and Slave

In addressing the matter of Onesimus' status on his return to Philemon's household and whether Philemon should accept Onesimus, Paul raises the issues of equality and freedom within the context of empire. Bearing in mind that the members of the house church and the household are the same set of persons, the reality of the situation is this: in the house church Philemon and Onesimus are co-equals but in the household they are socially unequal. What needs moral clarity is whether Onesimus can be both brother and slave and Philemon both slave master and brother. For Philemon to accept Onesimus as co-equal would mean freedom for Onesimus. Equality would have given freedom but freedom would not have necessarily given equality. One can be free but not equal; but one cannot be equal without being free. Thus, it is the issues of equality and freedom that are central to Paul's moral guidance such that his perspective on slavery in the Roman Empire is exposed.

But with slavery having some three levels, according to Patterson, one needs clarity pertaining to the level on which to judge Paul's moral stance.[47] For Patterson, the levels of slavery are the personal, institutional and systemic.[48] On the personal level one is dealing with a dominated, oppressed and natally alienated individual.[49] On the institutional level with the mechanisms – laws, violence, manumission, peculium – used to maintain a relation of absolute domination of persons conceived as natally alienated;[50] and on the systemic level with structural dependence on the institution of slavery.[51]

For Patterson, Paul dealt on the personal level; and sought all legal means for manumission.[52] But is not the individual part of the nexus of relationships in society, that no man is an island? The personal cannot be divorced from the institutional and systemic. Any attempt to do so leads to accommodation to and complicity with the status quo. However, as Paul asked Philemon to do more than asked, that is, to accept Onesimus as no longer a slave but a beloved brother, and addressing the letter not only to Philemon himself, meant that Paul's view on slavery impinges on both Patterson's institutional and systemic levels. Patterson's conclusion, therefore, is not without challenge.

Paul's perspective on slavery, nevertheless, is the subject of much debate. The arguments range from whether Paul sanctions slavery as an institution,[53] to the ambiguity of his counsel in 1 Cor. 7:20–24.[54] Also included in the range of arguments is whether moral judgement is limited to the personal, institutional or systemic,[55] to whether his seeming indifference is "sheer pragmatic realism"[56] or belief in the Parousia.[57]

For this work, however, the understanding of Paul's view on slavery is formed from Gal. 3:23–29, 1 Cor. 7:20–24 and Philemon, among the seven authentic or undisputed Pauline letters (the others are 1 Thessalonians, 1 and 2 Corinthians, Romans, Philippians). This means that this work accepts the view that the Deutero-Pauline Epistles (Colossians, Ephesians, Peter, Titus, 1 and 2 Timothy), written after 70 CE, reflect attempts to restore patriarchy and promote the view that Christianity was not a threat to the status quo.[58] As such, these Deutero-Pauline Epistles do not influence the perspective herein articulated. The emphases in Gal. 3:26–28, 1 Cor. 7:20–24 and Philemon are on social equality, co-equality and freedom. With these emphases, one must conclude that Philemon and Onesimus are brothers, not master and slave. In contrast, for the Deutero-Pauline Epistles, with their emphases on submission, obedience, patience and endurance, it is neither irreconcilable nor incompatible for master and slave to be brothers.

Nonetheless, a further analysis of scholarly thinking concerning Paul's perspective on slavery is expressed below *vis-à-vis* his counsel in the letter to Philemon. Care is taken to discern how the issues of equality and freedom are adjudged and on what level – personal, institutional, and systemic – the discussion takes place.

Socio-political Ethics of God's Reign
For Patterson, Pauline Christianity is essentially dualistic, keeping each mode of existence, the house church and the household, separate.[59] In this separation, the interior and the otherworldly focus of the house church is

kept distinct from the social realities and forces of the household. What the slave lost in the society is regained in the church. What causes this separation is the dualistic ethic of judgement and the justified sinner in the conception of Jesus as Messiah and Saviour.[60] This is seen in two ways. First, for the ethic of judgement Jesus Christ is seen as the Messiah who punishes the wicked and rewards the righteous. Jesus Christ as Messiah saves by divine enslavement, not by ending social injustice.[61] Second, the demands of Jesus Christ as Messiah are for watchfulness, obedience and stoic acceptance of the status quo. So, for the ethic of the justified sinner, Jesus is the liberator from enslavement to sin. As such, both master and slave can experience justification through the same crucified Jesus who died for all.[62] Therefore, reconciliation between master and slave is a matter of right relationships (righteousness), not right relations (justice). It is not that Patterson agrees with this dualism in Pauline Christianity. Rather, he contends "Christianity, after Paul, had already constructed an extraordinarily shrewd creed with a built-in flexibility that made it possible for emperor and slave to worship the same god without threatening the system, but also without denying all dignity to the oppressed".[63]

Patterson's dualistic view of Christianity is challenged by the view taken by David Bosch who was brought up in a Nationalist Afrikaner home in Apartheid South Africa. As such, Bosch was schooled in the ways of racial, economic, cultural, linguistic and religious distinctiveness. Bosch contends that in Paul's day, there was no dualistic distinction between a conception of political and religious hopes as "all reality was of a piece".[64] The issue for Bosch is that Paul is read through the prism of Augustine and Martin Luther. He contends Augustine is responding to Pelagianism and Donatism and thereby, on the one hand, individualized salvation and, on the other, centred salvation in the church or sacristy. Martin Luther saw Paul as stressing that salvation comes through justification by grace through faith and hence the view of Paul's disinterest in secular activities. For Bosch, Paul needs reading through the lens of the reconciling work of Jesus Christ who destroyed all barriers that divide humankind.[65] In the reconciling work of Jesus Christ, there is no polarity and racial, ethnic, social and economic distinctions are wiped out.[66] While Bosch advocates for reconciliation to be the alternative vision of reality that the church must incarnate, Bosch fails to advance the political implications of reconciliation in Apartheid South Africa. Even so, reading Paul this way still makes it possible to relate to the same person as both one's inferior and one's equal,[67] that is, though brothers and sisters yet still master and slave.

In sum, what this dualistic ethic does is to make it possible for Christianity to practise a complicit and accommodating role in the society such that institutionalized injustice is never under revolutionary challenge. The issues of equality and freedom are dealt with on the personal level, not the institutional and systemic.

However, whereas Patterson and Bosch see the dualistic ethic as reinforcing the status quo, Derek Tidball, who lectures in pastoral theology at the London school of theology but with training as a sociologist, sees it as manipulationist: a reinterpretation of the world which holds that things are not as bad as they seem, and so provide a way to cope. Tidball states it thus:

> *What Paul offers to Christian slaves is a totally new appreciation of their value as persons.* They are no longer "things" but people who have standing and status before God (1 Corinthians 7:20-24). In Christ, the slave is a freeman. God has demonstrated their worth by forfeiting the life of his son through crucifixion. If only, Paul argues, they grasped this greater fact, slavery itself *becomes inconsequential. A slave can remain happily a slave and still serve the Lord in spite of his social limitations.* Such a view affects not only the slave's self esteem but the actual pattern of relationships which exist between Christian masters and slaves.[68]

This view, merely promotes servile obedience. How can slavery become inconsequential when it is a fact of daily experience? Here for Tidball, despite his training in sociology, religion is more opiate than an instrument for social change. Seemingly, Tidball's pastoral instincts and inclinations are stronger than his sociological orientation. In effect, it is quite acceptable for the brother to be a slave and the slave master a brother, whatever the social limitations.

Furthermore, for some commentators, it is Paul's belief in the Parousia, the coming reign of God that will bring about social justice, which renders the abolition of slavery of comparative unimportance.[69] But J. Christian Beker, professor of biblical theology at Princeton theological seminary, argues that those who take Paul's understanding of the Parousia as an invitation to ethical passivity and quietism, or an appeal to ethical irresponsibility or fatalism or even withdrawal from the world have misunderstood Paul.[70] For Paul, advocates Becker, the Parousia motivates and challenges believers "to move God's creation toward that future triumph of God".[71] Moving the future into the present, therefore, cannot come about by passivity, quietism, irresponsibility or withdrawal.

On the contrary, social activism is demanded of those who believe in the Parousia. Social activism recovers God's coming triumph from doom and gloom theology from speculation and an escapist understanding of salvation. This means that the issues of co-equality and social inequality need settling in this present life. In fact, to settle in this present life the issues of social justice between master and slave are signs of the presence of God's kingdom in the midst of life.

Likewise, understanding the Parousia as present reality, J. Paul Sampley, Professor of New Testament at the Boston University School of Theology, looks at the issue from another angle. Through Christ's death and resurrection, God has destroyed the forces of death and evil and "already has begun the new creation in the midst of the old (Rom. 8:21; 2 Cor. 5:17, 15:14–28; Gal. 6:15)".[72] Even so, what is now or already is also not yet. To be in Christ is to be already sharing in the fullness of life, which is still to come in all its fullness. In other words, that which is hoped for is already possessed. So, disciples must become that which in reality they already are, or strive for the goal for which they are destined".[73] In reality, the issues of co-equality and social inequality should not even arise. Social inequality has no place in the kingdom of God.

But the reign of God in reality is yet to be. So, Bosch posits that Christ's coming inaugurates a new era, a different historical period, which, though not the final age, is different from the previous age.[74] The new age is neither the closure nor the completion of the present. Rather, it is that the death-resurrection of Christ is tangible evidence in the present of the future triumph of God over history.[75] The time between the ages calls for hope-full involvement in historical realities. By establishing systems and structures of social justice, master and slave as brothers are not without hope in this present life.

In contrast, while Becker and Sampley urge social activism, John Knox, a Scottish religious Reformer along Calvinist lines, advocated patience. Knox understood, on the basis of Rom. 13:1–7, that "the power of the state, so soon to be superseded, was meantime to be patiently accepted, even by the deprived".[76] Additionally, Knox posited that to conform to the status quo, however oppressive, is to preserve a tolerable order and peace whereas the alternative would be civil war.[77] Here Knox's Calvinist beliefs in the sovereignty of God in all things shone through. Calvinists believe in Predestination in which one's fate is determined in advance by God's infallible prescience. Knox's argument in favour of patience is a not so disguised justification for the status quo whether it be oppressive or not. While the reign of God is awaited, servile obedience will never turn exploitation into justice and domination into emancipation. Humanizing oppressive and exploitative systems and structures will. As such, if the brother patiently exercises servile obedience, the brother will forever remain a slave; and should the slave master devotedly encourage obedient servitude, he will never become a brother.

The views on the Parousia expressed by Beker and Sampley are in effect a realized eschatological perspective.[78] Horsley contends that a realized eschatological perspective depoliticizes Paul or "pulls Paul's political punches" and advocates a theory of functionalism.[79] Functionalism ensures that groups work to fit the system and thereby embrace the status quo and reinforce group solidarity.[80] The goal of functionalism is to reform and perfect the social system. The situation where Philemon and Onesimus are brothers but also master and slave reflects circumstances of tension and conflict owing to their varied interests and relations to the means of production. Relations of domination-submission are caused. They come about on account of conflicting relations to social production. Any changes, therefore, that tend towards social justice and equality would of necessity be structural in nature. To accept the theory of functionalism, however, is to accept the slave and the slave master as brothers.

Yet another interpretation regards Paul's attitude towards the issues of equality and freedom inherent in slavery as pragmatic, tactical and common-sensical. Taylor and Patterson reckon that there is nothing an infant community of faith could effectively or affectively do to revolutionize a system and structure so deeply entrenched in imperial Graeco-Roman society.[81] B. Gerhardsson sees Paul's socio-political liberation programme, in the given circumstances, as tactical and common-sensical. Tactical in that provoking the authorities might bring about greater hardships for the enslaved; and common-sensical as slaves were not in the position of power necessary to affect social change.[82]

Nevertheless, one cannot accept that Paul's letter to Philemon is a personal matter as it was addressed also to Apphia, Archippus and the church that met in Philemon's house. To the contrary, Paul's letter, though personal, when read closely has wider social implications beyond an individual household economy. To this end, as the household economy is the basis or microcosm of the state, to address, if not to redress, the issues of equality and freedom as they pertain to the Philemon household economy is, by implication, to do so in the Politea or the Graeco-Roman Empire.

One should add to the argument that liberation must be integral for both master and slave, if they are to be truly brothers in this life. Integral liberation is the freedom of the whole person and all persons in all the oppressed and subjected dimensions of their lives.[83] In other words, economic (from material poverty), political (from social oppression) and religious (from sin) liberation do not come one after the other, in different stages and times, but all together. For as Boff contends, the struggle for economic liberation is also a struggle for political and religious liberation,[84] "justice and grace are affairs of economics too".[85]

What the foregoing analysis of the social structures and systems of imperial Graeco-Roman society and Pauline theopolitics and slavery demonstrates is the impossibility of dealing with slavery or matters of equality and freedom, on a purely personal level. The individual is also a social being, a member of a community. To deal with mechanisms that regulate that individual's life in community is to deal with the structures and systems that constitute that very community. Put another way, to reconcile master and slave as brothers is not simply a matter of removing social distinctions or restoring the slave to his or her natal origins. Rather, it is so to alter the relations to productions that mechanisms and structures and systems of that society allow for self-definition and self-determination. After all, what good are rights without social power or the means to empower?

Socio-historic Environment of Philemon

From the foregoing, the portrait of life in imperial Graeco-Roman society is one in which households were more political than domestic units or economies; it was more a question of industry than morality; and the social system was the opposite of what it really was.

Household Economy, more Political than Domestic

In the socio-economic pyramid of imperial Graeco-Roman society, one was defined, determined and characterized by one's relationship to the social forces and processes of production. This was a relationship that was unlikely to change since it was decided by the accident of birth in the first instance. In these social relations of power, the rulers' primary concern was the maximizing of productivity and profitability and for the ruled, the minimizing of output. The end result was a balancing act between enforcing submission and corresponding resistance,[86] especially in the absence of a middle class. With little means of social mobility, and hence no chance even of economic advancement on the part of the ruled, not only were lines of interests clearly defined but the likelihood of redefining relationships to production were virtually nil. But does this mean that the ruled were doomed forever to be at the mercy and benevolence of the rulers?[87] This study submits that Onesimus' action of running away says that the answer is no. No power can halt the quest for freedom.

Industry and Morality

Moreover, in imperial Graeco-Roman society, slaves were defined as property.[88] As property, it meant that they were priced and displaced – bought, sold, traded, leased, bequeathed, presented as gifts and pledged for debt.[89] Slaves, therefore, had no independent social existence.[90] What is not denied here is that whatever the definition of a slave, the slave was still a person, a human being, possessing human capacities and therefore in need of protection against indignity, injustice and dishonour. This makes it impossible, if not incongruous, to regard the slave as a person and thing at one and the same time. Yet, this was the case in Paul's day. What the understanding of the slave as a person and thing says, nevertheless, is that in that day slavery was more a question of industry than morality.[91] In whatever era, is not industry a moral issue as well? Can the two exist separately?

In his letter to Philemon, Paul sees this issue of industry and morality at play in Onesimus' name, which means "useful". Paul is debating or is unable to make up his mind as to what is the most industrious (useful) use to put Onesimus. In other words, is the most industrious (useful) use of Onesimus to remain with Paul as a mission-partner, for which Paul needs Philemon's consent (vv. 13–14)? Or is it for Onesimus to return to Philemon no longer as a slave but as more than a slave, a beloved brother (v. 16)? At stake here is the fact that Onesimus is a person, not a thing, not an item of trade. Thus, the issue is more about the morality of industry than being limited to a question of industry only. When the moral question is addressed then the issue becomes Onesimus' right to self-definition and self-determination.

Opposites in the Society

Despite the dominance of the ruler, several aspects of imperial Graeco-Roman society's socio-economic and political structure show that, in many ways, the system seemed the opposite of what it really was. To begin with, the slave master's point of independence and lordship was also a point of dependence.[92] The slave owner's domination rested on that which was not guaranteed, submission of the slave, in spite of recourse to force. Onesimus' act of running away shows the fragility of the dominance of the slave master. Governors can only rule with the consent of the governed.

Furthermore, it is bondage that gives birth to freedom. Ironically, without slavery, freedom was never conceived. It was the promise of redemption or eventual freedom that was used to keep the slave in bondage.[93] So, freedom as a motivating force was more powerful than the whip. In other words, "slavery was a self-correcting institution: what it denied the slave, it utilised as the means of motivating him".[94] If Onesimus had never been enslaved, he would have had no need to run away.

And lastly, within imperial Graeco-Roman society, as noted previously by Patterson, there were three levels of freedom operating. On one level, there was personal freedom, which is expressed negatively and positively.[95] Negatively, it is the refusal to exercise absolute power over another; whereas positively, it is the implicit recognition and acceptance that one has the liberty to live as one pleases "so far as one can".[96] On another level, freedom is sovereignal.[97] This is the power to censure and muzzle the expression of another's will, whether in print or speech.[98] And finally, civic freedom is realized where adult members of a community play a part in the decision-making processes in their community of birth or in which they are recognized.[99] So for civic freedom, it is acknowledged that everyone has rights and obligations.

With reference, to the master and slave as brothers in Philemon, these levels of freedom mean that there is a struggle for personal freedom *from* within a context of the dominance of sovereignal freedom *for* the full realization of civic freedom. This is a struggle that is not confined to Onesimus only but to all slaves within imperial Graeco-Roman society, and oppressed people everywhere resisting against domination and exploitation.

Eisegetics and Exegetics

Hermeneutic of Domination-Resistance

The basic question that arises out of the "brothers" but master and slave issue, is how does the structural and systemic character (mutuality, egalitarian, liberated, social justice) of the house church challenge, redefine, revolutionize the structural and systemic character (authoritarian, oppressive, exploitative, profit oriented) of the household?[100] The dilemma here is that the structural systemic characters of the household and house church are fundamentally different. The challenge that comes with this dilemma is how fundamentally to turn the vision of a new creation into reality or build a liberated community,[101] using the Bible as the hermeneutical tool, in this case Philemon.

Clearly, in the letter to Philemon, there was a clash of interests, a social struggle, between Philemon as oppressor and Onesimus as oppressed, evolving into social relationships of inequality and exploitation. The solution lies in structural and systemic change in the household. The household is the locus of the oppression, the cause of the structural and systemic injustice. What needs to come about is a new kind of relationship in which social justice and socialization of the means of power take priority so that existence in the household is characterized by partnership and participation.[102] Onesimus is a brother when he is a partner in the ownership of the means of production and active participant in the decision-making process of the household. It is this egalitarian system and structure of social relations independent of social distinctions that already exist in the house church (v.1). Where there is no such partnership and participation, their will always be the need to resist, or to "run away" in Philemon's case (v. 12).

Consequently, the phrase "run away" ought to be understood from a different viewpoint. The term "sending back" (v. 12) cannot be understood as "run away".[103] Run away implies that Onesimus was "on the run" from the law or justice. If Onesimus was on the run, it was from injustice for justice, rather than from justice. Onesimus' running away brought him on stage in his own personae as an activist in his own liberation, as an agent of his own destiny, not being represented but representing himself.[104] In other words, Onesimus was not in Philemon's house making one tactical manoeuvre after another against the slave system, that is, opposing the system of slavery from within. Rather, in running away, Onesimus was standing outside the system of slavery, thereby resisting it. As Richard D. E. Barton, professor of African and Asian studies at the University of Sussex, England, points out "resistance requires an 'elsewhere' from which the system may be perceived and grasped as a whole and from which a coherent strategy may be elaborated".[105] Running away was Onesimus' "elsewhere", acting in his own interest for a new kind of household.

Conclusion

In imperial Graeco-Roman society, it is relations to the forces and systems of production that define and determine relationships and the quality of life. To focus on the personal nature and character of these relationships is to make adjustments and accommodate to the status quo. But to concentrate on the systemic and structural aspects, that is, the casual relationships, is to see the need to remove social injustices and inequalities so that a new and transformed social order result and the right to self-definition and self-determination are restored. Since the letter to Philemon was not addressed to Philemon alone, Paul does not expect the restoration of Onesimus to be a matter settled between Philemon and Onesimus by themselves.

Any appeal to Philemon personalized the issue of unequal relationships between the oppressor (ruling class of imperial Rome and its appointees) and the oppressed (Onesimus and all the dominated). Calling on Philemon to act fairly without bringing about social transformation is to appeal to his moral convictions and seek thereby to transform the system from within. Appeals to moral convictions "end up with good individuals with pure intentions who put up with oppressive institutions and allow power structures to remain unaltered. The struggle seems to be not against structures but within oneself".[106] In effect, the appeal to Philemon is to ask for the impossible. To do so is to request that Philemon oppose, indeed resist, the very system from which he was profiting. Further, it points to the fact that "resistance is not about being a protector of the weak but a protester against the social system that perpetuates injustice and inequality".[107]

More precisely, Philemon's place is finding a liberating praxis for justice and effective change in a society of domination and oppression. But whether Paul wanted the full social implications of the (casual) relationship between Philemon and Onesimus realized is open to debate, as Paul's letter lacks specificity.[108]

It is, therefore, to an examination of how Philemon is interpreted that this work now turns. This examination is to determine whether interpreters see and understand Philemon as a site of struggle or a product of social forces, ideology and struggles taking place in its context (behind the text); or whether interpreters concentrate on the rhetorical features of the text/letter (on/in the text); or indeed whether interpreters allow their contextual experiences and influences to shape their interpretation (in front of the text). Put another way, I am interested in finding out what gives agency to their "readings" of Philemon; and where they locate resistance as occurring in the letter.

Notes

1. Musa W. Dube, "Saviour of the World But not of This World: Postcolonial Reading of Spatial Construction in John", in Sugirtharajah ed., *The Post Colonial Bible*, p. 131.
2. Mosala, *Biblical Hermeneutics*, p. 115.

3. G. E. M. de Ste Croix, *The Class Struggle in The Ancient Greek World* (London: Duckworth, 1981), p. 120.
4. Sean Freyne, *Galilee: From Alexander to Hadrian* (Notre Dame, IN: University of Indiana Press, 1980), p. 156.
5. Ibid.
6. Freyne, *Galilee*, p. 158.
7. Martin Hengel, *Judaism and Hellenism* (London: SCM Press, 1974), p. 13.
8. Mosala, *Biblical Hermeneutics*, p. 157.
9. Carolyn Osiek, R.S.C.J., *What are They Saying About the Social Setting of The New Testament* (New York: Paulist Press, 1992), p. 41.
10. Gerd Theissen, "The Social Structure of Pauline Communities: Some Critical Remarks on J. J. Meggit – Paul, Poverty, Survival", *Journal For The Study of the New Testament* 84 (2001): 73.
11. Norman K. Gottwald, "Social Classes as an Analytical and Hermeneutical Category in Biblical Studies" *Journal of Biblical Literature* 112 (1), (Spring 1993): 4.
12. Itumeleng Mosala, *Biblical Hermeneutics and Black Theology in South Africa* (Grand Rapids, MI: William B. Eerdmans Publishing Co., 1990), p. 103.
13. Osiek, *What are They Saying About the Social Setting*, p. 41.
14. Derek Tidball, *The Social Context of the New Testament* (Exeter: The Paternoster Press, 1983), p. 79.
15. Craig S. de Vos, "Once a Slave Always a Slave – Manumission and Relational Patterns in Paul's Letter to Philemon" *Journal For The Study of the New Testament* 82 (2001): 95.
16. Horsley, *Sociology and the Jesus Movement*, p. 69.
17. Dimitris J. Kyrtatas, *The Social Structure of Early Christian Communities* (London, New York: Verso, 1987), p. 30.
18. John Dominic Crossan, *The Birth of Christianity* (Edinburgh: T. & T. Clark, 1998), p. 181.
19. Orlando Patterson, *Slavery and Social Death* (Cambridge, MA: Harvard University Press, 1982), p. 28; Richard A. Horsley, "The Slave Systems of Classical Antiquity and their Reluctant Recognition by Modern Scholars" pp. 19–59 and Dexter E. Callender, Jr., "Servants of God(s) and Servants as Kings in Israel and the Ancient Near East" pp. 67–80, *Semeia 83/84 Slavery in Text and Interpretation*, Atlanta, GA: Society of Biblical Literature; Moses I. Finley, *Ancient Slavery*, p. 97.
20. Moses I. Finley, *Ancient Slavery*, pp. 74–75.
21. Ibid.
22. Orlando Patterson, *Slavery and Social Death*, p. 28.
23. Orlando Patterson, *Slavery and Social Death*, p. 7.
24. Ibid.
25. Ibid.
26. Finley, *Ancient Slavery*, pp. 95–96.
27. Patterson, *Slavery as Social Death*, p. 74; See also Jennifer A. Glancy, "Slaves and Slavery in the Matthean Parables" *Journal of Biblical Literature*, 119 (1) (Spring 2000): 67–90 who has emphasized the vulnerability of the enslaved body to violence and showed the kind of abuses suffered by slaves in the first century.
28. Patterson, *Slavery as Social Death*, pp. 209–14.
29. Patterson, *Slavery as Social Death*, p. 211.
30. Kyrtatas, *The Social Structure*, p. 61.

31. See Patterson, *Slavery and Social Death*, pp. 209–14.
32. Callahan, *The Slavery of New Testament Studies*, p. 6.
33. Horsley, *The Slave System of Classical Antiquity*, p. 50.
34. Crossan, *The Birth of Christianity*, p. 181.
35. Crossan, *The Birth of Christianity*, p. 181.
36. See Daube, *Saviour of the World*, p. 131.
37. Callender, Jr., *Servants of God(s) and Servants as Kings*, p. 78.
38. Moses I. Finley ed. *Slavery in Classical Antiquity – Views and Controversies* (Cambridge: Heffer, 1968), pp. 68–69.
39. Moses I. Finley, *Ancient Slavery and Modern Ideology* (London: Chatto & Windus, 1980), p. 90.
40. Richard A. Horsley, *Sociology and the Jesus Movement* (New York: Continuum, 1989), p. 69.
41. John H. Kautsky, *The Politics of Aristocratic Empires* (New Brunswick, London: Transaction Publishers, 1997, rev. ed.), p. 72.
42. Allan Callahan, "The Slavery of New Testament Studies" in *Semeia 83/84 Slavery in Text and Interpretation*, p. 5.
43. Mosala, *Biblical Hermeneutics*, pp. 159–60.
44. Ibid.
45. J. B. Lightfoot, *Saint Paul's Epistles to the Colossians and to Philemon* (London: Macmillan & Co. Ltd., 1912), pp. 309–10.
46. Leonardo Boff, O.F.M., *Faith On the Edge – Religion and Marginalized Existence* (San Francisco, CA: Harper & Row Publishers, 1989), p. 7.
47. Orlando Patterson, "Paul, Slavery and Freedom: Personal and Social-historical Reflections", *Semeia 83/84 1998, Slavery in Text and Interpretation*, p. 267.
48. Ibid.
49. Ibid.
50. Op. cit. p. 268.
51. Ibid.
52. Ibid.
53. Views here have taken into consideration the disputed Pauline letters of Colossians, Ephesians, Titus, Peter; John Knox, "Paul Among the Liberals" *Religion In Life* 49 (Winter 1980): 416–21.
54. Will Deming, "A Diatribe Pattern in 1 Corinthians 7:21-22: A New Perspective on Paul's Direction to Slaves", *Novum Testamentum*, XXXVII, FASC (2 April 1995): 131–37.
55. Patterson, *Paul, Slavery and Freedom*, pp. 263–79.
56. C. J. Cadoux, *The Early Church and the World* (Edinburgh: T. & T. Clark, 1st edn 1925 reprinted 1955), pp 132–33; Burchell Taylor, "Onesimus: The Voiceless, Powerless Initiator of the Liberating Process", in Howard Gregory ed. *Caribbean Theology – Preparing for the Challenges Ahead* (Barbados: Cedar Press, 1995), p. 18; Biot ed. 1840, pp. 125–26, 140–41.
57. J. Christian Beker, *Paul's Apocalyptic Gospel – The Coming Triumph of God* (Philadelphia, PA: Fortress Press, 1982), pp. 111–15; J. Paul Samply, *Walking Between the Times – Paul's Moral Reasoning* (Minneapolis, MN: Fortress Press, 1991), p. 9.
58. Clarice J. Martin, "The Haustafeln (Household codes) in African American Biblical Interpretation: 'Free Slaves' and 'Subordinate Women' in Cain Hope Felder ed.

Stony the Road We Trod: African American Biblical Interpretation (Minneapolis, MN: Fortress Press, 1991), pp. 207–10; see also Richard A. Horsley, *Paul and Empire: Religion and Power in Roman Imperial Society* (Harrisburg, PA: Trinity Press International, 1997), pp. 228–31.

59. Patterson, *Slavery and Social Death*, pp. 75–76.
60. Ibid.
61. Ibid.
62. Ibid.
63. Ibid., p. 76.
64. David Bosch, "Paul on Human Hopes" *Journal of Theology for Southern Africa*, 67 (June 1989): 4.
65. David Bosch, "Mission and the Alternative Community: How My Mind Changed" *Journal of Theology For Southern Africa* 41 (December, 1982): 9.
66. David Bosch, "The Churches as the Alternative Community" *Journal of Theology For Southern Africa* 13 (December, 1975): 3–11.
67. Bosch, *Paul on Human Hopes*, p. 8.
68. Tidball, *The Social Context of the New Testament*, p. 116.
69. Cadoux, *The Early Church and the World*, p. 133.
70. Beker, *Paul's Apocalyptic Gospel*, p. 111.
71. Ibid.
72. Sampley, *Walking Between the Times*, p. 9.
73. Frank C. Porter, "The Place of Apocalyptic Conceptions in the Thought of Paul" *Journal of Biblical Literature* XLI (1992): 204.
74. 59 Bosch, *Paul on Human Hopes*, p. 6.
75. Ibid.
76. John Knox, "Paul and the Liberals" *Religion In Life* 49 (Winter 1980): 418.
77. Ibid.
78. C. H. Dodd took the lead in the development of the realized eschatological perspective. Dodd held that the Christ-event is the realization of the rule of God in this present world. As such, every aspect of the age to come is fulfilled in the present. 1 Thessalonians, 1 Corinthians 10, 2 Cor. 5:17, Matt 13:37–43 and 25:31–46 are key texts for Dodd. See C. H. Dodd *New Testament Studies* (Manchester: University of Manchester, 1953), pp. 54–57, 108–18; and *The Meaning of Paul for Today* (Cleveland, OH: World Publishing Co., 1957).
79. Horsley, *Paul and Empire*, p. 142.
80. Horsley, *Paul and Empire*, p. 143.
81. Taylor, *Onesimus*, p. 18; Patterson, *Paul, Slavery and Freedom*, p. 266.
82. Berger Gerhardsson, "Eleutheria (Freedom) in the Bible", in Barry P. Thompson ed. *Scripture: Method and Meaning, Essays Presented to Anthony Tyrell Hanson on his 70th Birthday* (Hull: Hull University Press, 1987), pp. 3–23.
83. Boff, O.F.M., *Faith On The Edge*, p. 60.
84. Ibid.
85. Ibid.
86. Ibid., p. 73.
87. Calypsonian Rudder, a calypso entitled "Rally Round the West Indies" asks a similar question: "are we doom forever to be at somebody's mercy...?"
88. Finley, *Ancient Slavery*, pp. 73–75; Patterson, *Slavery and Social Death*, p. 28.

89. David Brion Davis, *The Problem of Slavery in Western Culture* (New York, Oxford: Oxford University Press, 1966), p. 10.
90. Patterson, *Slavery and Social Death*, p. 5.
91. Finley, *Ancient Slavery*, p. 32.
92. Patterson, *Slavery and Social Death*, p. 98.
93. Patterson, *Slavery and Social Death*, p. 101.
94. Ibid.
95. Orlando Patterson, *Freedom Vol. 1 Freedom in the Making of Western Culture* (London: I. B. Tauris & Co. Ltd., 1991), p. 3.
96. Ibid.
97. Patterson, *Freedom in the Making*, p. 4.
98. Ibid.
99. Ibid.
100. John Dominic Crossan and Jonathan L. Reed, *In Search of Paul – How Jesus' Apostle Opposed Rome's Empire with God's Kingdom* (London: SPCK, 2004), p. 12.
101. Crossan and Reed, *In Search of Paul*, p. xi.
102. Boff, *Faith On The Edge*, p. 73.
103. See J. B. Lightfoot, *Saint Paul's Epistles to the Colossians and to Philemon* (London: Macmillan & Co. Ltd., 1912); John M. G. Barclay "Paul, Philemon and the Dilemma of Christian Slave-ownership", *New Testament Studies* 37 (2) (April 1991): 161–86; Joseph A. Fitzmyer, S.J. *The Anchor Bible: The Letter to Philemon, A New Translation with Introduction and Commentary* (New York: Doubleday, 2000); Norman K. Petersen, *Rediscovering Paul, Philemon and the Sociology of Paul's Narrative World* (Philadelphia, PA: Fortress Press, 1985); John D. Nordling "Onesimus Fugitivus: A Defence of the Runaway Slave Hypothesis in Philemon" *Journal for the Study of the New Testament* 41 (February 1991), 97–119.
104. *"Fan The Flame* by Tim Hector", *Outlet Newspaper* (19 January 2001): 5.
105. Richard D. E. Barton, *Afro-Creole, Power, Opposition and Play in the Caribbean* (Ithaca, NY and London: Cornell University Press, 1997): 50:
106. R. S. Sugirtharajah, *Postcolonial Criticism and Biblical Interpretation* (Oxford: Oxford University Press, 2000), p. 90.
107. Ibid., p. 91.
108. John M. G. Barclay "Paul, Philemon and the Dilemma of Christian Slave-ownership" *New Testament Studies* 37 (2) (April 1991): 183.

Chapter 4

"Readings" of Philemon

Introduction

Any analysis or interpretation of biblical text that does not take into account the socio-historic environment of the Bible tells more about the interpreter than the interpretation. As C. L. R. James, world-renowned social commentator from the Caribbean, notes "any extended cricket analysis which is not based on historical facts ... tells more about the writer than what he is writing about".[1] In support of this perspective James states "Who will write a biography of Sir Donald Bradman must be able to write a history of Australia in the same period".[2] Essentially, in any attempt to "read" biblical text, one cannot ignore the socio-historical praxis of those who compose biblical texts. To attempt this brings more into focus the context, presupposition, hermeneutical suspicion and social location of the interpreter than the biblical text. This is not to say that the interpreter is more important than the text. No. Rather, interpretive strategies are conditioned by the context, influences and experiences of the interpreter. A disinterested reader of biblical texts does not exist. Even so, if one is interpreting historical phenomena, then the circumstances of those phenomena cannot be ignored.

The task here, therefore, becomes one of discerning whether interpretations of Philemon were conditioned by the material circumstances out of which Philemon was produced or the context of the interpreter. The slavery and contemporary era are used as the context for interpreting Philemon. The aim will be to determine the arguments advanced and to discover the prevalent interpretive practices of the periods. My principal aim, though, is to learn what gives agency to interpreting Philemon during the era of slavery and the contemporary era.

The Era of Slavery

Accordingly, what becomes necessary here is to examine the nature of the discourses on the letter to Philemon. To facilitate this examination, the work of three pro-slavery proponents are appraised – bishops N. S. Wheaton, Protestant Episcopalian bishop of Connecticut, John Henry Hopkins, Protestant Episcopal bishop of Vermont and Rev. Raymund Harris, a Spanish-born Jesuit priest as well as three anti-slavery advocates – Rev. Thomas Atkins, an ordained Baptist minister who held pastorates in Pennsylvania, Virginia, Philadelphia and was secretary of the Eastern Baptists of Pennsylvania Colored Relief Protective Association, Olaudah Equiano, a native African and former slave and Frederick Douglass, an outspoken Abolitionist who was born into slavery in 1818, escaped in 1838 and was legally emancipated in 1846. How they used and understood Philemon in their advocacy for or against slavery is ascertained. In so doing, discovery is made as to whether their use or abuse of Philemon was more about the interpreter than the biblical text, that is, whether Philemon was abstracted from its socio-historic context. To abstract Philemon from its socio-historic origins, and thereby not give agency to the socio-ideological and theological agenda at work in its composition, is to abuse its use.

Racism is the domination of one race over another. Throughout the seventeenth and eighteenth centuries the socio-political-cultural-economic systems in the Caribbean and the Americas was structured around slavery. For Patterson, a noted Caribbean sociologist working at Harvard University, slavery is "the permanent, violent domination of natally alienated and generally dishonored persons".[3] It was the native Caribs, Arawaks and Mestisos, and then the Africans, brought against their will for the express purpose of providing free labour, who suffered the brunt of this system of violent domination and dishonour. These exploitative, dominating and discriminatory circumstances formed the socio-historical, economic, cultural and political context that the pro- and anti-slavery proponents and slaves inhabited. It is important to note this context. Having previously described the socio-historical context of Philemon, we are now in a position to see where agency is given in or what gives agency to the use or abuse of the letter.

Here, it is crucial to examine some of the arguments advanced by pro-slavery advocates.

The Black Race as Curse

To begin with, pro-slavery advocates claimed that there could be no social equality between the black and white races as Africans were fated to be under the thumb of whites by Divine order. One such proponent was bishop N. S. Wheaton whose views are derived from Genesis 9.

In a context of natal alienation, violent domination and the dishonouring of humanity, Wheaton stated "the inferior race must, by a law which we cannot control, remain under the same kind of subordination to the higher intellect of the Anglo Saxon, till it shall please God to lift up the curse, pronounced four thousand and five hundred years ago".[4] Similarly, Wheaton divided the human race into two groups, the sons of Ham, the Africans and the sons of Japheth, the Whites. So, Wheaton claimed "wherever the sons of Ham and the sons of Japheth have been brought into juxtaposition, the original of servitude, in some of its forms, has universally prevailed: a servant of servants shall be unto his brethren. I do not so much understand this in the light of a command that it should be so, as of a prophecy, it would be so".[5] Thus, the sons of Ham are deemed to be inferior and fated to slavery. Bondage in slavery is their divinely ordained destiny. In short, Genesis 9 is used to justify relations of domination-submission.

Further, Wheaton cited Pauline practice in Ephesians, Colossians, Titus and 1 Peter to promote servile obedience. Wheaton summed up his argument this way: "Divine mafter never taught Paul that the purchasing of slaves, servitude or bondage was an unnatural, iniquitous purfuit contrary to the spirit and practice of faith in God. If such was the case, then Paul would have feverely condemned the unjuftifiable conduct of Philemon in detaining Onesimus in criminal bondage".[6] And then Wheaton asked, "is not obedience in the slave, according to the Apostolic standard, made a duty as sacred as any other duty, sacred or moral".[7] As such, for him there was nothing morally wrong with slavery owing to the fact that Paul condoned the system of slavery and its practices. Wheaton is willing to stand on Paul's authority, never mind that Pauline authorship of Ephesians and Colossians is disputed and Titus and 1 Peter came from a context in which the church was accommodating to the status quo.

Essentially, Wheaton accepted that relations of domination-submission between master and slave were legitimate. For all that, however, there is also a remarkable and surprising acknowledgement by Wheaton, given his aforementioned views on race, that suggests that no power can halt the quest for freedom: "when bondage is made more stringent and oppressive, and when it is seen that, in the event of their escape, there is no hope of recovery, in the aggrieved party, there is left rankling a sense of wrongs unaddressed – of intolerable insult, of a broken covenant – all tending to excite and foster a wish to separate forever from, and cease from all intercourse with, a people, who cannot or will not be held to any compact, however sacred".[8] In other words, no power or system can halt the quest for freedom.

Giving support to the view that the Black race is a curse was Bishop John Henry Hopkins. For Bishop Hopkins, in the relations between master and slave, there is no sin.[9] Sin was only committed in the treatment of slaves. As long as the slave masters treat the slaves with 'justice' and 'kindness', there are no sinners and sinned against. Treating slaves with "justice" and "kindness" is but to do what is scriptural and constitutional.[10] Bishop Hopkins took the view that slavery was a physical evil, rather than a moral evil. He claimed that Gen. 9:25, 11:14 and 6:9 showed that the Almighty God ordained slaves to servitude because "he judged it to be their fittest condition and all history proves how accurate the prediction has been accomplished, even to the present day".[11] Additionally, Bishop Hopkins dismissed Deut. 23:15–16 as reference to a foreign heathen master and not slaves of Israelites.[12] He built his argument further by interpreting Gen. 16:9 as the angel commanding the fugitive Hagar to return to her mistress and submit herself[13] and suggested that the Mosaic law (Exod. 20:17, Lev. 25:10) gave approval to possessing persons as property.[14] In other words, the domination of one race over another is of divine order.

On the back of such interpretation, Hopkins interpreted Philemon as Paul returning a fugitive turned convert to Christianity asking for forgiveness.[15] In so doing, Paul did nothing contrary to the practice of Christianity.

Rev. Thomas Atkins, however, challenged Hopkins' interpretations and offered alternative scriptural evidence. Atkins questioned Hopkins' exegesis of Genesis 9 arguing that at that time "whatever servitude existed was mild; families were not separated and only able bodied men were appointed to be hewers of wood and drawers of water for service of the Temple".[16] Still slaves though!! Additionally, the bondservants in Abraham's house "were the confidential and faithful domestics of Pharaoh's household and trained for defensive warfare by their masters".[17] In comparison, Atkins noted, slave masters did not instruct their slaves in the principles of Christian religion or in the use of arms. In fact, it was a penal offence to instruct slaves in reading and writing.[18] Also, Atkins observed that Hagar's condition and circumstances were different in degree and nature to American slaves. Hagar and her son Ishmael were not sold to strangers; instead they were granted personal liberty and given supplies for the journey.[19] Atkins considered the separation of families as an act of violence and a violation of the principles of natural justice.[20] As such, he was standing against the legitimization of domination by one race over another on the authority of the Bible arguing that, in biblical times, servitude was benign, slaves were in positions to exercise authority and the character of slavery in the New World was different.

Furthermore, Atkins contended that, though in a Graeco-Roman legal context wives, children and servants were the property of husband, fathers, masters, "they are not things, chattels, articles of lawful merchandizing; they are persons and by the law of revelation and nature are justly entitled to rights and privileges, civil and religious".[21] In short, for Atkins, the negation of the humanity of another human cannot be justified either by reference to the Bible or nature.

In sum, Wheaton purported that relations of domination-submission between master and slave were legitimate; Hopkins saw that though slavery was a physical evil it was not morally offensive, and that Onesimus was an outlaw. Contrary to both Wheaton and Hopkins, Atkins believed that one was hard-pressed to find any moral grounds for justifying or legitimizing slavery in the Bible and the natural order. All three interpreters, however, have gone completely outside the text of Philemon neglecting thereby the socio-historic environment in which the letter was produced to fashion their interpretation. Agency is not given to the socio-ideological interests and social practices out of which Philemon emerged. The question now becomes what reading strategy they used to arrive at this domination-submission theory.

Blame the Victim

Another position set forth by pro-slavery protagonists was to blame the victim. This thinking came from an interpretation of Philemon that saw Onesimus as the one who was wrong, not the one who was wronged. This was the perspective of the Rev. Raymund Harris. Harris held several views on slavery that brought out the racial tone of his argument. For Harris, the "rights" of masters over slaves were "facred and inviolabe"[22] and by implication this means that slaves have no "rights" over their masters. This "right" of masters over slaves is borne out by the fact that Paul sent Onesimus back to Philemon because he never had Philemon's "exprefs approbation and confent" to keep Onesimus.[23] Harris extended this argument by pointing out that Paul's refusal to assume Philemon's "right" was based on the fact that Jesus never condemned slavery as unjust. In fact, it was God who ordered the estate of Philemon, as master, and Onesimus, as slave. The race and class-based discrimination advanced by Harris stands indefensible.

Consequently, he regarded Philemon as a Christian of "distinguifsed merit" while Onesimus was charged with "defrauding his master of fome part of his master's property and eloped".[24] As such, Paul wrote, "to effect a reconciliation between Onesimus and Philemon and to obtain from the mafter the re-admission of his fugitive slave into his house and service",[25] that is, a return to servile fidelity. But as James G. Birney, who was secretary of the American antislavery society in 1837–38 and struggled to bring an end to slavery through constitutional and political means,[26] asked, "How could Onesimus wrong Philemon or be indebted to him when Philemon had absolute power over him"?[27] In other words, Onesimus did not have the wherewithal to wrong Philemon, except by running away.

Seemingly, Harris attempted to find scriptural evidence to dissemble his own arguments. He posited "all things whatsoever he would that men would do to you do the same for them" and thereby saw in this that "no person should reduce another to the condition of a slave and that every type of subordination ought to be suffered to continue in the world". He pointed out further that masters should treat their slaves "with the same tenderness, justice and humanity as he desired his slave to him". Yet he argued that the golden maxim "ferves to enforce masters and slaves reciprocal duties in their fpheres of life". In other word, he does not condemn slavery. In reality, slaves would never find themselves in a position to reciprocate.

Nonetheless, Olaudah Equiano, in robust riposte to Harris, disclaimed the view that Paul encouraged servile fidelity[28] and that slaves, who were not to be embittered by their oppressive lot, must submit to their masters. Equiano stood four-square against the domination-submission theory. For example, I refer here to the argument mounted by Olaudah Equiano in his response to Harris.[29] For Harris, bondage was compatible with Christianity. What was needed was patience under servitude. Equiano, in response, mounted his challenge on the grounds that the brotherly love of which Paul spoke when urging Onesimus' return to Philemon was subversive of slavery. For Equiano, slavery was irreconcilable with the values of dignity, compassion and equality of Christ's kingdom. Thus, for Paul to have denounced slavery was tantamount to advocating revolution over against personal reformation.[30] Consequently, slaves would have desired release from material bondage rather than redemption from personal sin.

Furthermore, Equiano also attacked the domination-submission theory. Equiano held that slavery was inconsistent with Christianity such that it was unacceptable in Christ's kingdom for one human being to hold another in bondage. Equiano stated "slavery was derogatory to the honour of Christianity for it was wrong that persons whom Christ redeemed to be regarded as slaves and property".[31] As such, slavery ran counter to the doctrine of the atonement – human beings could only be redeemed through the sacrificial death of Christ at Calvary. The situation, therefore, between Philemon and Onesimus, and by implication within the imperial Graeco-Roman world in general, was for Equiano, untenable.

Human Person as Property

A further argument advanced by pro-slavery proponents in coming to their interpretation of Philemon was the understanding of the human person as property. Here, it was the person who was the commodity, not the person's skills or labour. This made it possible to purchase and thereby own a person, which inevitably eliminated any rights the "possessed" person had.

Nevertheless, Rev. David Young, a Presbyterian minister who converted to Methodism in 1859 in Harrisburg, Ohio, objected to this argument. His objection concerned the actual or totality of power that one human had over another. For him, it was simply wrong and evil that one should wield that kind of power.[32] As such, Philemon's ownership of Onesimus as property was wrong. In this light, Young interpreted v.16 as Onesimus' opportunity to reclaim relations with relatives and fellow creatures and Christians[33] and took the position that "in the flesh" and "in the Lord" had to do with equality in personal and social relations.[34]

Hermeneutics of Plain Sense

The arguments and counter arguments mounted above reveal the reading strategies or the epistemologies of the interpreters, their way of knowing into the text/letter. Both Wheaton and Hopkins came to their interpretation of Philemon via an understanding of passages in the Old Testament that seemingly legitimize the domination of one race over another. They based their arguments on the Old Testament story of Ham in Genesis 9, yet dismissing Deut. 23:15–16, as well as on the disputed Pauline letters of Ephesians and Colossians as well as Titus and 1 Peter, all in an era when the nascent New Testament church was accommodating to the status quo. For example, Wheaton takes the position that the essential facts of the case in Paul's letter to Philemon are that Philemon is an exemplary Christian and Onesimus, as a converted fugitive, wants to return to his master.[35] From these "facts", Wheaton concluded that Paul never censored Philemon, made no appeal to Philemon's conscience and returned Onesimus to bondage despite the fact that Onesimus was already free.[36] Thus, slavery is just; and Onesimus' real freedom was his adoption into the house church that met in Philemon's household.

Bishop Hopkins, having argued that, within the Bible, there is nothing morally repugnant about slavery, he repudiated the view that a fugitive slave should not be returned to his former master. He suggested that Paul acted uprightly in returning Onesimus to Philemon. In other words, bondage in slavery is acceptable.

Hence, though reading into biblical texts or eisegesis is legitimate, by coming to their interpretation of Philemon through the Old Testament, both Wheaton and Hopkins engaged in proof-texting. Proof-texting is not eisegesis. Eisegesis takes place when the interpreter uses his or her socio-historical and contextual realities as an epistemological lens through which to interpret biblical texts. Neither Hopkins nor Wheaton came near to using the repugnance of slavery as an epistemological lens. And neither did they engage, even from a safe distance, the socio-ideological theological agenda at work in Philemon. As such, coming to Philemon neither out of their own contextual realities nor from circumstances that produced Philemon, they abstracted Philemon from its historical social context.

Hermeneutic of Human Rights

Coming from a completely different angle and experience, and more experience than angle, Frederick Douglass used mockery and ridicule in at least three of his speeches to challenge the domination-submission theory as an interpretive tool. In the eulogy he delivered on 14 April 1858 in New York for William Jay, he hailed the tenth clause of William Jay's last will and testament as the first bequest to a fugitivus. In part, the clause states, "I bequeath to my son one thousand dollars to be applied by him at his discretion in promoting the safety and comfort of fugitive slaves".[37] The bequest was no disguise in support for resisting the system of slavery and its practices. To the contrary, resistance was given tangible and open encouragement. It is difficult to miss the obvious reference to Philemon 10–19 used by conservative clergymen as an inspired commitment to obey the fugitive slave law of 1850. Onesimus did not run away in the sense of being an outlaw. Being "away", he was standing outside the system of slavery to challenge it. Douglass considered the attempts to control and overawe another by the force and authority of inhuman laws as futile and blasphemous,[38] calling wrong right and right wrong.

Likewise, in a speech on "the American Constitution and the Slave" given in Glasgow, Scotland on 26 March 1860, Douglass contested the view that both the American Constitution and the letter of Philemon in the Bible gave legitimacy to slavery. Whereas the American Constitution was interpreted to be pro-slavery, the Bible is seen as against liberty. But Douglass asks, with some amount of exaggeration, if not irony, "so you declare a thing is bad because it has been misused, abused and made bad use of? Do you throw it away on that account? No! You press it to your bosom all the more closely; you read it all the more diligently; and prove from its pages that it is on the side of liberty – and not on the side of slavery. So let us do with the constitution of the United States".[39] In other words, the bad use to which the Bible has been put in justifying slavery does not make the Bible bad. The mis-use of the Bible may be bad, though the Bible itself is not. Bad use does not make the Bible bad. So, for Douglass, just as the Constitution of the United States is not laid aside even when it is perceived that its use does not serve the purpose of liberty, so, too, the Bible must not be laid aside.

In similar fashion, in his speech on the Proclamation and the Negro Army, 6 February 1863, New York, Douglass challenged the view that slavery was of Divine appointment. He noted that, in the churches, it was taught that Jesus and the Apostles, despite full knowledge and experience of Roman slavery, never condemned slavery and encouraged obedience of slave to master. Then Douglass mockingly commented, "even to catch and return runaway slaves was in accordance with Apostolic example, and the main feature of the Fugitive Slave Bill was in harmony with Paul's Epistle to Philemon (laughter)".[40] For Douglass and his hearers, no slave would have been that stupid to return voluntarily to his master having escaped.

In sum, through satire, Douglass exposed and criticized the misuse and abuse of Paul's letter to Philemon as giving legitimacy to slavery. Nonetheless, even Douglass did not give agency to the socio-ideological and theological agenda at work in the letter to Philemon. Douglass gave agency to his experience of deprivation and dishonour, which provided the epistemological lens by which he read Philemon.

To summarize, Wheaton and Hopkins engaged in *proof-texting*; Douglass and Equiano relied on their personal *experiences* of the harsh realities of slavery and so spoke with righteous indignation; Harris employed *reverse psychology* wherein Onesimus ought to have felt guilty for running away; and Young used the *material conditions* of the composition of the letter. Each strategy served the interest of the particular interpreter. None was neutral.

Nevertheless, with the exception of Harris, Young and Equiano's response, the reading strategies of Wheaton, Hopkins and Douglass failed to deal with the socio-historic environment of the text/letter. Where Wheaton and Hopkins did give agency to the material conditions of the composition of the letter, it was never with the intent of effecting social transformation in the society they habited but rather to maintain the status quo and reinforce servile fidelity. It was Equiano, one who had experienced slavery in all its harsh and dehumanizing dimensions and thereby employed a different way of knowing into the letter, who gave agency to both the contextual realities and the socio-ideological and theological agenda at work in the letter, such that a social order of liberation was championed. The question is, why?

Exegetics and Eisegetics

The foregoing has raised two contradictory questions. One, why is it that Christians could use the Bible as an authority to support slavery and at the same time flout the teachings of the same Bible that persons whom Christ redeemed cannot be regarded as slaves and property? And two, why is it that Christians reading the same biblical text arrived at contradictory conclusions about slavery?

To begin with, Wheaton and Hopkins held privileged positions in the establishment and can thus be regarded as upholders of the status quo. Their social location within the socio-political structure and system was privileged. Therefore, they were not inclined to question, unlike Atkins, Douglass, Equiano and Young, the cause of the oppression, exploitation and inequalities within the society. Though Young's social location was also privileged, he was prepared to question the status quo, which came about because of the agency he gave to the letter as a product of the socio-ideological practices and systems of its context. This in turn raised his critical awareness in exposing the oppressive nature of the social system and practices.

However, the personal experience of slavery was the context out of which the reading strategies of Douglass and Equiano arose. Both were slaves. As such, it meant that both came out of a culture in which forbidding slaves to learn to read was a tool of oppression. Inevitably, in slave societies, the Bible was taught in accordance with ideas and vested interests of the ruling class. Slaves had to rely on listening and memory, the aural tradition. It was the reading strategy that had authority for the slaves, not just the biblical text. This meant that slaves had no loyalty to any official text, translation or interpretation and thereby were at liberty to remember, repeat, retell, and resist any narrative or portions of scripture that suited their interests or spoke to their struggles.[41] Slave hermeneutic, then, began with their experience of the reality of oppression by which they were enabled to measure what they were told against what they were experiencing and what they thought of themselves.[42] Social location, who we are and where we are from, and hermeneutical suspicion do condition interpretation.

In addition to social location and hermeneutical suspicion, all of which get mixed-up in what we believe about God and how we interpret the Bible, the understanding of biblical texts as products of their environment are also critical factors in exposing oppressive systems and practices in the context out of which one interprets and in which biblical texts were produced. Where interpretation does not privilege the underclass, it strengthens the status quo. Both Young and Equiano gave such a privilege to the underclass in the interpretive process. Nonetheless, it is not always the case that the oppressed and exploited will question, never mind challenge, the status quo.

The answer to the first contradictory question, then, is that where the materiality of the Bible – the socio-economic, political, cultural and ideological dimensions of the text – does not condition interpretation, then a disjuncture develops between the material conditions of the interpreter and the biblical texts. The material conditions of the biblical text play no critical part in interpreting the context, and in reality a disjuncture develops between faith and praxis. It is thus this disjuncture between the materiality of the interpreter and biblical texts that characterizes Caribbean biblical hermeneutical practice.

The second of the contradictions raised above is given to the same response of failure to give agency to the materiality of the Bible. Harris blamed the victim, not the system and structures, for the upheaval, dislocation and struggle within the society. Harris, with his reverse psychological reading strategy, saw Onesimus as the one who sinned, rather than the one sinned against. To see Onesimus as the one who sinned is to blind oneself to the violation of his person by the system and structures of the society. It is the system and structures that have infringed upon Onesimus' rights as a person. Where the few benefit from the labour of the many, and resources and power are used for the self-satisfaction of the few rather than the self-realization of the many, there is structural violence.[43] What structural violence does is to set in train a spiral of violence in three stages: oppression, resistance and repression.[44] In Philemon, all three stages are at work. How Onesimus' return is treated depends in large measure on whether Onesimus is seen as the one who had committed a wrong or the one who was wronged, and that requires an epistemology that is able to identify the real victim and read the letter from the victim's perspective.

However, while the perspective of whether Onesimus did wrong or wrong was done to him does not take Philemon out of its life context, interpreting the letter from the point of the view of the privileged Philemon reinforces the status quo or structural violence.

Furthermore, following the argument of J. Albert Harrill, while antislavery proponents viewed slavery from the moral – right and wrong, justice and injustice – point of view, the pro-slavery proponents saw it from the political perspective.[45] For anti-slavery proponents, the appeal to Christian morality is that of conscience over biblical authority,[46] which leads to a more critical reading of Scripture.

According to Harrill, there are three hermeneutical movements in the reading of Scripture by anti-slavery proponents. The first step is the development of the hermeneutic of immutable principles: an egalitarian reading of Jesus' Golden rule as opposed to a patriarchal reading.[47] Matthew 7:12 and Luke 6:31 are taken as the core principles of this epistemology.

The second step is the argument from conscience over biblical authority.[48] Here one could be wrong about the interpretation of a text yet maintain the morality of a cause. For Harrill, "the moral norms of the Bible were conditioned by social arrangements and cultural assumptions of a particular age and people".[49] So, one needs to determine what is the "word of God" and the "word of writers".

And the third step is the hermeneutic of typology (Rev. 6:15–16, 19:11–13) and apocalyptic theology that involves the actual use of force to bring about freedom.[50]

On the other hand, for the pro-slavery proponents, the political imperative is biblicism, a literary reading of Scripture. This manner of engaging the text is fuelled by the view that the New Testament does not condemn slavery and thereby signals an acceptance of an organic model of society for which subjection is essential.[51]

Harrill, therefore, makes two contributions to the discussion on the contradictory conclusions reached by Christians on the material conditions of slavery: one, that the contradictions are due to the Christians' understanding of morality and politics; and two, a literal, as opposed to an egalitarian, typological and conscientious reading strategy. Even so, besides ignoring the issues of social location and hermeneutical suspicion, Harrill does not give agency to the material conditions out which the text was produced.

In sum, the reading strategies – proof-texting, experience, reverse psychology and reason – of interpreters cited in the above came to an interpretation of Philemon via Genesis 9 and disputed Pauline letters from an era when the church was accommodating to the status quo. Besides, the interpreters concentrated on the struggle occurring in their context. While these reading strategies and concentration on the existential realities of the context are not brushed aside, my contention is that in Philemon a thoroughgoing social struggle is taking place for social control or social transformation. In effect, in Philemon, a socio-ideological and theological agenda was at work, and that agenda was neglected, which meant that the ruling class ideas and interests embedded in the letter were not identified.

Noticeably, where the materiality of both biblical texts and the context of the interpreter are ignored no challenge to the status quo ensues and a disjuncture between faith and praxis develops, as there is neither grounding nor impetus for an alternative social order. Mainly because of their personal experiences of the harsh realities of slavery but not without linking those experiences to the dehumanizing conditions in Philemon, it was only Douglass and Equiano who resisted the oppressive system of slavery. If there is no vision of and hope for an alternative social order coming out of praxis and the oppressive and repressive nature of the status quo, then resistance does not occur.

The discussion here highlights the critique concerning Caribbean biblical hermeneutical practice. Here it is seen in the interpretation of Young, Equiano and Douglass that it is necessary to do more than applying the interpretation of biblical texts to contextual realities in order to expose, challenge and resist oppressive systems and practices. Agency must be given to both the social forces and struggles of the context of readers of biblical texts and the environment out of which the biblical texts were produced for there to be any meaningful and effective challenge to the status quo on the authority of the Bible. Attempts to contextualize biblical texts without reference to their materiality become a pretext for social action, and carry no force for resisting any oppressive systems and practices.

The Contemporary Era

Now, one could argue or even attempt to excuse the anti- and pro-slavery proponents and slaves for allowing contextual and existential realities to inform and condition biblical reading practices. However, while the form of harsh, dehumanizing and exploitative conditions of oppressive intent have changed since the days of slavery, the character and purpose of oppressive intent have remained unchanged. The "leopard" of oppression has not changed its spots. Leopards of whatever description do not change spots. The question is, have biblical reading practices changed form or have they remained the same in character and intent from the days of slavery to the contemporary era? Or to put it another way, what gives agency to biblical reading practices in the contemporary era? Below, this question, from the perspectives of the liberal, liberationist and postcolonial biblical reading strategies, is examined for the period 1980 to the present.

Liberal Hermeneutics
With the liberal reading strategy, the attempt is to locate the site of struggle, whether in the material conditions of the letter to Philemon or within the social location or hermeneutical presupposition of the interpreters referenced. This searching aims to expose what is giving agency and where resistance is occurring. A liberal can be defined as one who holds to and emphasizes the expression of individual "rights", freedom, enterprise and rule of law in the building of society. Thus, within a liberal reading strategy, I am interested to see what individualistic, abstract and subjective aspects of the letter to Philemon are emphasized in the light of the socio-ideological and theological interests and social practices at work in the letter.

Within New Testament study a number of scholars, among them Gillian Feeley-Harnick, Norman K. Petersen, John M. Barclay and Chris Frilingos, centred the site of struggle in the letter on the weight of the influence that Philemon and Paul carried in the household and house church as well as on the need for Philemon and Onesimus to resolve their personal conflicts. Others who share this understanding are B. M. Rapske, Ralph P. Martin, N. H. Taylor, Joseph A. Fitzmyer, John D. Nordling and Carolyn Osiek, Cain Hope Felder and S.C. Winter.

Authority: Individualizing Social Struggle
According to Gillian Feeley-Harnick Paul's intention in Philemon is to establish his authority, to find a way of making Philemon honour his request.[52] So, the letter to Philemon is about how one transforms power into authority.[53] The centre of contention is no longer the conflict between Philemon and Onesimus but who has power to command whom. In structuring her argument around the issue of authority in the letter, Feeley-Harnick regards Onesimus as the gift, the instrument of God's larger design,[54] which is to settle the authority issue between Paul and Philemon. Put another way, it means that Onesimus is just a pawn, caught in the middle of the debate as to who is the chief executive. To support her

contention Feeley-Harnick argues that Paul was not observing Deut. 23:16 in the breach in spite of the fact that it is the case in Roman law that all fugitives must be returned to their masters.[55] And that vv.18–19 depicts a covert strategy by Paul to gain the advantage over Philemon, especially since "there might not have been any debts to repay as Onesimus may have run away on account of maltreatment".[56] Thus, while struggle is cited here it is not between contending socio-ideological interests and practices within the system, but between individuals.

This same tendency to individualize the social struggle occurring in the socio-historic environment is evident in the work of Norman K. Petersen, John M. Barclay and Chris Frilingos. Whatever the nature of the struggle they identified, the argument drifts to the issue of individual authority.

Though Norman K. Petersen recognizes that by running away Onesimus threatened slavery as an institution,[57] he sees the letter/text as more about Paul's authority. Petersen notes the nature of the social relations between Philemon and Onesimus in the social structure of the society and church.[58] In the world, Philemon is master, Onesimus slave; but in the church, Philemon has no role as master and none is superior or inferior, they are both equals.[59] On Onesimus' return, Philemon has three possible options: remain Onesimus' master and "justly" inflict punishment, lend Onesimus to another master, perhaps Paul, or liberate Onesimus.[60] These are all legitimate within the social structure of the imperial Graeco-Roman world.

In the church, however, Philemon only has one choice: receive Onesimus as brother either out of obedience to Paul or out of goodness.[61] In the church, Philemon can no longer live the double life of master and brother, for being master conflicts with or is incompatible with being brother. According to Petersen, "it is logically and socially impossible to relate to one and the same person as both one's inferior and as one's equal".[62] In effect, Onesimus being a brother to Philemon means that he cannot also be a slave to Philemon in any domain. In other words, "being in Christ is a state of social being that governs the relationships between believers even outside the spatial and temporary boundaries of the church".[63] Given, therefore, Philemon and Onesimus's state of being, the course of action open to Philemon is to "liberate" Onesimus". In short, the issue here is reduced to the identities of Philemon and Onesimus as equals before God.

However, whatever option Philemon takes has social implications. If he does not receive Onesimus as brother, will he expel himself from his own house? Will he undermine the value of equality on which the budding church is founded and thereby begin to unravel the social fabric of the community? Here Philemon's dilemma is in thinking "not in terms of his role as master but of relinquishing it",[64] to move from thoughts of punishment to freedom.

Yet Petersen does not see the letter as developing along this line of thinking. Rather he sees the letter as plotted around the theme of indebtedness – Onesimus to Philemon (in the world) and Philemon to Paul (in the church). Thus, the letter turns on the authority of Paul. Logically, if Paul has the authority to command Philemon's obedience, then he has the authority to discipline.[65] The matter now concerns who has the executive power and authority to command obedience.

In sum, for Petersen, Onesimus's desire to return poses the issue of equality of identity; and Paul's intervention centres on the issue on authority.[66] So, the letter exhibits a movement from equality of identity to authority. The dilemma here is that in a slave society such as imperial Graeco-Rome, master and slave are not brothers and thereby there is no equality of identity; and authority is the exercise of total control by the master over the slave as his property. As a result, with all attention focused on authority, Onesimus is decoded out of the letter and the economic and social relations that concern the household and house church are hidden.

Similarly, Barclay sees the issue as being not only about who decides Onesimus' future but also when that future should come about. Barclay takes the central tension in Philemon as the fact that in the house church, Philemon and Onesimus are co-equals but in the household they are socially unequal.[67] This tension raises the question as to whether Onesimus' status as a convert to Christianity should lead now or in the future to his liberation from slavery.

On the one hand, if Philemon decides to grant Onesimus his freedom, then this undermines the socio-economic structure of imperial Graeco-Roman society.[68] Thus freedom would be seen as a reward for running away, which might encourage other slaves to become converts to Christianity to gain their freedom. Even so, this leaves unsettled the issue of who pays the price of manumission and limits, if not the ruin, then certainly the ability of wealthier masters to maintain both household and house church.[69]

On the other hand, if Philemon accepts Onesimus as both co-equal and socially equal, then there are implications for both the house church and the household. In the context of the house church, it raises such questions as who is host, the slave or the master? Who is the leader? Is the offering taken as a contribution towards manumission? Are the household rules active in fellowship? What does brotherhood mean? Is brotherhood about parity in personal or spiritual and material relationships?[70] And in the context of the household, the issues of disobedience, insubordination and disrespect cast very long shadows. For who punishes whom, and for what? Who gives orders to whom, and who obeys?

Essentially, Barclay sees no relief of the central tension: can Philemon be both master and "brother" and Onesimus both slave and "brother"? Can Philemon and Onesimus be both co-equals and yet socially unequal? In other words, in whom does the power reside to determine Onesimus's destiny and when shall that decision take effect? The upshot of this position is that Onesimus becomes the object, not the subject, of his own destiny. Onesimus's destiny is decided for him, not by him.

Unlike Petersen and Barclay, Chris Frilingos contends that it is Paul who has the power to decide Onesimus' destiny, even while confining the issue of authority to Philemon's household. The battleground is in the household. If Philemon accedes to Paul's request, then Paul implicitly has administrative influence in Philemon's household.[71] Again, Onesimus is a pawn; this time as a sign of Paul's domestic power in Philemon's household.[72]

To support his argument, Frilingos cites the fact that the imperial Graeco-Roman household was a place of social, economic and political intercourse, not simply a place of residence.[73] Moreover, in the letter, Paul uses family language to displace Philemon's authority and stake his claims to Onesimus.[74] Onesimus is Paul's child and thereby Paul has paternal rights (vv. 10, 12,). As Paul's child, Onesimus is now an industrious servant as Paul's envoy (vv. 11, 13, 17). According to Frilingos, this "ownership" of Onesimus means that Paul is now superior to Philemon. Thus, for Frilingos, it is Paul who has the power to determine Onesimus' destiny. But is not running away a determination of one's own destiny? The position taken in this work is that it is. And will Onesimus go back simply on Paul's say so? I think not! Arguing that it is Paul who has the power to decide Onesimus' future is to overlook the fact that the act of running away, dangerous and daring though it was in Imperial Graeco-Rome, is itself an exercise of power no less.

What Feely-Harnick, Petersen, Barclay and Frilingos have done is to centre the social struggle depicted in the letter to Philemon in individuals – Philemon and Onesimus – rather than in the socio-economic structure. But, should the issue be confined to a determination of who has authority? Even if confining the issue to individuals is allowed, should it not be about Onesimus' freedom? It was Onesimus after all who was oppressed. Any focus on individuals will ultimately function to the favour of the status quo, which means that the system and its practices remain entrenched. To read Philemon from the point of view of authority is to read the letter from the point of view of the status quo, and hence there will be a failure to deal with the systemic and structural issues. What is at issue here is not right relationships (righteousness) but right relations (justice). What the liberals have failed to recognize is that power is primarily a product of relation to the means of production,[75] and is derived, therefore, from ownership of the means of production.

Reconciliation: Unchanging Oppressive Structures and Systems

The readings of B. M. Rapske, Ralph P. Martin, N. H. Taylor, Joseph A. Fitzmyer, John D. Nordling and Carolyn Osiek also limit the social struggle in the letter to Philemon to that which existed between Philemon and Onesimus, but from the point of view of reconciliation. Reconciliation, however, is dealt with on the personal level, which means that the social implications are neglected.

Rapske sees the letter of Philemon as being about putting aside punishment for any material injury, not exercising the right to administer punishment for the crime of running away.[76] In the same vein, Martin sees the request of vv. 8–20 as having to do with Philemon taking back Onesimus but with clemency.[77] This argument is built around v. 15. Here Onesimus' action in running away is providential. As such, Onesimus must not receive punishment. In this light, v. 21 is understood as manumission in view of v. 17, which means, "give him full acceptance" as a Christian.[78]

Though Taylor takes the issue from the point of view of re-socialization, the basic issues of forgiveness and acceptance have not changed. For Taylor, when Onesimus absconded he became de-socialized from the house church.[79] Therefore, he seeks Paul's mediation for reinstatement "not only as a slave of the household but as a brother in the house-church".[80] The essence of conversion here is re-socialization wherein the fugitivus theory and the case for manumission are dismissed. Onesimus could not be a fugitivus. As a fugitivus, he would not willingly desire to return to the inhuman treatment that awaits him. And Taylor, therefore, sees manumission as diminishing Philemon's obligation without increasing Onesimus' well being and security.[81]

Taylor concludes that "on balance, it would seem more likely that Paul is petitioning for Onesimus' restoration to his previous position in Philemon's household, complimented by his new relationship of Christian brotherhood with Philemon".[82] In short, servitude in the household sweetened by brotherhood in the house church, which means nothing changed – Philemon is still master and Onesimus is still a slave.

Fitzmyer's understanding of reconciliation is also based on the notion that nothing changed in the social structure. Basing his argument on vv. 15–16, Fitzmyer sees three options open to Philemon: take Onesimus back without punishment, take Onesimus back and restore him to the familia and servility; and emancipate Onesimus and return him to Paul as mission-partner. Each of the choices here, however, implies that Onesimus remains a slave. Even though Fitzmyer points out that the emphasis in the letter is on love (vv. 7, 20) such that there is no longer a master–slave relationship between Philemon and Onesimus but a brotherly one (v.16), this only means that Onesimus is now regarded as a Christian.

The arguments advanced by Rapske, Martin, Taylor and Fitzmyer amount to the fact that the social structure would not be challenged. After punishment was put aside, clemency was enacted and re-socialization was thoroughgoing, the socio-economic structure would have remained just as Onesimus had it. Liberals are seemingly not interested in socio-economic and political analysis of systems and structures, however blatantly oppressive and unjust. Rather, their priority ostensibly is in reconciliation between individuals rather than social justice.

Similarly, the arguments of Nordling and Osiek, though not dealing with forgoing punishment, do little to change the understanding of reconciliation. For Nordling, the radical nature of Christian forgiveness is pitted against the harsh laws of the world.[83] Nordling admits that manumission does not bring about affective change in the material/structural and legal relations between slave and master. Even so, he still contends that Paul's concern appears to have been perceptional and relational rather than structural.[84] Nordling centres his argument on vv. 16 and 17. He interprets "in the flesh" to refer to the household and "in the Lord" to the house church.[85] Though two entirely different domains, Paul wants the same treatment for slaves in both realms. As such, Onesimus could act independently, based on his own volition, refuse to carry out commands and determine punishment for any in the household where and whenever necessary. Thus, Onesimus is accorded privilege and honour. Further, v. 17 draws on the language of hospitality. The one received becomes a friend. But Nordling notes that in that society "friendship could only have existed between social equals and hospitality was only offered between social equals".[86]

What Paul wants, then, is that Philemon treat Onesimus as a social equal. However, social equality, for Nordling, has to do with refusal to insult or degrade, offering protection and respecting the honour and dignity of the slave.[87] Nonetheless, social equality is only one side of the social justice system. Social inequality is not a separate issue. Both social equality and social inequality affect the same person within the same social justice system.

In short, Nordling sees Paul as wanting a filial relationship between Philemon and Onesimus, a change in the nature and quality of the relationship, which however leaves the socio-economic structures unchanged or untouched.

Osiek also takes up the relational issue, albeit on a personal rather than a structural level. Osiek perceives that while Paul wants Onesimus as mission-partner, he needs to procure the approval of Philemon which of necessity means reconciliation between Philemon and Onesimus.[88] So, being a mission-partner is conditioned by reconciliation. Osiek takes v. 16 as the verse on which the letter hangs.[89] Here "in the flesh" means what Philemon and Onesimus are as human beings in their historically conditioned status; and "in the Lord" removes all social distinctions or the status of master and slave.[90] As such, social distinctions are no more, for conversion changes the nature of the relationship between Philemon and Onesimus. As a consequence of this change in social distinctions, Philemon can now accept Onesimus as a social equal (v. 17) and forgive and reconcile rather than exact justice (v. 18).[91] Even so, nothing is done to address social inequality, which remains entrenched.

So far, the liberal "readings" of Philemon centre the struggle that is taking place in the letter in the personal relationship between Philemon and Onesimus, not the system and its structures and practices. By doing so, the liberal "readings" suggest that Onesimus's destiny rests on Philemon's graciousness.[92] What puts Onesimus in a right relationship within the household economy is Philemon's unmerited love towards Onesimus, not a new order of social equality. However, the struggle in the personal relationship is caused by the system. Without resolving the struggle in the system, the struggle in the personal relationship will remain. To attempt to deal with the personal apart from the systemic is to attempt to deal with the symptom and not the cause.

Reconciliation: Avoiding Systemic Evils
However, whereas the arguments in the foregoing understand that reconciliation depends on the graciousness of Philemon, Cain Hope Felder and S. C. Winter comprehend reconciliation as the out-working of the inward change wrought by God in conversion. For Felder, Paul's focus in the text/letter is on the power of the Gospel to transform human relationships and bring about reconciliation, regardless of class or other

distinctions.[93] Where the power of the Gospel is active, families are created (*brother* in vv. 1, 7, 16, 20; *sister* in v.2 and *"my child … whose father I have become"* v.10); partnership develops, which implies and involves acceptance, trust, regard, divisions of responsibility and equality in sharing (v.17); and relationships are formed based on love and not on any legal demands (v.16).[94] Here the changes that come about in the outworking of reconciliation are taking place in personal relationships, not within the system.

For Winter, the change in the relationship is brought about by the fundamental change in his being that Onesimus has experienced through baptism (v. 16).[95] Baptism has invalidated the "ownership" institutionalized in slavery (vv. 15–16) and any rights bequeathed by slavery (vv. 17–20).[96] Together vv. 15–16 and 17–20 demonstrates that Paul does not acknowledge the authority of a Christian master over a Christian slave. Among the baptized, "slavery is not only wrong but invalid".[97]

Moreover, Paul replaces the relationship between "owner" and "owned", recognized in the imperial Graeco-Roman legal system with a relationship of indebtedness through parenthood in baptism.[98] The intent of the argument here is that "a transformation in relations between individuals occasions a change in social status".[99] Nonetheless, the argument is confined to social equality, or what is taking place in personal relationships, and is not about social inequality, or what ought to be taking place in the system.

In complete contrast to Felder and Winter, Craig S. De Vos perceives that it is a change in perception that is required, not a change in personal relationships or within the system. De Vos holds to the thesis that on account of the stigma associated with slavery in an imperial Graeco-Roman society that was male-dominated, servile in culture and had a group-determined identity, neither reconciliation nor manumission may have affected the relationship between Philemon and Onesimus.[100] Even where manumission was gifted or earned, it did not substantially alter a person's basic character or behaviour. Added to this, is the fact that a patron-client relationship, which reflects inequality of social power, still flourished. Essentially, the structural change of manumission had no effect on personal relationships.[101]

Hence, what Paul suggests is a fundamental change in relationship wherein Onesimus is treated as a brother or even as an honoured guest, that is, no longer as slave, so that the male-dominated, servile culture and group-determined identity values of imperial Graeco-Roman society are effectively undermined.[102] In other words, the essence of Paul's recommendation is a change in perception or the challenging of a stereotype.[103] If you can change how an individual is perceived, then you can affect how that individual is related to. Therefore, for De Vos, to change perception is to change relations. Again, there is no direct onslaught on the system. What happens in personal relationships is the fulcrum of the struggle.

In sum, Felder, Winter and De Vos turn the argument inward, that is, into an abstraction and thereby void the letter of its socio-economic and political dimensions. Focusing on abstract notions is but to sanction an oppressive social system and justify oppression.

What those who have been identified with liberal hermeneutics here have failed to do is to link reconciliation with liberation. There is no reconciliation without liberation. Reconciliation is that which takes place on both the personal and communal levels. While on the personal level, reconciliation permits the "master" to also be as "brother", it does not also allow this on the communal level. On the communal level, systems and structures and their practices are taking effect. As such, liberation has to do with freedom from that which is oppressive and repressive in the system. In other words, not only must the oppressed go free but the social systems or structures and practices that oppress must also change.[104] Freedom without material/social power is hallowing. To bring a new order into existence is but to destroy the system that oppresses. Ultimately, reconciliation takes place where humans are at liberty to affirm who they are (self-definition) and what they want to become (self-determination).

Altogether, the foregoing understands the socio-ideological and theological agenda at work in Philemon as taking place in personal relationships, not within the system. But Richard Horsley sees it differently. Horsley contends that the issue is not only about social equality but social inequality. Horsley challenges the notion that the issue of social inequality was ever hidden, just neglected. And so, Horsley asks "how come that it is only with the conversion of Onesimus that the problem (of social inequality) arose for the first time?[105] Why had not the problem come when Philemon was converted?[106] After all, Philemon got converted before Onesimus!! Was there no problem with a member of the siblinghood remaining a slave-master as long as the slave himself does not belong?[107] Conversion notwithstanding, social inequality was always there in the system. It is in the system that the real struggle is taking place. Here Horsley genuinely conjoins reconciliation with liberation. It is in this conjunction between reconciliation and liberation that social struggle is located or fought.

In short, the liberal view represented here focused on executive power or the struggle for power. This means that the struggle takes place or is located in the upper echelons or among the executives of the socio-economic and political structure of imperial Graeco-Roman society. The site of struggle in the letter of Philemon, however, is in the socio-economic and political structure and its practices, not in who administers the system. In other words, whereas liberal hermeneutics emphasizes charity, prioritizes reconciliation over social injustice and accentuates individualism,[108] it also takes little interest in social analyses and thereby gives absolutely no agency to the socio-ideological dimensions of biblical texts.

Liberationist Hermeneutics

The question now becomes, where is the site of struggle in the letter of Philemon for liberation hermeneutics, that is, how does the socio-ideological and theological agenda that shaped Philemon determine the "readings" of liberationists? Did they champion the cause for a new social order for all, not just for free persons? To have free persons without a new order only means that the system that enslaves is still entrenched. So then, where is the site of struggle located for liberationists? Liberation is taken here to mean freedom from structural and systemic bondage, which operates on three levels: analysis of lived realities (socio-analytical), theological reading of lived realities (hermeneutical) and commitment to, and involvement in, social realities (pastoral). As such, Liberation hermeneutics is used in the sense of interpreting social processes with the principal intention of realizing human freedom from all kinds of structural and systemic oppression and injustices.[109]

In what follows, an analysis of the "readings" of Philemon by Theo Preiss, Amos Jones Jr., Robert E. Dunham, Clarice J. Martin and Sabine Biebersstein, as representative of liberation hermeneutics, which I have grouped under the liberation perspective is undertaken. This grouping reflects the interest of the interpreters in what is taking place in the social system and structures and practices in Philemon.

Coequality and Social Inequality in the Household
While Preiss and Jones Jr.'s focus on the removal of social distinctions does not emphasize effecting change in the social system and structure, their position still enables them to hold in tension the struggle between house church and household. For Preiss, the emphasis is not on what Onesimus did but on what Onesimus became.[110] Where Preiss misses the mark, however, is in not elaborating on the meaning and implications of what Onesimus did and became. I would contend that the emphasis is indeed

on what Onesimus did. What Onesimus did by stepping outside the system was to resist it, which in turn determined what he became; not only a convert to Christianity but free. Nonetheless, in contending that it is a free person that Philemon is to receive back, Preiss has identified the struggle that would ensue between house church and household.[111] In other words, the issue is not only about co-equality but also social inequality.

Where Preiss sees the removal of social distinctions as critical, Jones Jr. perceives social status as most critical. For Jones Jr., the issue of equality has to do with a complete change in the concrete social status of the slave, and not just on equality before God or in the budding church.[112] However, Jones Jr. deals with the issue in light of his understanding of ecclesia (Rom. 12:2; 1 Cor. 7:29–31, 2 Cor. 11:32–33; Phil. 2:12–13, 3:20; Acts 17:7) where membership guarantees freedom from sin and servitude.[113] In the church, as Jones Jr. as understands church, slaves were no longer under any obligation to their masters. The ecclesia, then, is a community of equals.[114] There is neither master nor slave. Nevertheless, though the social distinctions may be removed, what of change in the social system and the structures that perpetuate the distinctions? What is of most importance, change in social status or the social system and structure?

What Preiss and Jones Jr. fail to deal with is the categories of master and slave as social classes. Being a slave placed Onesimus in a social class, which meant that he had a master, Philemon. Master, also, is a social category in society. How can the issue, then, be confined to the removal of social status and social incongruity, and not also incorporate the struggle between social classes. Indeed, it is class structure that led to slavery, the necessity of dominant classes in society to create and maintain those social structures and institutions that ensure their positions of privilege and power.[115] To take away the class structure is to dismantle the power base of the dominant and bring about a more participatory role in the decision-making process and relations to production by the dominated.

The issue of class structure is determinative in Dunham's "reading". Dunham perception is that Philemon, as master and brother in the world must come to terms with a slave who has become a brother.[116] In this regard, what are the steps Philemon must take from mercy to justice? Dunham lists two steps. In the first place, Philemon needs to realize that through conversion the old social distinctions of identities and status are no more.[117] Dunham comes to this perspective from his interpretation of Gal. 3:27–28, where social distinctions are no longer determinative in the community of the baptized.[118] And second, Philemon "must relinquish rights *(person as property)* in favour of what is right" *(right to self-determination and self-definition).*[119] At once, social distinctions and social inequality are removed and thereby the old oppressive order is transformed into a new order of liberation.

Co-equality and Social Inequality in the House Church

All the arguments concentrate, so far, on the structures and practices within the system. But Clarice J. Martin and Sabine Biebersstein look at what took place outside the system. In this regard, Martin takes running away as an act of self-determination and self-definition and thereby examines the praxis of resistance and equality in the faith community that meets in Philemon's house.

Martin holds that both Paul and Onesimus share the same social location – imprisonment. However, Paul has the privileged status as seen in his advocacy for Onesimus. Nevertheless, Onesimus sees his humanity and religiosity as different from Paul's. Consequently, Onesimus regarded even a dangerous freedom as superior to Christianized slavery, and ran away.[120] Where social location is not a consequence of class structure, praxis may yet be different. Social location is not necessarily a result of praxis.

Biebersstein poses the question: how is slavery to be reconciled with the liberating message of the Gospel?[121] Before arriving at an answer, she places the letter of Philemon in its socio-political context. For Biebersstein, the community of believers that met in Philemon's house were members of the minority Jewish community living under the dominating system of the Roman Empire. In the Roman Empire, the society was divided between the free and the unfree. In writing to this community, Paul uses familial terminology in addressing the recipients of the letter (vv. 1–2), to describe the relationship between himself and Onesimus (vv. 10–13) and the desired relationship between Philemon and Onesimus (v. 16).[122] With the use of such language, Paul creates, without stating it explicitly, a new social reality: "a model of egalitarian structures of relations independent of rank, status and gender" (cf. Galatians 3:27–28).[123]

Moreover, Paul employs economic terminology in describing the relationship between himself and Philemon by giving it a material basis (vv. 17–22).[124] Philemon came to faith in Christ through the influence or witness of Paul and thereby "owes himself" to Paul. Between Paul and Philemon, there is a creditor-debtor relationship. Out of this business partnership, or the brotherhood between all three, Paul "directs" Philemon to do "more than I ask".[125] Brotherhood makes sense only when material livelihood is assured; or where there is social equality.[126] Co-equality makes for brotherhood.

In sum, what Biebersstein has done is to see the community of believers that met in Philemon's house, the household economy, as a microcosm of the Roman state and the house church as a community of freedom. In the Roman state slavery was accepted as the order of society. Consequently, society is divided between the ruler and the ruled. Here, the runaway is pursued and punished. But in the house church a way must be found, or allowed, in cases of the subversive action of a runaway, for the Gospel praxis of resistance and equality. Herein lies the answer to the question Biebersstein posed earlier (how is slavery to be reconciled with the liberating message of the Gospel?): through praxis of resistance and subversion by the dominated within dominating systems and structures that degrade and dishonour human beings.

From the interpretation of those identified under the liberation perspective, it is observed that an interest in institutional practices and the ideology that undergird those practices characterized liberation hermeneutics. This interest of liberation hermeneutics is demonstrated in concern shown for victims of institutional practices, the transformation of unjust and oppressive institutional practices, socio-structural analysis of, or the detection of, oppression and oppressors, exploitation and exploiters in biblical texts and the class and ideological position and commitment of interpreters. In short, liberation hermeneutics is about "creating a new person and a qualitatively different society"[127] as it challenges systemic and structural inequalities and emphazises that equality and justice are attainable in this life.[128]

This characterization of liberation hermeneutics has foregrounded the fact that the "readings" of Philemon were done from within a specific perspective. However, Jones Jr. is an African-American and both Clarice J. Martin and Sabine Biebersstein are feminist theologians, which mean that their "readings" of Philemon arose not only from their particular perspectives but also from their specific experience of oppression and domination. Thus, the plight of Onesimus, the conflicts and injustices in the system and the consequent need for the transformation of that social order received favoured concern. Presuppositions and hermeneutical suspicion conditioned their "readings" of Philemon and thereby established a link between social location and interpretation.

Consequently, the resistant "readings" of especially Martin and Biebersstein resulted from their experience of marginality and oppression and vision of and hope for an alternative social order grounded in the identification of oppressive ruling class interests and power in the structure of the social system.

Postcolonial Type

Postcolonial is a contentious term or theory borrowed from literary studies and used in manifold ways.[129] The leading light of Postcolonial usage within the context of biblical studies is R. S. Sugirtharajah.[130] As a critical discourse within biblical studies, Sugirtharajah employs Postcolonial theory to uncover suppressed voices, interrogate and expose the political and ideological agenda of interpreters and reveal imperial assumptions and intentions in biblical texts and their interpretation. As such, the postcolonial perspective concentrates on the biblical text and its interpretation as well as the interpreter. Within the context of this work, postcolonial criticism to biblical studies is used, therefore, to show the suppression of Onesimus' voice, reread Philemon from the perspective of Onesimus, the dominated 'other' and to expose the consequences of imperial ideology and oppressive intentions in the letter.

To demonstrate the characteristics of postcolonial criticism to biblical studies, an analysis is undertaken of the "readings" of Philemon by Valentina Alexander, a female Caribbean theologian in the Diaspora, Renita J. Weems, a feminist African American theologian and Burchell Taylor, a male Caribbean theologian.

Rereading Philemon from the Perspective of the Oppressed

Alexander puts herself in the place of Onesimus and writes a letter to Philemon. She writes to Philemon as a brother, one who no longer exists under dominating and oppressive material conditions "not because you are my master but because you are my brother".[131] Further, she is writing to explain, rather than to beg back, her subversive action of running away and to voice her disagreement with Paul's plea for reconciliation between herself and Philemon: "I must write to you now to contest Paul's request, not that you should welcome me as a brother, but rather that you should still expect me to be your slave".[132] Alexander's focus is on cause – domination and exploitation; on hermeneutical suspicion: why are there still master and slave relations? Why are the oppressed subjects to oppression? So, her focus is on the system, structures and ideology that caused slavery to exist.

Consequently, for Alexander, the brother matter is concomitant with issues of partnership and participation. There can be no brotherhood without participation and partnership. That's what the 'hood' – the place of abode of brothers – is all about. So the real division within the social structure is not between master and slave but between master and brother. The antithesis or antonym of master is not slave but brother. For Alexander, reconciliation is neither the real issue nor the solution. Reconciliation does not remove the dominating and oppressive material conditions of slavery. In this regard, Alexander advances three reasons for Onesimus running away.

First, Alexander posits that she was tired of oppression. "When I ran away from you all those weeks ago, I felt tired, embittered and a resentful man".[133] Tiredness is a revolutionary impulse. Rosa Parks, civil rights activist in the United States of America, also felt tired of the injustices of racism and so refused to move to the back of the bus.

Second, Alexander holds to the conviction that human beings are not property but endowed with the inalienable right to self-determination and self-definition. Alexander declared, "no matter how much kindness that you showed me, something in my heart continually reaffirmed that it was not right that I belong to you and that I do not belong to myself".[134] There is no such thing as a free slave.

Third, Alexander contends that reconciliation and bondage are untenable. So Alexander posits:

> in his great love, Christ has removed my chains and set me free ... I have something greater than ever belonging to myself now that he has made me his child and I belong to him ... what an affront that would be to the Almighty God that should set me free and you should choose to enslave me again ... Christ has come to set us free from our chains ... we cannot let ourselves be chained again, neither our spirits, nor our bodies, nor our minds.[135]

In other words, while conversion does not disembody the converted, the freedom one experiences in Christ is not one-dimensional. It is holistic. It embraces the social, economic and political as well as the spiritual.

Exposing Oppressive Systems and Practices
Weems rereads Philemon from within her interpretive community of an African American woman. By so doing, she raises three points. First, she locates the central tension or site of struggle in the text/letter is the fact that a religious leader, Paul, is sending back a slave to a slaveholding Christian friend.[136] Here Weems has juxtaposed the class interests (Philemon) and the destiny (Onesimus) of the protagonists in the text/letter and Paul's complicity in protecting "the reputation of the budding church movement from being seen as a threat to the social and economic fibre of the Roman Empire".[137] In so doing, Weems has identified the socio-ideological and theological interest and agenda at work in Philemon, and has posited that social inequality engenders social conflict.

Second, Weems does not see Onesimus as a runaway, a fugitive from justice. On the contrary, Weems contends that Onesimus has escaped "because he did not want to remain a slave, even the slave of a Christian.[138] As a result of having escaped his harsh and oppressive condition, Onesimus, "despite his conversion or perhaps because of it, is not returning to his slave master freely".[139] Escape is the voice of the oppressed, an act of self-determination and self-definition.

Third, Weems regards Paul's social location as privileged. For Weems, Paul's birthright as a "Hebrew among Hebrews" means that for Paul, a male, education and being a Benjaminite do not result from his birthright; and as a Roman citizen, Paul had social and political privileges (Acts 23:22–29).[140] Hence, Weems holds that Onesimus, who was not so privileged, understood his humanity and religiosity as different from Paul's, and would not return freely to an oppressive context.

Silence Speaks

Taylor, too, sees Onesimus as one who takes matters, his liberation, into his own hands. While Onesimus is not given a voice in the text, Taylor holds that vv. 10–13, 16, 21 give a different picture.[141] Through running away, the maximum possible protest/action he could take in the prevailing social context, Onesimus speaks. In other words, Onesimus's action in running away speaks louder than words. Taylor reckons that Onesimus

> was simply not accepting slavery as something to which he must be subjected.
> He did not think that he was fated to be a slave by virtue of his class or any
> other feature of his humanity. This act of running away was protest action.
> It was an act of defiance and rebellion of the human spirit against oppression
> and indignity.[142]

As such, Taylor went on to declare "oppression in any form cannot be benevolent and cannot be reformed to make it truly acceptable to the human spirit".[143] In this light, Taylor takes v.16 as Onesimus' condition for return.[144] Here is the voice of silence. As Taylor puts it "Onesimus is the voiceless, powerless initiator of a liberating process".[145]

However, where Taylor sees protest, I see subversion. While protest can and does mushroom into large-scale civil action, it is usually about or has its origin in individual or group grievances and seeks to redress these wrongs. Not so with Onesimus' action of running away. In fact, running away is akin to maroonage, as practised by many slaves in the Caribbean during slavery. With particular reference to Jamaica, maroonage has three phases.[146] There were the individual acts of resistance such as the Tacky revolt.[147]

Further, there were premeditated acts of revolt not against the system but undertaken to gain personal or group freedom from institutional bondage while leaving the system intact.[148] And lastly, there were frontal attacks on the institution and system of oppression so that there was freedom for all, a new social justice system and every individual was accepted as a moral, cultural and social equal.[149] Onesimus' act of running away, though an individual act (this is only one case of many possible instances that was canonized) had wider social implications for social justice and equality, not only for the religio-household economy of the Philemon estate but for the Roman Politea in general.

One implication is whether runaway is an oppositional stance or an act of resistance. According to Barton, there is a difference between opposition and resistance. Opposition contests the structures of power from within the system.[150] Resistance takes a stand against the system from outside the system.[151] Onesimus being away from the household economy meant that he was standing outside the system. It is praxis of resistance that is most effective in bringing about systemic change. Standing outside the system offers little or no opportunity for neutralization and control by absorption into the structures of power.

What we see here in Postcolonial hermeneutics is that Philemon is reread from the particularity and peculiarity of the interpreter – African American woman, a Black woman in the Diaspora and an Afro-Caribbean male – and that Onesimus, silenced in the letter of Philemon, speaks. This manner of rereading reconstructs biblical texts as well as giving agency to both the context of the interpreter and the material circumstances out of which biblical texts emerged. Rereading or reconstructing is a necessity, especially for the marginalized or subaltern, because biblical texts came out of various colonial contexts – Egyptian, Persian, Assyrian, Hellenistic, Roman – and were composed within royal courts.[152]

What rereading biblical texts in this manner reveals is that reports of divine-human encounter, values and struggles in biblical texts come from the perspective of those in power. As Weems notes "the voices that get embedded in the text of the Bible are for the most part male, elitist, patriarchal and legitimated".[153] And Weems further cautions against aligning oneself with the voice embedded in the text for in so doing one may be unwittingly identifying oneself with the socio-ideological position and class interest of that voice.[154] Consequently, Sugirtharajah charges that before texts can be exegeted for their liberative potential or for existential relevance, their ruling class interest, ideology, stigmatization and portrayal in content, plot and characterization need investigating.[155]

Exegetics and Eisegetics

What needs clarifying now is where liberal, liberation and postcolonial perspectives locate the site of struggle, and the socio-ideological and theological agenda at work in Philemon. The liberal perspective situates the site of struggle as taking place between individuals over who has executive power, not in the socio-economic and political system. Even where socio-ideological interest and social practices were identified, especially in the case of Petersen and Barclay, the argument or attention drifts to the issue of authority.

The liberation perspective positions the site of struggle more in the systems, structures and practices of the context and less in the biblical text. Here the text is taken as production, a message to be received, understood and applied or a medium to be analysed. In other words, emphasis is placed on its contextual relevance. However, there is a danger here. A contextual approach suggests that the text is only ideological in its application.[156] On the contrary, given the fact that some texts were composed in royal courts this means that they do have socio-ideological roots, albeit in oppressive practices.

For the postcolonial perspective, a socio-ideological and theological agenda is always at work both in the biblical texts and their interpretations. Taking the Bible as product bases the site of struggle in the economic, social, ideological and cultural dimensions of the text. But what postcolonialism goes on to do is to search for and investigate how the socio-ideological and theological agenda of biblical texts gets re-inscribed in stigmatization and portrayals in narratives and characterization.[157] What is said in the biblical text and what is said about what is written in the biblical text requires tracking.

To track what is said in and about the biblical text, the interpreter needs to follow the lines of inquiry adopted by Alexander, Weems and Taylor who asked from *whose point of view* is the text written? What in the text is oppressive? Where in the text does oppression lie? If one is coming to the text from the interpretive stance of the particularities and peculiarities of one's context, then much care is needed not to identify with the dominant voices and ruling class ideas embedded in the text, considering that biblical texts have their ideological roots in oppressive practices and ruling class interests.

Conclusion

The foregoing has revealed several hermeneutical insights from both the era of slavery and the contemporary era.

From the era of slavery:

- Where one's social location within the social structure is privileged, one is less inclined to question the causes of structural oppression.
- Where agency is given to the material conditions that produced biblical texts, critical awareness is raised.
- Where the reading strategy is not conditioned by the particularities and peculiarities of one's contextual realities, there is neither questioning nor challenging of the status quo.
- Where one comes to biblical text out of a concrete commitment to social struggle for justice or praxis, both the reading strategy and the material conditions out of which biblical texts were produced have authority or agency.
- Where the materiality of biblical texts does not condition interpretation, then a disjuncture develops between faith and praxis.

From the contemporary era:

- It takes more than social location to bring about a praxis of resistance.
- It is through a praxis of resistance and subversion by the dominated that dominating systems and structures are dismantled or changed.
- Presupposition and hermeneutical suspicion establish the link between social location and interpretation.
- Rereading biblical texts from the particularities and peculiarities of one's context leads to a reconstruction of biblical texts.

Altogether, the foregoing examination of how historical phenomena have been interpreted demonstrated that a reading strategy from the particularities and peculiarities of one's context, out of concrete commitment to social justice and the giving of agency to both the materiality of biblical texts and the context of the interpreter result in resistance. If a biblical hermeneutic is not developed that gives agency to the materiality of biblical texts and the context of interpreters, and reads biblical texts from the particularities and peculiarities of one's context and from a position of concrete social engagement and commitment, then that unforced error of contextualization in Caribbean biblical hermeneutical practice is set to continue.

The proposition, which meets the requirements of reading biblical texts from the particularities and peculiarities of the Caribbean context and giving agency to both materiality and praxis, is a biblical resistant hermeneutic within a Caribbean context. This resistant hermeneutic aims to eliminate the unforced error of contextualization in Caribbean biblical hermeneutical practice and enables Caribbean hermeneutes to interpret the Bible from the particularity and peculiarity of their own experience of domination, exploitation, survival and the struggle for sovereignty.

Notes

1. See, C. L. R. James, *Beyond A Boundary* (London: Stanley Paul & Co., 1963), p. 182, for a discussion on the influence of W. G. Grace's influence on popular life in pre-industrial England.
2. C. L. R. James, *Beyond A Boundary* (London: Stanley Paul & Co., 1963), p. 182.
3. Orlando Patterson, *Slavery and Social Death* (Cambridge, MA: Harvard University Press, 1982), p. 13.
4. N. S. Wheaton, *Discourse on St. Paul's Epistle to Philemon* (Hartford, CT: Press of Case, Tiffany and Company, 1851), p. 23.
5. Ibid.
6. Op. cit., p. 12.
7. Ibid.
8. Ibid., p. 28.
9. Bishop John Henry Hopkins, *The Bible View of Slavery: A Letter From the Bishop of Vermont, New England to the Bishop of Pennsylvania* (London: Saunders, Ottley & Co., 1863), p. 7.
10. Ibid., p. 8.
11. Bishop John Henry Hopkins, *Scriptural, Ecclesiastical and Historical View of Slavery: From the Days of Patriarch Abraham to the Nineteenth Century* (New York: Pooley & Co., 1864), p. 7.
12. Ibid., p. 11.
13. Ibid.
14. Ibid.
15. Op. cit., p. 14.
16. Atkins, *American Slavery ... A Reply*, p. 4.
17. Atkins, *American Slavery ... A Reply*, p. 6.
18. Atkins, *American Slavery ... A Reply*, p. 7.
19. Ibid.
20. Atkins, *American Slavery ... A Reply*, p. 8.
21. Atkins, *American Slavery ... A Reply*, p. 9.
22. Raymund Harris, *Scriptural Researches on the Licitness of the Slave Trade* (London: 1788), p. 69.
23. Ibid.
24. p. 65.
25. Harris, *Scriptural Researches*, p. 66.
26. See *Dictionary of American Biography* (London: Oxford University Press, 1929, Vol. 2), p. 293.
27. James G. Birney, *Sinfulness of Slaveholding in all Circumstances: Tested by Reason and Scripture* (Detroit, MI: Charles Wilcox, 1846), p. 51.

28. Olaudah Equiano, *The Interesting Narrative and Other Writings – Letter to the Rev. Raymund Harris, author of "Scriptural Researches on the Licitness of the Slave Trade"* (London: Penguin Books, 1993), p. 336.
29. Ibid.
30. Ibid.
31. Equiano, *The Interesting Narrative*, p. 336.
32. Rev. David Young, *Slavery Forbidden by the Word of God* (Aberdeen: G. & R. King, 1847), p. 5.
33. Young, *Slavery Forbidden*, p. 10.
34. Ibid.
35. Wheaton, *Discourse on St Paul*, p. 8.
36. Ibid.
37. John W. Blassingame, ed., *Frederick Douglass Papers, Series on: Speeches, Debates, Interviews, Vol. 3, 1855-63* (New Haven, CT: Yale University Press, 1985), p. 258.
38. Ibid.
39. Blassingame (ed.), *Frederick Douglass Papers*, p. 363.
40. Blassingame (ed.), *Frederick Douglass Papers*, p. 559.
41. Renita J. Weems, "Reading Her Way Through the Struggle: African American Women and the Bible" in Norman K. Gottwald and Richard A. Horsley, *The Bible and Liberation – Political and Social Hermeneutics*, revised edition (Maryknoll, NY: Orbis Books, 1993), p. 34.
42. Ibid., p. 38.
43. See Thomas Merton, *Faith and Violence* (Notre Dame, IN: University of Notre Dame Press, 1968), pp. 7–8; and the *Report on the Consultation on "Violence, Non-Violence and the Struggle for Social Justice"* (Geneva: World Council of Churches, 1972), p. 6.
44. Richard A. Horsley, *Jesus and the Spiral of Violence – Popular Jewish Resistance in Roman Palestine* (Minneapolis, MN: Fortress Press, 1933), p. 22.
45. J. Albert Harrill, "The Use of the New Testament in the American Slave Controversy: A Case History in the Hermeneutical Tension Between Biblical Criticism and Christian Moral Debate", *Religion And American Culture*, 10 (2) (Summer 2000): 149–86.
46. Harrill, p. 149.
47. Harrill, p. 174.
48. Ibid.
49. Ibid.
50. Ibid.
51. Ibid.
52. Gillian Feeley-Harnik, "Is Historical Anthropology Possible? The Case of the Runaway Slave" in, Gene M. Tucker and Douglas A. Knight (eds) *Humanizing America's Iconic Book*, Society of Biblical Literature Centennial Addresses, 1980, p. 117.
53. Ibid., p. 120.
54. Ibid., p. 120.
55. Ibid., p. 120.
56. Ibid., p. 121.
57. Norman K Petersen, *Rediscovering Paul – Philemon and the Sociology of Paul's Narrative World* (Philadelphia, PA: Fortress Press, 1985), p. 94.

58. Ibid., p. 97.
59. Ibid., p. 97.
60. Ibid., p. 98.
61. Ibid., p. 98.
62. Petersen, *Rediscovering Paul*, p. 289.
63. Ibid., p. 289.
64. Ibid., p. 290.
65. Ibid., p. 292.
66. Ibid., p. 301.
67. John M. Barclay, "Paul, Philemon and the Dilemma of Christian Slave-ownership" *New Testament Studies,* 37 (2) April 1991, p. 183.
68. Ibid., p. 177.
69. Ibid., p. 177.
70. Ibid., p. 182.
71. Chris Frilingos, "For My Child Onesimus: Paul and Domestic Power in Philemon" *Journal of Biblical Literature,* 19 (1) Spring 2000, p. 104.
72. Ibid., p. 104.
73. Ibid., p. 95.
74. Ibid., p. 100–02.
75. Max Weber, *The Theory of Social and Economic Organisation* (London: Free Press, 1964), p. 152.
76. B. M. Rapske, "The Prisoner Paul in the Eyes of Onesimus" in *New Testament Studies,* 37 (2) April 1991, p. 192.
77. Ralph P. Martin, *Interpretation – A Bible Commentary for Teaching and Preaching – Ephesians, Colossians and Philemon* (Atlanta, GA: John Knox Press, 1991), p. 134.
78. Ibid., p. 144.
79. N. H. Taylor, "Onesimus – A Case Study of Slave Conversion in Early Christianity", *Religion and Theology,* 3 (3) 1996, p. 279.
80. Ibid., p. 274.
81. Ibid., p. 271.
82. Ibid., p. 270.
83. John D. Nordling, "Onesimus Fugitivus: A Defence of the Runaway Slave Hypothesis in Philemon", *Journal Study of the New Testament,* 41 February 1991, p. 118.
84. Ibid., p. 102.
85. Ibid., p. 102.
86. Ibid., p. 102.
87. Ibid., p. 102.
88. Carolyn Osiek, *Philippians and Philemon* (Nashville, TN: Abingdon Press, 2000), p. 127.
89. Ibid., p. 139.
90. Ibid., p. 140.
91. Ibid., p. 140.
92. R. S. Sugirtharajah, *Postcolonial Criticism and Biblical Interpretation* (Oxford: Oxford University Press, 2002), p. 112.
93. Cain Hope Felder, "The Letter to Philemon" in *The New Interpreter's Bible* (Nashville, TN: Abingdon Press, 2000), p. 885.

94. Ibid., pp. 889–901.
95. S. C. Winter, "Philemon" in Elizabeth Schussler Fiorenza, *Searching the Scriptures – A Feminist Commentary* (London: SCM Press Ltd. 1995), p. 307.
96. Ibid., p. 307.
97. Ibid., p. 307.
98. Ibid., p. 307.
99. Ibid., p. 308.
100. Craig S. De Vos, "Once a Slave Always a Slave? Slavery, Manumission and Relational Patterns in Paul's Letter to Philemon", *Journal for the Study of the New Testament* 82 (2001) 101.
101. Ibid., p. 92.
102. Ibid, p. 102.
103. Ibid., p. 103.
104. J. Deotis Roberts, *A Black Political Theology* (Louisville, KY: Westminster John Knox Press, 1974, reprinted 2005), p. 140.
105. Richard Horsley, "Paul and Slavery: A Critical Alternative to Recent Readings", *Semeia* 83/84 (1998) Slavery in Text and Interpretation, p. 179.
106. Ibid.
107. Ibid.
108. Taken from class notes on lecture delivered by R. S. Sugitharajah on "Liberal and Liberation Hermeneutics", 23 February 2005.
109. Juan Luis Segundo, *Liberation of Theology* (New York: Orbis Books, 1976), pp. 7–38.
110. Theo Preiss, "Life in Christ and Social Ethics in the Epistle to Philemon", in *Studies in Biblical Theology* No. 13, *Life in Christ* (London: SCM Press, 1952), p. 34.
111. Ibid., p. 34.
112. Amos Jones Jr., "Paul's Message of Freedom" in Norman K. Gottwald and Richard A. Horsley eds. *The Bible and Liberation* (Maryknoll, NY: Orbis Books, 1993), p. 504.
113. Ibid., pp. 512–14.
114. Ibid., p. 520.
115. Tim Hector "Hopes and Aspiration at and After Emancipation" Fan The Flame *Outlet Newspaper* 24 April 1998.
116. Robert E. Dunham, "Between Text and Sermon: Philemon 1-25", *Interpretation* 52 (2) April 1998, p. 191.
117. Ibid., p. 193.
118. Ibid., p. 193.
119. Ibid., p. 193.
120. Clarice J. Martin, "Womanist Interpretation of the New Testament: The Quest for Holistic and Inclusive Translation and Interpretation" in James A. Cone and Gayraud Gilmore, eds. *Black Theology – A Documentary History*, (Maryknoll, NY: Orbis Books, 1993), pp. 226–36.
121. Sabine Biebersstein, "Disrupting the Normal Reality of Slavery: A Feminist Reading of the Letter to Philemon", *Journal For The Study of the New Testament* 79, September 2000, p. 106.
122. Ibid., p. 113.
123. Ibid., p. 112.

124. Ibid., p. 114.
125. Ibid., p. 114.
126. Ibid., p. 114.
127. R. S. Sugitharajah, *Postcolonial Criticism and Biblical Interpretation* (New York: Oxford University Press, 2002), p. 65.
128. Taken from class notes on lecture delivered by R. S. Sugitharajah on "Liberal and Liberation Hermeneutics", 23 February 2005.
129. See Bill Ashcroft, Gareth Griffiths and Helen Tiffin, *The Postcolonial Studies Reader* (New York: Routledge, 1995).
130. See R. S. Sugirtharajah, *The Bible and The Third World: Precolonial, Colonial and Postcolonial Encounters* (Cambridge: Cambridge University Press, 2001); *Postcolonial Criticism and Biblical Interpretation* (Oxford: Oxford University Press, 2002); *Postcolonial Reconfigurations: An Alternative Way of Reading the Bible and Doing Theology* (London: SCM Press, 2003).
131. Valentina Alexander, "Onesimus's Letter to Philemon" in *Black Theology in Britain* 4, May 2000, p. 61.
132. Ibid., p. 61.
133. Ibid., p. 61.
134. Ibid., p. 62.
135. Ibid., p. 62.
136. Weems, *Reading Her Way Through the Struggle*, p. 43.
137. Ibid., p. 43.
138. Ibid., p. 43.
139. Ibid., p. 43.
140. Ibid., p. 43.
141. Burchell Taylor, "Onesimus: The Voiceless, Powerless Initiator of the Liberating Process" in Howard Gregory, ed. *Caribbean Theology – Preparing for the Challenge Ahead* (Barbados: Cedar Press, 1995), p. 18.
142. Ibid., p. 20.
143. Ibid., p. 20.
144. Ibid.
145. Ibid.
146. Don Robotham, "The Development of Black Ethnicity in Jamaica" in Rupert Lewis and Patrick Bryan *Garvey: His Work and Impact* (Lawrenceville, NJ: Africa World Press, Inc., 1994 2nd edition), p. 32.
147. Ibid., p. 32.
148. Ibid., p. 34 for example, The Maroon-British Treaty of 1739.
149. Ibid., p. 35 for example, the Sam Sharpe led rebellion in St James in 1832.
150. Barton, *Afro-Creole*, p. 50.
151. Ibid., p. 50.
152. R. S. Sugirtharajah, *The Bible and the Third World – Precolonial, Colonial and Postcolonial Encounters* (Cambridge, UK: Cambridge University Press, 2001), p. 251.
153. Weems, *Reading Her Way Through the Struggle*, p. 45.
154. Ibid., p. 42.
155. Sugirtharajah, *The Bible and the Third World*, p. 251.
156. Itumeleng J. Mosala, "Biblical Hermeneutics and Black Theology in South Africa, The Use of the Bible" in Gottwald and Horsley, *The Bible and Liberation*, p. 56.
157. Sugirtharajah, *The Bible and the Third World* p. 252.

Chapter 5

TOWARDS A BIBLICAL RESISTANT HERMENEUTIC WITHIN A CARIBBEAN CONTEXT

Introduction

Struggles for survival and sovereignty characterized, and continue to characterize, the existence of the Caribbean peoples, despite the advent of political independence for many Caribbean islands. Since the early days of colonialism in the fifteenth century the Europeans wiped out the indigenous population. Africans, without their consent, and later Asians were transplanted from their homelands to people the islands for purposes of exploiting labour. The transplanted peoples were bound to resist, rebel and subvert. Thus, the "masters" of the transplanted peoples had to dominate violently and "civilize" their subjects in order to fulfil their exploitative purposes. With abiding effects, this dominating and "civilizing" project of the "masters" resulted in structures of spirituality and theologies rooted in an alien culture and experience transported but not transposed both of which suffer from a penetrating sense of unreality and unrelatedness.[1] It is this unreality and unrelatedness from such structures of spirituality and theologies that were experienced in the weekly worship experience in my village chapel, and which continue to need resisting and transforming.

In exploiting, dominating and "civilizing" circumstances, resistance becomes the way of being for those who struggle for self-definition and self-determination. Admittedly, not every person, who is culturally and spiritually enslaved to imposed foreign structures and systems, wants to resist and subvert such foreign patterns. Many formerly colonized peoples living in circumstances dominated and exploited by foreign powers and cultural imperialism like it so. In such circumstances of domination and exploitation, a resistant hermeneutic, with the Bible as a cultural weapon, provides Caribbean peoples with a means of talking back in their own voice, and exposing and challenging any new order of colonialism.

Accordingly, three tasks are performed. One, formulate a biblical resistant hermeneutic entitled "towards a biblical resistant hermeneutic within a Caribbean context". The use of "towards" in the title for the biblical resistant hermeneutic implies that the resistant biblical hermeneutic is neither the final nor the definitive reading strategy in biblical hermeneutics within a Caribbean context. The word "towards" points to the dynamic and ongoing development of biblical interpretation within the Caribbean context. Two, offer a resistant reading of Philemon; and three, draw possible inferences from the resistant biblical reading strategy.

Component Parts of a Biblical Resistant Hermeneutic

There are five dimensions to this resistant biblical hermeneutic: cultural-literacy consciousness, praxis of resistance, culture as "text", text as cultural construction and context. All together, the five dimensions highlight the socially constructed nature of biblical texts and their interpretation. The intention of this biblical resistant hermeneutic is to raise an alternative consciousness and show how oppressive systems and practices can be challenged and exposed so that such systems and practices are reconfigured for socio-economic transformation or an order for liberation.

The discussion on these five dimensions will flow in the direction of the arrows. Each part is not separate and distinct from each other. The parts do overlap and interact and are only separated for discussion purposes.

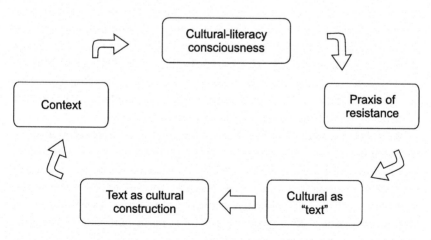

Figure 5.1: A biblical resistant hermeneutic reading strategy

Cultural-literacy Consciousness

Cultural-literacy consciousness is not knowledge about the vernacular, dance, music and rhythm of a people, that is, the form or medium of expression of a culture but the cultural meaning and experience of these forms and media. In other words, how they affect cost of living; instruct, educate and raise consciousness; and inspire to challenge or resist unjust systems. Concern about form and media are secondary issues. The primary issue is what *is* to be celebrated, and how and why what is to be celebrated *is* experienced.[2] Thus the issue is not about indigenization or cultural renewal but cultural meaning or the experience of culture, not a cultural experience (this is for tourism).

Essentially, cultural-literacy consciousness is a knowing about ourselves as Caribbean peoples – who we are and can become, why we are under-resourced and under-developed. It is being about, "how to be", about geography and history, constructing a new way of being. It is to assess and know our place, socio-geographic space, in the world.[3] Garfield Sobers, the world's greatest all-round cricketer, by playing cricket in racist Rhodesia in 1970 showed little or none of this consciousness or knowledge of place unlike Vivian Richards, arguably the world's greatest batsman, in the 1980s, when he refused to play in apartheid South Africa for millions of dollars. In an assessment of the action of both cricketers, Hilary Beckles, a Caribbean social historian, opines that Sobers "was not attuned to the historical and ideological nature of his social location within West Indies cricket".[4]

Seeing the physical world in its right size and proportion enables a people to identify their place (country) in the world. On the maps of the world, many of the Caribbean countries are mere dots and many more are simply not identified. Failure to see ourselves as having a place in the world can lead to a devaluing of self and a lack of understanding of our past such that we do not know who we are today. As such, cultural-literacy consciousness is a movement towards roots – a desire to establish identity, an awareness of the process by which the region was peopled and the process of history, politics and economics at work in the region.[5]

What is being acknowledged here is that the socio-geographic space of the Caribbean reader of biblical texts is plural in nature and is a hotly and highly contested and problematized area of social existence. Cultural-literacy consciousness takes into account the historical differences, pluralistic cultural sensibilities, multiple ethnicities and religions of Caribbean peoples. Even so, within ethnic, class, gender and religious differences, there are divided interests.

For instance, within the socio-geographic space of any interpretive faith community of the Caribbean, there would be those who belonged to marginalized subject positions[6] and those to dominant subject positions.[7] In other words, you could have decision-makers, the unemployed, abused women, underpaid factory workers, non-nationals, struggling banana farmers, persons of African, Chinese or Indian descent, etc. as members of one interpretive faith community at any one time. Now, those belonging to the marginalized subject positions and thereby suffering from the injustices of the system may see the system as oppressive, and structured and controlled to maintain power and privilege. For those within the dominant subject positions, there are two groups – those benefiting from the system and those disadvantaged.[8] Inevitably, those benefiting from the system will want the system to survive so that their power and privilege remain intact. And those disadvantaged by the system will contest and critique its practices and agitate to bring about a just social order.

The trouble is that both the benefactors and disadvantaged belong to the same village community, play for the same village community sports team, shop at the same community supermarket, are members of the same faith community and are interpreting the same faith text. What is needed here is not the cultural-literacy consciousness that merely knows that one plus one does not necessarily make eleven or even that one subtracted from ten leaves nought. Rather, it is the consciousness that comes from knowing what are the dominating and exploitative influences and agenda at work in the socio-geographic space.

Moreover, if we only know our class position, marginalized identity and status, we know very little. The shape of persons' indignity are known if the cultural meaning of persons' class position, marginalized identity and status is known, that is, why persons are unable to find employment, excluded, unable to pay bills, discriminated against. Indignities flow from persons' class position, marginalized identity and status. It is experienced indignities that form the bridge between persons' condition and consciousness, and which lead to resistance.

For instance, when Douglass' slave master put a stop to his mistress teaching him to read because it would make him "unfit to be a slave", Douglass developed the consciousness that "the pathway from slavery to freedom" was literacy.[9] Or take Roper's view that while Pentecostalism and Evangelicalism are in essence the people's church, they are of the poor without being for the poor as they do not wrestle with the fundamental issues of alienation and powerlessness.[10] Another example concerns a well-known rural Hindu priest of Guyana who, at a cricket match between the

West Indies and India in 1953, "unleashed a string of popular Hindu curse words, punched the air, uncoiled his sacred turban, turned to the crowd and waived it triumphantly" because Ramchand, an Indian bowler, bowled Pairaudeau, a white Guyanese batsman from Georgetown who was representing the West Indies.[11] Thus, he was identifying with Indian despite his Guyanese nationality. Such understanding and public display of emotion were not being simply conscious of African and Indian heritage and tradition or what characterized one as African or Indian. To the contrary, it is a cultural-literacy consciousness that knows the causes of oppression and exploitation.

To ground the elements of cultural-literacy consciousness put forward above, namely experienced indignities, the raising of consciousness and resistance, let me share extracts from the stories of Malcolm "Jai" Kernahan and Terrence Thornhill, both of Trinidad who became involved in resistance movements in Trinidad during the popular political upsurge of the 1970s, as told to Brian Meeks,[12] a Jamaican political scientist.

Extract 1

Experienced indignities

Brian Meeks: Tell me a little bit about yourself. Where are you from?

How would you describe yourself?

Malcolm "Jai": Well, my father was an oil field worker, production department.

Kernahan: We used to live in company quarters ... near to Fyzabad. In 1953 when I was about four or five years old, he got blind and the company throw we out the house. Well, from that we become dirt poor, you know, because he had spent some money to buy some land and then he come and got blind. While working, some steel thing damage the eye and he lost his sight. He couldn't work again; they didn't need his service, so they told him to leave the house in a month's time. Well, we just become poor after that, you know. He went to one and two Obeah man to try and get back his sight – you the masses.

BM: How many of you were in the family?

MJK: Three boys. Yeah, well, then we started to live by family. We had to go by uncle and live a little time. But one of the agreements we had come to with the oil company is that when we reach of age, the children would get work in the oil field. So we all knew that when we were of age we would get work in the oil field. But my father was a real militant oil field worker. I remember when I was a little fella they used to tell me how they used to beat people who used to break strike – scabs, no? – So I never got work in the oil field.

Malcolm formed his identity from the indignities or the discrimination his father suffered at the hands of the social system. He linked the poverty his family experienced to the social system.

Extract 2

Consolidating consciousness

BM: So what did they tell you?

MJK: Well, they just push me around, you know? "come back so and so, ... come back so and so ...". I get to hate the oil company and the white people and t'ing in them times, you know, so it was easy for me to fall into the Black Power Movement when that time came around. In 1967 ... they had a consciousness movement was building ... a lot of progressive literature started to find its way in Trinidad. Eldridge Cleaver's *Soul on Ice,* Walter Rodney's *Groundings With My Brothers,* and I started to read books. As a matter of fact, I have been in the struggle since '67.

BM: What happened in '67?

MJK: Well, I always used to look at the Oil Field Workers' Trade Union as kind of militant organization. I admired George Weeks. Well, they had a fella by the name of Clive ... who went to Cuba and he came back and said, "the only solution was armed revolution". I found that concept was nice and romantic and I get to like it, you know? ... an' then '69 came around and St James had an organisation named WOLF – Western United Liberation Front – that was some soldiers ... during this time too a dance troupe...came from Uganda and they had their hair in Afro with a part, and from that everyone used to wear dashikis and part of their hair in a certain style. And a kind of consciousness started to come along, a kind a blackness; and then we came and got involved with NJAC, but I was never a member of NJAC.

BM: Why?

MJK: I thought they were middle class. Talking about the dashikis and sandal ... culturally, I couldn't deal with them ... As far as the "black man" was concerned, NJAC was middle class. Them fellas wasn't ready. They were only talking ... But we still supported the movement. We marched with them, you know? And then from 1969–1970 we started to get *Peking Review* on the block and Errol Balfour he come around and started to talk about Marxism, and suddenly we started to see the struggle in terms of class.

Malcolm's level of awareness was raised when he was unable to find employment and through his commitment and involvement in social justice movements and causes.

Extract 3

Resistance

BM: I want to come back to what was going on in your mind. That transition is a serious one, to decide to take up arms and fight the government. How easy was that decision?

MJK: ... My life was hard, real tough. So I say that I would rather die than live under the system. I don't want to live under the system anymore. Because you getting turn back everywhere you go to look for jobs; your name not recognised; you is nobody; you ain't living nowhere; you poor. If death come, no big thing ... To be honest, based on the vibes we had taken at that time, we couldn't do anything else. I believe that if I hadn't picked up a gun and gone to armed struggle I would be a mad or a vagrant. I couldn't fit into nothing in the society ... I think that the 1970 Revolution saved me.

For Malcolm, armed struggle against an unjust social system was "salvation". In traditional Christian understanding, salvation is understood as the forgiveness of some wrong committed against another. For Malcolm, "salvation" is not about the forgiveness of those who sinned. Rather, it is personal involvement in and commitment to the social struggle for justice to deliver those who were sinned against.

Extract 4

Social location

Brian Meeks: Tell me a little bit about yourself?

Terrence Thornhill: I was born July 27, 1949 in Glencoe. It was a residential area in a middle class setting ... My father was one of the first black men to get degrees at university in England along with Eric Williams. His was in English at Cambridge. Both parents were teachers. My father was a head teacher and my mother was a common-entrance teacher. It was a middle class family. As far as

> I can remember, we always had a car; the house had
> hot and cold water. I went to Tranquillity Primary
> School and later to Queen's Royal College.

Extract 5

Consolidating consciousness

BM: How did you become involved with the 'movement'?

TT: I did track and field in school and went to the US in 1969 on a track
scholarship to study at the Catholic University in Washington,
DC. While there, seeing how black people were treated, I went
through some changes in my life ... then I started to see the
sufferings of black people and identified with them. We started to
talk about the Lord, Jesus Christ, how he was real and what they
did to him; he went about trying to help and the suffering he
experienced. And I was able to link His suffering to that of black
people and see where the system always oppresses those who are
good. That was November 23, 1970 and that day it came to me very
strongly that my life wouldn't be just to continue in school like
this, but to search for that truth which Jesus brought to mankind
and help somebody in the way of life.

Unlike Malcolm, Terrence perceives his identity as formed from social
location of privilege. However, despite Terrence's middle class privileges,
he was neither blind nor insensitive to the indignities of the oppressed.

Extract 6

Resistance

By May 1971, my teachers were asking me if I was still in their class ... When
I returned to Trinidad in June 1971, it was under a state of emergence. Guy
Harewood was my good friend from primary school days ... in those days, we
had Mao's *Little Red Book*. One of his sayings was that "the political man is
the real man". So as far as Guy and a few others were concerned, NJAC was
only talking, theorising, but not willing to put their life on the line for the
cause in the way that we thought it should be, in terms of guerrilla warfare.
So Guy and them were branching off from NJAC, and just a little group
talking among themselves. So I came back and met that. I started to go
around with them. I had access to cars and so I used to go and purchase
weapons with them, because the cars I had would be "cool". So I got involved,
though I used to tell them, this set of revolutionary thing is not me, because
I am for Jesus, which is peace. But then I listened to them, noted their
sincerity and I was on a search for truth also. And there were slogans on the
walls, like "armed revolution is the only solution" and "the voice of the people

is the voice of God", and it was slowly coming to me that armed revolution is the way. I went back to the Bible because my whole experience was Bible oriented and every time I opened it I would read where Moses saw the Egyptians advantaging the Hebrews and he took a sword and killed an Egyptian. So my interpretation was that maybe we should take up the gun, because the people are being advantaged.

Though Terrence had conflicting identities and enjoyed middle class privileges, he nevertheless got involved in the struggle for social justice because it was not about the privileges he had or enjoyed. Rather, it was about how the system deprivileges people.

What we see in these narratives is that for both Malcolm and Terrence it was not so much their class positions and marginalized identity and status that led them to join resistance movements. Instead, it was the cultural meaning of the indignity of being pushed around to find employment, unemployed, penniless, socially dead and the awareness to link such particularities of the sociality of their existence with aspects of the biblical agenda and practice that were the impetus and epistemological lens that resulted in their joining resistance movements.

In sum, cultural-literacy consciousness deals with causal particularities rather than with universalities. It is not about the givens of one's social location but what causes the social circumstances of that social location. In other words, it seeks responses to such questions as: what are the axes of power and privilege? How does causality run? How am I shaped by my location and how can I shape my location? Cultural-literacy consciousness takes marginality as a site of radical possibility, a space of resistance and refusal[13] as it begins with seeing social reality from the outside in. Thus, cultural-literacy consciousness avoids been pawned by the socio-ideological agenda of others and rescues from unreality and unrelatedness.

The cultural meaning of the sociality of existence in our socio-geographic space must condition Caribbean biblical hermeneutical practice even if it is not necessarily the first step in biblical interpretation. It is the cultural meaning of the sociality of our existence that provides the epistemological lens, our way of knowing into the biblical texts, that is so critical for the reading of biblical texts from the particularity and peculiarity of one's social location. Those from whom I gathered empirical evidence would not interpret Philemon without the consciousness of their history of slavery. Besides, it provides the ground and impetus, raising of an alternative consciousness, for concrete commitment and involvement in social struggle, which inevitably leads to challenging and resisting oppressive systems and practices.

Praxis of Resistance

Praxis of resistance is acting as subjects for freedom, social equality and just social relations, rather than being acted against, as objects, in ways that are oppressive and unjust. In other words, praxis of resistance is a strategy for social transformation, in which biblical texts are read within the context of struggle and out of a commitment to social justice. What is meant by praxis of resistance, then, is a subjective commitment, taking sides in the "action", taking the side of those who struggle against oppression for social justice.

Praxis of resistance does not refer to Anansi style praxis of resistance as found in Caribbean folklore, which is tantamount to hideology: "preserving an inner freedom beneath the mask of compliance".[14] In Caribbean folklore, Anansi is reflective of a mode of resistance and a personality of the oppressed. Anansi survives by his wits and cunning; defeats animals and human beings in contest of wits and generally triumphs; always gains the plaudits of those without power, even in defeat, and the approbation of the powerful.[15]

Anansi's exploits, argues Rawick, empowers the oppressed, an empowerment which those in control of the decision-making process would neither confer nor enable.[16] In such circumstances, Genovese sees Anansi as both victim and an exponent of spiritual resistance that accepts the limits of the politically possible.[17] Vicariously, the oppressed are enabled to assert themselves and their humanity and overcome their mental slavery, the internal reflection of their objective circumstances.[18] So for Rawick, Anansi, qua oppressed, is engaged in an individualistic campaign – struggles in concrete ways "in his own activities on behalf of himself"[19] – not to revolutionalize oppressive systems – but rather "to change his circumstances and thereby gain enough footing to rebel".[20]

However, Barton contends that though Anansi outwitted Massa and was never caught even after all of Anansi's exploits and triumphs, the system and structure that ensured Massa's power and privilege remain entrenched.[21] While the system was undermined and structures were exposed, Anansi ultimately functions to affirm the existing order. His actions being individualistic and not collective meant that Anansi was no more than a rebel, not a revolutionary.[22]

In essence, Anansi opposed the system. He did not resist it. Anansi stayed within the system, employing strategic moves. Anansi never moved outside the system to seek to transform it. What the Anansi style praxis of resistance demonstrates is that with opposition, the underlying structures of the system, though challenged, remain unchanged. In other words, the praxis of resistance is ideologically different from psychosocial resistance because the objective of resistance is to change the system and practices of the structures.

Praxis of resistance also does not mean an analysis of the human situation out of which existential questions of faith are raised or the ways symbols of the Christian message are used – the Cross, Holy Spirit, Resurrection and Sacrament of Holy Communion – to respond to such concerns and questions. Analysing the human situation by asking existential questions of faith and using symbols of the Christian message is nothing short of an exercise in contextualizing the Christian message. As such, contextualizing amounts to a private exercise that can be done from the safety of the study or office, manse or rectory, weekly Bible study in the church building, where the socio-economic and political issues are neglected and where discussion takes place within the realm of ideas or private existential categories or theodicy. Through contextualizing, the world is interpreted. The praxis of resistance is out of a concrete commitment to struggle for social transformation by which the unjust social systems and practices of society are transformed and faith in God is expressed and interpreted out of concrete commitment to struggle.

In addition, neither does praxis of resistance mean, "to be where the action is". On the contrary, praxis of resistance is a practical response to the "action", to the conditions of life. "To be where the action is" may not necessarily arise from any understanding of the cultural meaning of the sociality of existence or derivative of any clear ideological stance and commitment or from any analysis that oppression is caused by the social system. One is part of the "action" to liberate the oppressed and the oppressive social order. "To be part of the action" must issue from social strategy, not personal agendas.

Furthermore, the interviewees, or for that matter the weekly Sunday worshippers, the Caribbean pulpit, and the group that assembles weekly for Bible Study, could not have come to an interpretation of Philemon from a position of concrete commitment and involvement in social struggle for justice and spiritualized the understanding of freedom, slavery and reconciliation, shaving them of their materiality. Seldom do we gather around the Bible in the Caribbean out of praxis of resistance. When we do gather, we do so to mine biblical texts for their spiritual meaning and for personal spiritual development, not intending to re-engage with the sociality of existence, to identify and resist oppressive systems and practices and to denounce such practices as opposite to God's justice.

Culture as *"Text"*

Culture as "text" acknowledges that readers of biblical text do not drop from the sky. Even if they do, they will "land" and "settle", if alive, in some socio-geographic space, which has or will soon develop its own history. Likewise, it recognizes that words function to create a "world" or a version of reality. So, in biblical texts, both the text and text-maker are not only saying but also doing something, generating a "world" that exists in rhetorical presentation.[23]

Now, one of the observations this study makes is that Caribbean biblical hermeneutical practice seeks to know the socio-historical realities in which God is revealed. Furthermore, the study is developing a reading strategy that makes contact between the "readings" of social reality of both the authors of biblical texts and Caribbean readers. What is being argued is that the influences and experiences of one's socio-geographic space are a legitimate "text", a version, too, of social reality.

Consequently, the "canon" of the socio-historical praxis of the people of God is not confined to the 66 books of the Bible. Though the biblical canon is closed, revelation continues in the unfolding story of God in the socio-historical praxis of humanity. This unfolding story means that the version of reality depicted by biblical writers is not the only legitimate version of social reality. The biblical version of reality is only *one window* on or a way to view the world; *one mirror* or one reflection of life/ourselves; *one lens* or one means of allowing us to see what otherwise will not be seen. In other words, culture as "text" views the Bible as not being *from* God but *about* God. That is, it sees the Bible not from a top down perspective – from God to humanity – but from the bottom up – human efforts to understand what they can about God.

What, therefore, are the influences and experiences, the socio-historical realities, which shaped and are shaping the version of reality of the Caribbean reader of biblical texts? What is the wellspring of the influences and experiences that form and inform Caribbean peoples' ways of viewing the world or biblical texts? What are those influences and experiences in Caribbean social history that hold insights for biblical interpretation? What are those influences and experiences that reflect and impact Caribbean peoples' social life? What are the means by which Caribbean peoples discover themselves? What are those influences and experiences of Caribbean peoples in which the praxis of resistance is operative?

This work submits that those influences and experiences are found in the socio-cultural history of Caribbean peoples. Hence, as is noted previously, Mulrain uses *jumbie stories and laughter* as an interpretive lens by which to interpret biblical texts, without the texts losing their mythology, and to subvert despair and inspire confidence to face the future; Gossai employs the *game of cricket* to appropriate the issue of identity in the Old Testament book of Ruth; Jagessar probes into *Caribbean literature* to discover how writers utilize biblical theological traditions and constructs to invert their meaning in the light of the influences and experiences of Caribbean peoples; Middleton works with *Caribbean music* to contemporize and extend stories in biblical texts to include Caribbean socio-historical realities; and Spencer Miller engages with *popular Caribbean aphorisms* to identify power relations in biblical texts.

The argument for culture as "text" can be extended by relating an experience of a house-group of some 15–20 persons led by Father Leslie Lett that met often for prayers and Bible Study in an Anglican parish in the Caribbean island of St Vincent.[24] This experience demonstrates how culture is "text" and theology gets done. The text chosen for study was 2 Cor. 4:7–16a. Earlier in the day, a peaceful demonstration was broken up by state violence with tear gas pumped indiscriminately through the city. Father Lett resisted the group's insistence that he should publicly denounce state terror during the Sunday Mass until after the following conversation:

> Ellisson: "But Father, the Mass is the right place to speak out; people done start to lose jobs and who going to feed their children ... we have to share our food with them so they can fight for justice, for in the Mass Jesus teach us how to share bread and the cup that all may have to eat and drink and nobody get weak and perish."

> Thomas: "And, too, Jesus teach us in the Mass how to struggle for justice and against oppression, for in Mass he teach us how to have our bodies broken and our blood shed, like what happen this afternoon; the Mass is about Jesus struggling with us".

Then we agreed that the tear gas was the incense and that the Mass was truly celebrated in the street of the city that afternoon! The streets were the Sanctuary because wherever the people share, and wherever their blood is shed and their bodies broken in the struggle for justice for the weak in an oppressed community, there is the "real presence" of Jesus, there is the Sanctuary, the privilege locale of access to God.

The discussion then centred on the church's Sanctuary:

> Jane: "This means that we have to change up how we think about the church Mass – it's too holy-holy and don't help people to see what we are talking about here tonight".

Veronica: "I think that in the church Mass Jesus tries to make us learn how
to discern him; the trouble is people only learn how to discern
him in Bread and Wine, and they don't learn how to discern him
in poor people, in beat-up people, in the people who are down-
pressed. That is why St Paul said if people don't discern the Lord's
presence in the ordinary people in the community they eat and
drink damnation, not salvation, in the Mass."

Winston: "In other words, we need both Sanctuaries and they can't be
separated because in a way, they are one and the same."

Veronica: "Salvation and worship is about struggling for justice, like Jesus;
no wonder he said not all who say 'Lord, Lord, will enter the
Kingdom'. And the word that comes out of the Lord's mouth that
we must live by is the word of poor people, small people – if we
listen to them we hear Jesus' word".[25]

In this experience, it was the "tear gas as incense", "streets as Sanctuary"
and discerning Jesus in Bread and Wine, "in beat-up people, poor people
and down-pressed people", *the peoples' experiences and struggles*, that
became the primary "text" (a window, a mirror, a lens) for interpreting
2 Cor. 4:7–16a.

In other words, socio-cultural analysis conditions, shapes, informs,
influences biblical appropriation and that Caribbean jumbie stories,
laughter, cricket, Caribbean literature, Caribbean music and Caribbean
aphorisms as well as Caribbean peoples' struggles for justice, self-definition
and self-determination are legitimate windows, mirrors and lenses or
"texts" by which to undertake biblical interpretation. Even so, one cannot
lose sight of the cultural meaning of those socio-cultural influences and
experiences, the ideological stance and commitment of the reader or the
socio-ideological agenda and theology at work in biblical texts. The cultural
meaning of the social existence, ideological commitment and stance of the
reader and the socio-ideological and theological agenda of biblical texts
conjoin to form a reading strategy that resulted in resistance to oppressive
systems and practices. Or as Winston in the house-group conversation
above puts it "we need both Sanctuaries and they can't be separated".

In sum, culture as "text" is not just a matter of different readers using
different reading strategies. Rather, it is different readers reading in different
ways, owing to their multi-level social groupings that they represent and
to which they belong.[26] Such readings are constructs: that which is arrived
at by positioned and interested readers, reading from different and complex
social locations.[27] For this study, culture as "text" is about interpreting
biblical texts out of one's socio-cultural context.

Moreover, the incident cited above foregrounds the elements of the biblical resistant hermeneutic highlights the critique of Caribbean biblical hermeneutical practice. It is a cultural-literacy consciousness that understands tear gas as incense, the streets as sanctuary and the "real presence" of Jesus as experienced where blood is shed and bodies are broken in the struggle for justice and against oppression. It thereby provides the epistemological lens by which to interpret 2 Cor. 4:7–16a from the particularities of the context. Similarly, this understanding gives agency to both the materiality of the biblical texts and context of interpreters as well as ensuring that that the biblical text was approached from a position of praxis of resistance with a clear ideological stance and commitment. In addition, it eliminates the disjuncture between faith and praxis, as the street is neither the antithesis of sanctuary nor is the sanctuary the antithesis of the street. Out of the new understanding of body and blood, the Mass is no longer celebrated as unrelated to the sociality of existence.

In other words, the cultural meaning of the sociality of existence provides a way of knowing into biblical texts and thereby inspires concrete commitment to and involvement in the struggle for justice and against oppression. Besides, it makes resistance to oppressive systems and structures possible, with agency given to the materiality of biblical texts and context of interpreters.

Text as Cultural Construction

Text as cultural construction admits that biblical texts were not written in a vacuum; and neither does a reader come to biblical texts out of a vacuum. The Bible emerged from a particular socio-cultural environment and was written from some perspective. As such, biblical texts are merely "readings" of the social realities in which their authors lived. This means that the Bible is a "produced" text, a construction, and an account of a socio-historical practice. Here the biblical text is decentred, as the focus is not on the text per se but on the construction of "worlds".[28] It is as Catherine Hall states "a focus on history as constructed, not given; on the imagined community as created, rather than simply there; on identities brought into being through particular discursive work".[29]

The trouble is those "worlds" are constructed by the ruling classes, who also wrote biblical texts.[30] Thus the concern of biblical interpreters is whether and in what form a religious outlook finds expression in biblical texts or expresses the socio-economic relations and circumstances of a given society. Such a concern has bearing on what is called the "word of God". For what is called the "word of God" may be conversion into faith of ruling class interests that cut across social divisions. So, whose truth gets told in the Bible? The ruling classes' or God's? Is the portrayal of God in the Bible, therefore, reliable? And what one might ask is biblical truth?

As biblical texts have their ideological roots in oppressive practices, written as they were in royal courts and thereby dominated by ruling class ideas, interests and voices, the challenge of biblical hermeneutics is to identify those ideas, interests and voices embedded in the biblical text. For this biblical interpretive process, Weems indicates that hermeneutics is a process of two halves.[31] The first half is the reading process.[32] The action is between the text and the reader, in the quest for meaning of the biblical text. The socio-historic circumstances and rhetorical features of the text are examined in conjunction with the presupposition, social location and hermeneutical suspicion of the reader.

The second half of the biblical interpretive process concerns the actual biblical text. Weems contends that it is absolutely critical to identify the narrative voice of the text. This is in order to avoid aligning oneself with the ruling class interests and ideas embedded in the biblical text, which are elitist, patriarchal and legitimated.[33]

Even though Weems may have suggested that biblical interpretation is a process of two halves, each half is not independent of each other. Biblical hermeneutics is an ongoing process where one factor feeds into the next and there is continuous change of interpretation and meaning.

Altogether, the movement of a biblical resistant hermeneutic advanced in this chapter is *from* struggle against oppression *for* liberation and social equality *by* the creation of a community of interests in social development. In this community of interests labour power is not for the alien Other as Master but for the community as a whole. In addition, profits do not accumulate in fewer and fewer hands[34] as there is a new organization of production without exploitation and expropriation. Though we have been freed as a people in the Caribbean, a community has not been formed.[35] So, then, the issue of emancipation from socio-economic and political bondage is not abstract; it is the concrete ontological problem of *"how to be"*, of being in our particular socio-geographic space, called the Caribbean. Given the Caribbean's history of Colonialism and neo-colonialism, "how to be" emerges out of pain and suffering and underdevelopment.

Moreover, my resistant reading strategy does not privilege any one Bible reading strategy – behind the text, on/within the text or in front of the text.[36] To the contrary, it employs all three reading strategies so that the text is placed in real life contexts. In front of the text reading strategies involve cultural-literacy consciousness and praxis of resistance as the text is approached out of the ideological stance and concrete commitments of the reader. It also seeks answers to the questions: Who is the reader? How does the reader live? And where does the reader live? On the text reading strategies focus on the literary world of the text in a process of dialogue with the world of the reader. Behind the text reading strategies deal with the world from which biblical texts come. As a whole, the biblical resistant reading strategy enables a new way of knowing, seeing and being.

Consequently, by employing all three interpretive strategies, the biblical resistant hermeneutic yokes together the socio-ideological conditions of the text's production with the cultural meaning of social existence and the socio-ideological position and commitment of the reader. It also gives rise to the following *interpretive questions*:

- *What is the 'place' of the reader?*
  What are the class and ideological position and commitment of the reader? What is the reader's way of knowing into the text? Why are things (political, economic, historical) the way they are?

- *What is the 'place' of the text?*
  What are the socio-historical, political and economic circumstances that produced the text?

- *What is the text doing?*
  What class, ideological, gender or power interests does the text serve or challenge? What form does opposition or conflict take between the groups involved in the biblical text? How does the text resolve any opposition or conflict that may be taking place in the text? What religious perspective or understanding of God is expressed in the text? Whose voice dominates or is silenced? Does the text take sides?

- *What does the reader do in response to the biblical text?*
  Should the reader oppose, that is, stay within the social system and use strategic manoeuvres to challenge it? Or should the reader resist, that is, stand outside the social system, denounce it and announce an alternative social order? Or should the reader spiritualize the biblical text by disregarding the socio-economic and political dimensions of the text?

Table 5.1 shows a schematized resistant biblical hermeneutic by showing how it relates to the analytical reading strategies used in this study.

Table 5.1: A biblical resistant hermeneutic reading scheme

Analytical reading strategies	Aspects of resistant biblical hermeneutic	Consequence
In front of the text	• Praxis of resistance • Cultural-literacy consciousness • What is the "place" of the reader?	• What should the reader do in response to the biblical text? Oppose, resist (separate, denounce, announce), spiritualize understanding of text
On the text	• Literary world of the text • What is the text doing?	
Behind the text	• Text as cultural construction • Culture as "text" • What is the "place" of the text?	• New ways of seeing, knowing and being.

A Biblical Resistant Reading of Philemon

In this resistant reading of Philemon, agency is given to both the materiality of the letter as well as to the context of a Caribbean interpreter. In so doing, the gap identified in Caribbean biblical hermeneutical practice is being filled. Whether the letter is exegeted first and the cultural meaning second is established, the materiality of both text and context are still given agency. It is not about the sequence of the interpretive process or order but the agency that is or is not given to the material conditions of both the biblical text and the context of the interpreter.

All four interpretive questions in the biblical resistant hermeneutic are accounted for and expanded below.

What is the "Place" of the Reader?

First, Philemon is read from the perspective of hospitality worker(s), employed mainly in the hotel industry in the Caribbean thereby answering the question, *what is the "place" of the reader*? In the hotel industry in the Caribbean duties are carried out on a shift basis for most. Pay hovers above the minimum wage level and to ensure that there is enough money to meet family and personal expenses and commitments, employees work more than one shift, or extended shift hours, or do more than one job. It is from this social reality of long hours with little pay or exploitation that allows for the way of knowing (epistemology) into a reading of Philemon. The question to answer is: what is the cultural meaning of long hours of arduous work with little pay? To begin with, it is exploitative. There is an inequality between wage and labour to the advantage of the employer. Besides, with little pay, the quality of life for hospitality workers and their families is adversely affected since pay determines the quality of education the children receive, the quality of housing the family can afford and the quality of the goods and services the family can purchase. And further, both the exploitation suffered and the poorer quality of life experienced results in the indignity of not providing for families experiencing a better quality of life.

Such experiences of indignity are a direct consequence of the nature of relations to the means of production. In the Caribbean, with its history of a plantation economy and its current reliance on tourism, banking, government and offshore banking as the basis of the economy in the modern era, the mode of production is capitalist. In this capitalist system, the forces of production are land, the seas and skills (human resources); and in the socio-economic structure, hospitality workers neither play a part in the decision-making processes nor are part owners of anything in any establishment in the industry. They are simply members of the working class. In other words, defining and determining the quality of life is a function of relations to production.

Essentially, what we have in this socio-economic structure is an establishment exercising its economics (how many to employ and how much to pay and how long and often should they work) within the context of the economy of a country (policy of social security benefits, employment benefits and tax structure) that is over-determined by the ideology of the ruling class, subservient to foreign influences and interests. Any contest or conflict between the hospitality workers, which leads to strike action, is not limited to that which is personal (employer and employee) but structural (employer/employee and socio-economic structure). Put another way, by striking, the hospitality workers are not simply resisting the economics of an establishment but are protesting against the socio-economic structure of an industry.

In effect, striking is praxis. In this regard, one is acting as a subject for social transformation instead of being acted against, as an object, in ways that will exacerbate one's exploitative working conditions.

Furthermore, striking carries with it several social implications as it affects not just an establishment but also the socio-economic structure of an industry and the foreign influences and interests to which that industry is tied. Striking is an exercise of social power and the virtual politics of the exploited class. In striking one resists power by evading its reach and thereby limiting its material and symbolic claims.[37] More precisely, striking is the "elsewhere"[38] of the exploited class from which to defy and register disgust for domination. What's more, striking is the "body-politics" of the exploited class, that is, removing oneself physically from or out of the exploitative working conditions, gaining, in so doing, a large measure of bargaining power. In essence, "though the body is never free from the grasping reach of official power, it remains a site where power can be most contested on nearly equal terms".[39] Ultimately, to strike is to reclaim one's dignity, defend one's (physical) body against the abusive and extractive claims of an industry and totter that industry without violent and direct confrontation.[40]

What is being established here, through cultural-literacy consciousness, *is* an alternative consciousness of what it means to work hard and long with little pay and be marginalized by the social system. From this epistemology, one sees as the cause of social injustice, the socio-economic structure, system and practices, not a single establishment.

Just as significantly, the issues of the sociality of existence with matters of faith are being established. "Body-politics", the abusive, extractive and exploitative claims of the ruling class, are as socio-economic and political as they are theological. Such claims despoil God's creational purposes for the well-being of human beings or destroy the Divine image in which humans are made. Undermining ruling class vested interests and injustices, therefore, builds God's kingdom of righteousness and justice in the here and now.

What is the "Place" of the Text?

Second, *"place"* in the letter to Philemon is outlined in detail in Chapter 3 above. However, we discussed then that the economics of Philemon's household are integrated into the household economy structure of imperial Graeco-Rome. The socio-economic structure of imperial Graeco-Roman society is constituted of two classes: the ruling class and the dominated class. What compounds the issue in Philemon is that the household is at the same time the house church, which foregrounds the issue of social inequality (in the household economy) and social equality (in the house church). As such, the household economy structure of imperial Graeco-Rome forms the socio-cultural environment out of which the Philemon text emerged; and social inequality and social equality are the socio-economic relations and circumstances through which religious faith finds expression in the text.

What is the Text Doing?

Third, the letter turns on how to interpret Onesimus' (slave in the household, brother in the house church) action of running away and what Paul means by entreating Philemon (master of the household, brother in the house church) to accept Onesimus "no longer as a slave but a brother" (v. 16). In other words, the letter now seeks to answer the question, *what is the text doing*? As it stands, the letter begs interpretation from the perspective of Philemon so that there is a focus on his graciousness in forgiving Onesimus for having the temerity to run away; or from the perspective of Paul the mediator focusing on his skills as negotiator in bringing about reconciliation between two opposing parties. Both perspectives arise from a position of privilege. Without an epistemology that takes seriously Onesimus' marginalized position, which is given very little mention in the letter and therefore seems insignificant, interpretation will not arise from this perspective. And yet, the letter is bound up with both the vertical and horizontal material relationships between Philemon and Onesimus.

In the vertical position, that is, Philemon's and Onesimus' relationship in the house church, the conflicting and exploitative nature of the relationship between the ruler and ruled stands stark naked with all its dominating practices, class injustices and vested interests exposed. On the horizontal plane, that is, Philemon's and Onesimus' relationship in the household, the incompatible difference between master and brother in the household of faith cries out for redemption in all its need to incarnate righteousness and justice in the household economy.

Consequently, from the epistemology of the hospitality worker(s), Onesimus' action of running away is seen as anti-hegemonic, an "elsewhere" from which to express disapproval of the kind of socio-economic structure he does not desire to be part of. Conversely that "elsewhere" also makes known the nature of the alternative community he wants to live in: one in which he has the right to self-definition and self-determination. By his "body-politics", Onesimus may not have brought about social equality in the Roman Empire; however, social equality in that imperial context is not about how impossible it is to be realized but exposing an unjust social system and practice so that the door to social justice is cracked open.

What Does the Reader Do in Response to the Interpretation of the Biblical Text?

And finally, with the cultural meaning of long hours of hard work with little pay and striking explained and an analogous and dialogical link made with Philemon, the hospitality workers are now in a position to re-engage with the sociality of their existence, that is, *what does the reader do in response to the interpretation of the biblical text.* Far from taking the Bible as simply an account of the socio-historical praxis of a particular time, of a particular people in their quest to be the people of God, the Bible now becomes a weapon in the struggle against exploitation, for dignity, a better quality of life and an authentic existence.

The hospitality workers do not resist the socio-economic system by going to work every day without agitating for better working conditions and adequate wages. It is resisted in three ways. First, by refusing to work under exploitative conditions which are non-beneficial, non-participatory and where they have no stake, the hospitality workers thereby separate themselves from the socio-economic system. Second, denounce the socio-economic system as unjust having discerned the cultural meaning of hard work for little pay and linked and analysed such exploitation with the biblical text; or abandon the struggle for social justice perhaps out of fear of victimization or repression or in favour of praying about it. Third, announce an alternative vision of workers' participation in the decision-making processes and having a stake in the benefits that accrue by continuing the struggle to establish a just social order. While go slow tactics (opposition) may pass as also resistant, if the desired intention is to transform or bring about a new order of justice, then one must resist, not simply oppose. However, should there in reality be victimization and repression, it means that camps of interest are established – on the one hand, the establishment and industry acting to protect vested interests and privilege and on the other hand, the hospitality workers agitating to construct a just social order; and the struggle continues.

Even so, in effect, there are three options before the readers as they make a conscious choice to resist or change dominant and oppressive social structures. One, survival or finding a way to accept injustices while maintaining one's self-hood; two, rebellion – continued subversive activities aimed at transforming the oppressive social system; and three, revolution, outright overthrow of the ruling oppressive system.[41]

Brothers or "Slaves" of Caribbean "Masters"

Two of the inferences to draw from the above are, one, that fundamental principles of justice, dignity, self-definition and self-determination do not change with time and circumstances; and two, since the Caribbean is a "created" community, the perpetual struggle of Caribbean people has always been to emancipate themselves from the imposed trapping of foreign values, customs and control. Now, what we have seen in imperial Graeco-Roman society and Pauline theo-politics and slavery are the following: first, relations to production determine and define subject positions and the quality of life in the socio-economic structure and system; second, economic interests decide how persons are treated; third, mechanisms of "freedom" set up by the dominant class in society only serve to reinforce bondage, oppression and exploitation; and fourth, creating systems and structures of social justice between master and slave is a sign of the presence of the reign of God. Over time, these principles of rights, justice and freedom remained unchanged, despite changes in regimes of culture in society.

Matters of social equality, social justice, freedom, domination, servile fidelity, which are raised in the duality of brothers, but master and slave relationships in Philemon, are not without interest to the Caribbean context. Admittedly, with the exception of the islands of Montserrat and the British Virgin Islands (still British dependencies), the Dutch dependencies of St Martin (St Maarten), St Eustatius, Curacao, Aruba and Bonaire; the French territories of Guadeloupe and Martinique; and the American territories of Puerto Rico and the United States Virgin Islands of St Thomas/St John and St Croix, the other Caribbean islands have raised, individually, their flag of political independence from their former European colonizers. Each has its own Governor, Prime Minister, Parliament and Senate, Mr Speaker or Madam Speaker, national anthem, national flag, national dress, electoral democracy and standing army as evidence of "independence".

Yet, who owns and controls the financial sector and telecommunications networks? And is it not true that the largest slice of the budget cake goes towards repayment of the national debt? It is true! Despite the political and economic advancement made, through the sacrifices and courage of our heroes, dead and alive, it is still obvious that our real "masters" sit in offices and boardrooms of continental Europe and North America. Are we brothers with our former "masters"? Or are we still "Slaves"? In fact, up to and throughout the 1980s and early 1990s, North America was called "Big Brother",[42] and may still be so, if not in name then definitely in practice. Evidently, the duality of "brothers" but master and slave is as relevant to first century imperial Graeco-Roman society as it is to the present day Caribbean.

In the Caribbean, neither slaves nor their descendants presided over the process of abolition.[43] Abolition was presided over by the establishment by parliamentary means.[44] As such, only the system of exploiting labour was changed. Property relations were never altered. It is still the case. Until property relations are changed such that descendants of slaves are not mere propertyless wage earners who are divorced from the ownership of property but capable of producing wealth, the social revolution of abolition is still in the making.

Conclusion

In sum, in biblical hermeneutical practices within a Caribbean context, the Bible has functioned mainly as a weapon of criticism. Such a use is borne out by the fact, as rightly charged by Spencer Miller, that biblical study is undertaken within the context of denominational agendas and thereby predominantly as a faith exercise, and rarely guided by a need to seek either justice or liberation.[45] The necessary corrective to this state of affairs is a resistant reading strategy wherein readers are culturally literate and committed, and the socio-structural issues in both context and biblical text are identified and engaged. Here the hermeneutical movement is not first and foremost from biblical text to context. Rather, it is one that seeks to discover the cultural meaning of the reader in context, points to the need for the reader to come to the biblical text out of a commitment and from within the perspective of the reader's social reality and with the patience to divine the socio-ideological and theological agenda at work in the biblical text. In so doing, "reading" of the Bible is done not to gain knowledge or for spiritual formation or to critique behaviours but to arm the reader with the discoveries necessary to interpret and defend life.

Fundamentally, the biblical resistant hermeneutic "first discover the questions of which the biblical texts are answers and identifies the problems of which the biblical texts are solutions".[46] To read biblical texts in this way gives agency to both the material conditions that produced biblical texts and the context out of which they are interpreted. True, the Bible may yet be the answer or the solution but what is the question or the problem? Without this congruence in socio-structural analysis of biblical text and context of the interpreter, the possibility of exposing, challenging and resisting oppressive social structures and practices are greatly reduced or virtually nil.

Notes

1. Idris Hamid (ed.), *Troubling of The Waters* (San Fernando: Rahaman Printery Ltd., 1973), pp. 6–8.

2. Hamid, *Troubling of The Waters*, p. 161.
3. David I. Mitchell (ed.), *With Eyes Wide Open – A Collection of Papers by Caribbean Scholars on Caribbean Christian Concern* (Barbados: CADEC, 1973), p. 107.
4. Hilary Beckles "The Political Ideology of West Indies Cricket Culture" in Hilary Beckles and Brian Stoddart (eds), *Liberation Cricket, West Indies Cricket Culture* (Manchester and New York: Manchester University Press, 1995), p. 156.
5. Ibid., p. 107.
6. I take "subject positions" to mean identities. See Mary Ann Tolbert, "Reading For Liberation" in Fernando and Tolbert, *Reading From This Place*, p. 266.
7. Ibid., p. 266.
8. Ibid., p. 266.
9. Frederick Douglass, *Narrative of the Life of Frederick Douglass* (Boston, MA: Bedford/St Martin's, 1993), pp. 40–41.
10. Roper, *The Impact of Evangelicalism and Fundamentalism*, p. 43.
11. C. Shiwcharan, "The Tiger of Port Mourant – R. B. Kanhai" in F. Birbalsingh and C. Shiwcharan (eds) *Indo-West Indian Cricketers* (London: Hansib Publishing Ltd., 1988), p. 54.
12. Brian Meeks, *Narratives of Resistance – Jamaica, Trinidad, The Caribbean* (Jamaica: University of the West Indies Press, 2000), pp. 62–67.
13. bell hooks "marginality as a site of resistance" in Russell Ferguson, Martha Givens *et al. Out There: Marginalisation and Contemporary Culture* (New York: The MIT Press, 1990), pp. 341–43.
14. Richard D. E. Barton, *Afro-Creole, Power, Opposition and Play in the Caribbean* (Ithaca and London: Cornell University Press, 1997), p. 49.
15. Martha Beckwith, *Jamaica Anansi Stories* (New York: American Folklore Society, 1924), pp. xi–xii.
16. George P. Rawick, *From Sundown to Sunup, The Making of the Black Community* (Westport, CN: Greenwood Publishing Company, 1972), p. 100.
17. Eugene D. Genovese, *Roll Jordan Roll, The World the Slaves Made* (New York: Vintage Books, 1976), p. 254.
18. Rawick, *From Sundown to Sunup*, p. 100.
19. Ibid., p. 100.
20. Ibid., p. 100.
21. Barton, *Afro-Creole*, p. 62.
22. Ibid., p. 62.
23. Walter Brueggemann, "That The World May be Redescribed", *Interpretation*, 56 (4) October 2002, p. 361.
24. Father Leslie Lett, *Third World Theology, The Struggle for the Kingdom*, Jubilee Research Centre, 1986, pp. 7–8
25. Father Lett, *Third World Theology*, pp. 6–8.
26. Segovia and Tolbert, *Reading From This Place*, pp. 28–31.
27. Ibid.
28. Vincent L. Wimbush "Reading Texts Through Worlds, Worlds Through Texts", Semeia 62 (1993), *Textual Determinacy*, Part 1, p. 139.
29. Catherine Hall, *Civilising Subjects* (Cambridge: Polity Press, 2002), p. 9.
30. Robert B. Coote and Mary P. Coote, *Power, Politics and the Making of the Bible, An Introduction* (Minneapolis, MN: Fortress Press, 1990), pp. 4–11.
31. Weems, *Reading Her Way Through*, p. 36.

32. Ibid., p. 36.
33. Ibid., p. 45.
34. Leonard Tim Hector, "Hopes and Aspirations At and After Emancipation", *Outlet Newspaper*, 17 April 1998.
35. Leonard Tim Hector, "Ralph Gonsalves and the New Idea of a Caribbean Civilisation", *Outlet Newspaper*, 9 March 2001.
36. Gerald West, *The Academy of the Poor – Towards A Dialogical Reading of the Bible* (Sheffield: Sheffield Academic Press, 1999), pp. 124–42.
37. Obika Gray "Discovering the Social Power of the Poor", *Social and Economic Studies* 43 (3) (1994), p. 184.
38. Barton, *Afro-Creole*, p. 50.
39. Obika Gray, *Discovering the Social Power*, p. 186.
40. Ibid.
41. Stephen Duncombe, *Cultural Resistance Reader* (London, New York: Verso, 2002), pp. 7–8.
42. Bible study on 2 Kings 18: 17–37 by William Watty, "Big Brother and Weaker States" in Allan Kirton and William Watty (eds), *Consultation for Ministry in a New Decade* (Barbados: CADEC, 1985), pp. 9–18.
43. Richard Hart, *Slaves Who Abolished Slavery* (Barbados, Jamaica, Trinidad and Tobago: University Press of the West Indies, 1985, 2002), p. 336.
44. Ibid., p. 336.
45. Althea Spencer Miller "Lucy Bailey Meets the Feminists" in Kathleen O'Brien, Musa W. Dube, *et al.* (eds), *Feminist New Testament Studies – Global and Future Perspectives* (New York: Palgrave Macmillan, 2005), p. 221.
46. Mosala, *Biblical Hermeneutics*, p. 192.

Chapter 6

IMPLICATIONS OF A BIBLICAL RESISTANT HERMENEUTIC WITHIN A CARIBBEAN CONTEXT

Introduction

Whatever the interpretive starting point of biblical hermeneutics – context of the biblical text or context of the interpreter – knowledge of place is a necessity. Above, the argument is made for knowledge of place in terms of understanding the socio-ideological, economic, political and theological circumstances that produced the biblical text as well as for the understanding of the socio-cultural, ideological and economic meaning of the social realities out of which the interpreter "reads" for both to have agency in interpreting biblical texts. It is the practice of the reading of biblical texts in specific social contexts that brings about the recognition of meaning of biblical texts.[1] The biblical text cannot interpret itself. From this argument, it can be seen that resistance to oppressive social systems and structures results when such material and cultural understanding are given agency, and especially when this occurs alongside approaching biblical text out of a concrete commitment to and involvement in the struggle for social justice. What, therefore, are the implications for the specific context, in this case the Caribbean, for reading biblical texts as products? More precisely, what are the meaning-effects of a Caribbean biblical resistant hermeneutic?

Below, it is suggested that a Caribbean biblical resistant hermeneutic has some six implications: how one defines the Bible, "reads" the Bible; what are sites for doing theology, for understanding the ground and structure of Caribbean religions, the way in which the spirituality of Caribbean peoples is structured against resistance, for example, worship and salvation, and the relationship between culture and theology.

Defining the Bible

In bringing together the world out of which the biblical texts are produced with the world out of which the reader "reads", the nature of biblical literature becomes a critical issue. Besides the examples cited above (see Introduction (pp. 1–17) on JEPD and the Gospels), let me refer to other instances of the nature of the material conditions out of which biblical texts emerged to reinforce the point that biblical texts are already an interpretation, an "action", a record of involvement in God's call whether to obedience or disobedience.[2]

For instance, one does not have to look far or long in the Bible to see that biblical texts are already an interpretation. At the very beginning of the Bible, Chapters 1 and 2, there are two accounts of the one creation story (Gen. 1–2:4a and 2:4b–24). Effectively, in the Bible, there are differences not only between books but also within books.[3] In Gen. 1–2:4a, we have the creation of vegetation, animals before Adam, then man, and then long after woman; but in Genesis 2:4b–24 Adam is created before vegetation, animals after Adam and man and woman created together on the sixth day. What we have here is not a factual account as to the origin of the world but an understanding of worlds, the meaning of life or how life is seen.

In Israel's theological traditions, Gen. 1–2:4a is assigned to the Priestly account, with its emphasis on order, blessing and Sabbath and is dated to the time of exile in Babylon, 586–538 BCE.[4] Exile was a time of crisis in the life of Israel as they were without temple, monarch and land. When symbolic systems are lost, up-rootedness, despair and hopelessness are experienced. Theologically, loss of the temple meant that God chose to abandon Israel or God was powerless. The loss of the monarchy meant that Yahweh had broken promises of land and becoming a great nation or was not strong enough to keep promises; and the loss of the land indicated that Yahweh abandoned his promise or could not make it happen. As such, Genesis 1–2:4a is understood as the Priestly account, a re-imagination of what humanity is in the light of exile[5] as God's cosmic intent remains empowerment and well-being for all humanity (Genesis 1:28). Genesis 2:4b–24 is assigned to the Yahwist or J account, justifying King David's rule. With reference to the creation story, the point to note is the presence of the Serpent and how the man and the woman were cursed and expelled from the garden, condemned to hard labour, having gained the power "to know".[6] The point of the story is that all must share in the hard work of building the Davidic Empire.

Similarly, Hugo Assmann cited the case of various New Testament writers' ideological appropriation of Jesus' own earthly programme.[7] Assmann has noted the tendency of New Testament writers to link Jesus' earthly programme with Isaiah 61:1–7. But Isaiah 61:1–7 is about the class interests of the exiled Judean ruling class in Babylon. What the exiled Judean ruling class did in this passage is to transcribe the ideology of the Exodus of liberation of captives and the oppressed to suit their own ideology of return.[8] So, the text is about the luxury and privilege that can be anticipated in Zion,[9] not liberation, which makes it antithetical to Jesus' own earthly programme.

Therefore, biblical texts are a complex of different positions and groups, representing varying and contradictory traditions over a long period of history and out of a variety of situations.[10] Such varied positions, groups and traditions make it possible for the existence of "not a biblical message" but "biblical messages", not a biblical God but "biblical Gods".[11] What becomes important is for readers not to embrace, own and claim, too readily, the "message" and the "God" of the Bible without understanding biblical texts, the socio-ideological agenda and the context. To do otherwise makes it possible for the oppressed to collude with the oppressors in their own oppression.

Biblical texts, then, are not without problems. The writers of the Bible cannot be excused for the contribution they continue to make to the oppression of women, abuse of children (Genesis 22), the rape of the environment and the glorification of war (Revelation), on the basis that such problems are due to interpretation over the years, and not to the biblical texts themselves.[12] Given the way biblical texts have been written, they fail us sometimes through patriarchal bias (Genesis 22), or the glorification of violence (2 Sam. 12:11). So, as Fretheim notes, "to save the Bible from complicity in patriarchy and violence, and thereby to maintain the authority of the Bible in the face of such challenges, we engaged in exegetical egg-dances and the scissors and paste approach by using texts that have a positive appeal to control the interpretation of troubling texts".[13] But to try and save the Bible from complicity is to disallow the sinfulness and finitude of biblical writers and to suggest that human failings and frailties do not reveal themselves in biblical texts. They do. One needs to problematize the commonly held view of inspiration, which allows for the fact that the human mind – sinful and finite – will not understand everything about God. Human beings will not always get it right and full. In other words, the problem is not always at the feet of the interpreter, and never the biblical text.

What happens in Caribbean biblical hermeneutical practice is a willingness to not take biblical texts as already encapsulating an interpretation, as already being ideological. For instance, Jennings defines the Bible as the "record of and witness to the primordial revelation of God, especially in the particularity of Yahweh, God of Israel, and in Jesus of Nazareth".[14] The one universal message of the biblical text is taken and applied to Caribbean existential realities. Where such is done, it means that the Bible is only ideological in its interpretation. But the Bible is already ideological; it was written from some particular perspective and understanding and out of specific contextual circumstances. To cause the universal to fit the particular is impossible. In effect, what we try to do is to force the biblical text to conform to our own understanding of the biblical text, as truth is claimed in advance. It is only where and when the particular interprets the universal or is understood in the light of the universal that contextualization takes place.

As such, I posit that the particularities of the Caribbean experience can be seen in the light of the word of God (the particular) but the word of God (the universal) cannot be seen in light of the particularities of Caribbean experience. The word of God is not bottled up and confined to the Bible. The word of God is also in the particularity of Caribbean experiences, which is also "text".

Consequently, the Bible as the word of God is an abstract starting point for Caribbean biblical hermeneutics. However, even if one begins the hermeneutical task with the particularity of Caribbean experiences as the epistemological lens with which to read biblical texts, one must still come to the biblical texts and there identify the socio-ideological agenda at work.

What all this underscores is a distinction between the Bible and the word of God. The Bible is the revelation of the socio-historical praxis of God's intention and will for humanity as understood by a particular people, at a particular time and in a particular place. It is by engaging the particularities and peculiarities of the socio-historical realities of a particular context with discerning the theo-politics of biblical texts that the word of God is given birth. The Bible is not the word of God (dictation). The word of God is in the Bible (revelation).

"Reading" the Bible

Within a biblical resistant hermeneutic, culture is "text", which means that "reading" biblical texts begins with the lived realities of readers and cultural-literacy consciousness of those realities, not with the biblical text nor with the pastor or church leader as the repository of knowledge and meaning. As noted earlier, it is the drug and mug approach that is the existing reading practice of Caribbean biblical hermeneutics with, ostensibly, the gathering of knowledge for spiritual formation and faith development as the goal. Hence, with the drug and mug reading strategy, no agency is given to the material conditions of either biblical text or the context of interpreters. Equally, there is no intention of separating self or church from oppressive social systems and practices, deploring those systems and practices and proclaiming God's justice.

"Reading" for the biblical resistant hermeneutic is not about data co-creation, the accumulation of knowledge, but rather it has to do with constructing an alternative consciousness that leads to the building of a just world and society. For this to be achieved, there must be an explicit awareness of the cultural meaning of lived realities on the part of both teachers and members of the group as a prerequisite to being able to challenge the dominant power dynamics of a particular situation. So it is not just about accumulating "facts" but having an "activist" agenda.

This "activist" agenda necessitates the democratization of the interpretive process wherein interpreting biblical texts is done by communities of interests and in the interest of the community. I have in mind here, on the one hand, the pastor or church leader (privileged social location), and on the other hand, the community of interest (the marginalized, farmers, domestic workers, fishermen, construction workers, civil servants, abused women, etc.) that gather to study the Bible on a weekday in the village chapel. If this experience is to have an "activist" agenda, then those who gather cannot surrender the interpretation of biblical texts to the acknowledged "expert", the pastor or church leader, and thereby become passive consumers of his or her wisdom and discernment but must themselves become active participants in the encounter. To be active participants means to co-construct knowledge, as a joint production.

Furthermore, if the agenda is to become truly "activist", then farmers, domestic workers and fishermen, etc. need to study the Bible as differentiated groups rather than in a mixed group as is presently the case, which is non-productive and socially redundant. Interpreting biblical texts from the particularities and peculiarities of the lived realities of their specific group, a real-life social group, construction of knowledge,[15] will head in the direction of analysis of the cause of those realities and the pronouncement of judgement and organizing for different and just realities. Here the particular group would speak with and from their lived realities to biblical texts rather than biblical texts speaking to the particular group with their lived realities. In other words, the particular is speaking to the universal instead of the universal speaking to the particular.

Now, it is not that the pastor/leader does not have a role to play. He/she does. But he or she must become what Antonio Gramsci calls an "organic" intellectual.[16] For Gramsci, the "organic" intellectual works in organizing and constructing a contradictory consciousness of a social class,[17] which is to say that the organizing role of the pastor or church leader is also ideological. His or her teaching of the Bible is geared towards transgressing, educating as a practice of freedom.[18] For this to happen, the teaching approach needs to be constructivist,[19] which is a problem, meaning and dialogically based teaching approach. For the constructivist teaching approach educating is about constructing meaning from particular situations that aims to understand and transform social reality. The role of the pastor or teacher is that of a reflective practitioner.[20] With congregants, there is reflection-in-action and reflection-on-action such that for both parties knowing is "in action" or "praxis knowing". Further, the constructivist approach means that the pastor church leader does not only empathize with the group but is in solidarity with them in their daily struggle to live, survive and make ends meet, growing together with them in comprehending the lived realities they desperately need to transform into an order of social justice.

Admittedly, to challenge or change that which gives meaning to one's life or question the structures in which faith was created, can create a crisis of faith and, though liberating, can be quite challenging. In spite of that reality (or maybe in the face of that reality), if Caribbean biblical hermeneutics is to become truly liberating by resisting social systems and practices that oppress, then even that which is the bedrock of its experiences of faith, the Bible, must be "read" differently.

Doing Theology from Non-Traditional Sites

With biblical resistant hermeneutics' twin interest in the materiality of biblical texts and the context of interpreters, discourse about and in response to the activity of God, or theology, arises out of the socio-historical praxis of both the composers and interpreters of biblical texts. Traditionally, theological perspectives in the Caribbean take their departure from three points: God-Jesus-Holy Spirit, human beings, and world or culture or experience. The emphasis is in belief where the theological perspective locates the point of departure in God-Jesus-Holy Spirit, which makes it rather speculative. On the contrary, the biblical resistant hermeneutic inverts the points of departure for the theological perspectives: world or culture or experience, human beings and God-Jesus-Holy Spirit, and thereby raises the question, "what are the non-traditional sites for doing theology in the Caribbean"? As such, the biblical resistant hermeneutic is not attempting to do theology using Western academic categories but is privileging material conditions as authentic sites for doing theology.

Two of the neglected areas that do not get the attention they deserve, as veritable sites for doing theology, are *budgets* and *census*. Yet, it is in budgets that ruling class ideology or ideas take on material force, where public policies for human development are writ large and where the church's concern for the socio-economic needs of its members gets inscribed and its ministry to the whole person has its social referent. The interest is not only to discuss the issues from the political and economic angles but in what the church ought to do and say in the defence of life, in incarnating the love and justice of God among human beings.

Budgets

Budgets are quantitative instruments. Even so, while budgets may not be the most effective means of deriving qualitative conclusions, they do provide clues to qualitative realities – housing, health care, education, social services, and commitment to agricultural development. In effect, budgets link economic development and justice to religious values of justice (right relations between employer/employee, ruler/ruled) and righteousness (right relationships between employer/employee, ruler/ruled) and the common good to the bottom line. There is no antithesis between the practice of faith and economic justice. In reality, budgets are moral documents.[21]

Below, three questions are raised that will permit the foregrounding of theological issues that will advocate for social change and provide the basis for social transformation. In this regard, three pie charts of budgets for the years 2001 and 2006 for the Caribbean island of Antigua are provided for analysis (Figures 6.1–6.3).

The questions are:

- On the expenditure side of the budget, who or which sector of the economy gets the largest slice of the budget and why? What are the social implications?
- On the income side of the budget, who or which sector of the economy pays the larger portion of the budget and why? What are the social implications?

- In general, what is the negative and/or positive impact of the social justice concerns address by the budget? What are the economic justice issues (for example, spending cuts or increases in health, education, social services, taxes) raised in the budget?

Noticeably, the question of "who", on the expenditure side of the budget, refers to the fact that the largest slice of the budget is not contained within the national economy. If that were the case, it would have been a question of "which" sector within the national economy. The fact that it is an external entity that gets the largest share has nothing to do with either generosity or surplus. In reality, there is no surplus with which to be generous. Rather it reveals the reality of our dependence on foreign influences and forces such that we do not determine for ourselves our own response to those events that affect us. In effect, we give away that which we need. The two budgets shown in Figures 6.1 and 6.2 demonstrate the point.

In both budgets, public debt gets the largest slice, 20%; remarkably, it is the same percentage amount some five years apart, though under two different political administrations. Not much has changed. Instead of change in social and political and economic orientation and policies, there was only exchange of the political directorate. We have been borrowing to survive. Or to put it another way, we have been digging a hole in order to get ourselves out of a hole. Paying such a high price to foreign entities to

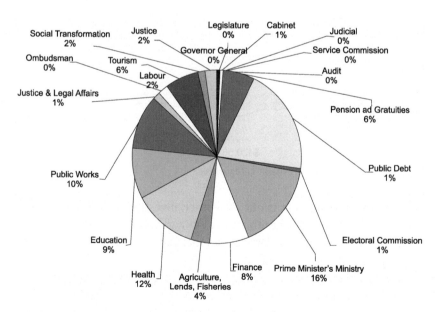

Figure 6.1: Budget for 2006 for the island of Antigua.

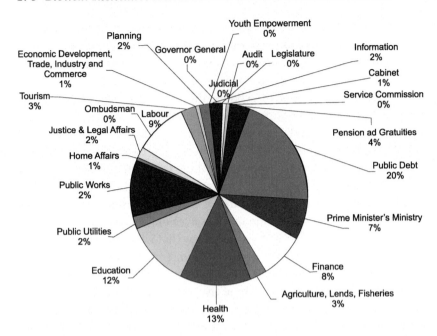

Figure 6.2: Budget for 2001 for the island of Antigua.

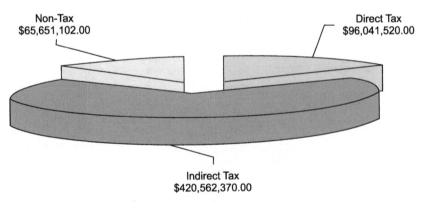

Figure 6.3: 2006 revenue by major categories.

survive cuts into, if not cuts out altogether, investments into human and economic development – health, education, agriculture and fisheries, which inevitably affect the quality of life for nationals, and for the worse. Effectively, we are paying for our oppression.

Similarly, the question of who or which sector pays the largest portion of the budget, on the income side of the budget, points to the fact that it may yet be some national grouping, as against a productive sector of the economy, contributing the larger share of the budget. The contributions here, however, may yet not be ploughed into national causes or projects as they are going into foreign hands. Take for example, the fact that over three-quarters of the revenue for the 2006 budget of Antigua is from indirect taxes with consumption and custom service taxes contributing more than 50% of the revenue. Now if we were to make a random selection of a basket of essential goods – Quaker Oats, Orchard pineapple juice, Jewell rice, Carnation milk, Purity flour, Peter Pan peanut butter, Maxwell House coffee, McCormick seasoning,[22] etc. – what we will see is that none of the labels indicate that they are "made in Antigua". It does not have a product, a style of its own. Even with the concessions made to consumers by the government of the day,[23] it still means that the cost of living is externally controlled, and dependence deepens. Besides, the high cost of living adversely affects the quality of life.

The issue being raised here is that quality of life and the cost of living are as much systemic and structural issues as they are theological. A wholesome quality of life and the root causes for a high cost of living are not antithetical to theology. With a biblical resistant hermeneutic, cultural-literacy consciousness will comprehend budgets as moral documents that have social implications for the quality of life of nationals, and ultimately hope. It also advances in the direction of biblical interpreters' critique, exposure and denouncement of that which does not contribute to the general well being of the community and organize for social justice and change.

Census

If budgets help us to draw qualitative conclusions, then quantitative conclusions are already drawn for us in the *census*. A nation's Census provides the raw material data about the living conditions of the people and thereby allows for the doing of theology from the perspective of the human condition, the lived realities of the people.

What needs to happen here is the building up of a social profile of a social class or a group or an area in terms of housing, health, crime, unemployment, education, marital/union status, etc. from the census data in order to identify areas of need, trends and possible causes of social problems. From here strategies can be developed to arrest difficulties, solve problems and thereby bring about just alleviation and relief as well as social well being. Building a social profile is not the same as stereotyping any class, group or area as the profile is not built on hunches but hard facts. For example, let us build a social profile of housing provisions in St John's city, Antigua from the 2001 census (Table 6.1).

Table 6:1: Housing provisions in St John's city, Antigua

	Total	Male	Female	Total	Percentage
Population	24,452	11,400	13,051		
Majority age group 35–39	2268	1022	1245		
Majority area – Grays Green		193	181		
Number of persons per household	6577			5	
Type of ownership – squatters	6577			14	
Construction material	6577			3582 wood; 1358 concrete	
Source of water supply	6577			1680 public stand-pile; 284 private	
Number of rooms per household	6577			2325 with 3 rooms	
Rented quarters	6577			2944	
Owned property	6577			3324	

What we are observing here, from the quality of the housing, are socially depressed communities in the environs of St John's city. This has social implications for health, crime, education of children, poverty and the general quality of life. In these circumstances, the path to well-being is not upward social mobility, as desirable or laudable as that may seem, but rather to construct a just social order. Communities of faith in these environs should not merely gather for worship of God that is centred on celebrating the Sacrament of the Lord's Supper and proclamation from the Bible that do not lead to agitating for a new social order. This is still the pattern. Such a lack of social activism brings to light the disjuncture between the structures of spirituality and the sociality of existence and redundancy of the biblical reading strategy. A biblical resistant hermeneutic that is grounded in people's lived realities has an "activist" agenda as its goal and would therefore serve to bridge the gap between the structures of spirituality and the sociality of existence and redundancy of the biblical reading strategy and resist those causes of the poor quality of life.

Understanding the Ground and Structure of Caribbean Religions

Given the material interest of a biblical resistant hermeneutic, it means that the ground of Caribbean people's experience of God did not arise from Caribbean socio-historical realities. Allow me to illuminate this point.

When Africans and later indentured labourers from India were forcibly brought to the Caribbean against their wills, they brought with them their religions. In Africa, the largely West Africans had a way of being, a structure of belief centred on a Supreme Being, gods, humans and the world.[24] Figure 6.4 represents that structure of being:

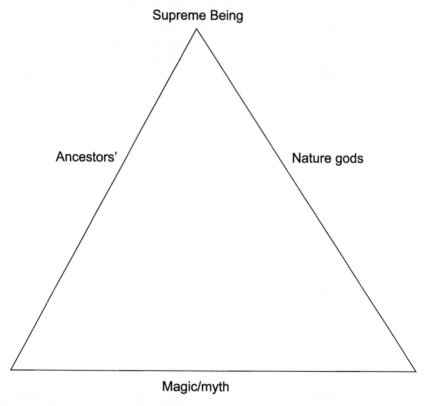

Figure 6.4: Structure of belief of West Africans

In the Caribbean, however, that structure of belief was destroyed. A number of strategies were employed to disrupt African spiritual and cultural organization. For example, the policy of separating persons from the same tribe and region was designed to prevent solidarity and organized activity to resist oppression. African nature gods, which belong to specific locales and tribes, also did not last long in the Caribbean.[25] As such, both the inability to come together as a tribal community and worship together as a tribe, made it impossible to re-ignite and re-knit their belief structure or way of being,[26] which is not to say that indigenous African religious ideas did not survive. Though significant changes were made, what survived and emerged had recognizable 'African' features – Obeah, Myalism, Rastafarianism, Revivalism, Shouters, Jordanites, Pocomania.

Consequently, the major loss was ontology, their way of being. In the Caribbean, therefore, spiritual relationships and the order of life and world-view were disrupted such that in Figure 6.4 the base became the apex. The way of being was magicized; the epistemological lens with which to see and interpret the world was now through magic. Magicization was centred in rituals for securing the assistance of evil powers in solving life problems and the struggle against oppression. The most expressive form of magicization was Obeah. For the Africans, spiritual agents were the cause of personal and societal acts of dehumanization, not the system under which one lives. So, the enemy was within, not without.

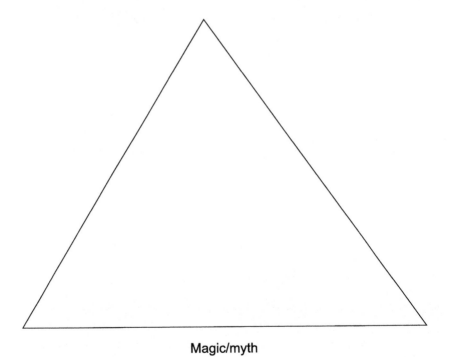

Magic/myth

Figure 6.5: Africans ontology in the Caribbean

For example, Mrs Flannigan relates the story she once heard as told by one of her servants to another. A slave's wife had mysteriously lost one of her gowns. Soon after the loss, the wife reportedly began to suffer odd sensations. The wife decided to consult an Obeah man to ascertain the possible cause of the distress. Upon seeing the wife, the Obeah man declared that the wife had "enemies" and it was from their intrigues that all her illness came. However, should she come again on another day and bring "all the money she could procure", he would conjure the evil things out of her. The servant who was listening asked if the wife received any benefit from the experience to which the storyteller replied "she say she do, but me no no; me no see she look better; hab to pay plenty money tho'; Obeah no like it if yo no gib much".[27]

Positioning a door key between the leaves of a Bible upon the eighteenth and nineteenth verses of the fiftieth Psalm was another way to "discover" who committed evil. Having secured the key in the closed Bible, both the accuser and the accused placed one of their fingers on the handle or bole of the key that is left exposed and repeated the incantation "By St Peter, by St Paul, you tief me fowl" (or whatever it was that was stolen) and the accused answers "By St Peter, by St Paul, me no tief you fowl". If the accused were guilty, the key would turn in the Bible.[28]

Thus, for slaves and ex-slaves, their "enemies" or the authors of their distress, whether in terms of the loss of personal effects, pains and tiredness from physical strain on the body, or deprivation, were not seen to be the oppressive social system and the Bible was employed as a conjuring book.

Besides Obeah, it was out of this alienated and divided existence that the neo-African religions of Myalism, Pocomania, Voodoo and Shango have their origins. They represent the Africanization of Christianity. My intention here, however, is not to privilege the socio-historical experience of Africans, as an ethnic group. This would be to exclude the faith expression of the indentured labourers from Asia, who were allowed to practise their Hindu and Muslim faith by the ruling elite, despite being subject to the same social experience of unreality and unrelatedness. So, my intention is not to engage in ethno-cultural hegemony. Even so, it is a fact that no other ethnic group suffered in the same degree the manipulation, discrimination and calculated denigration as Africans.

The plantocracy and missionaries preyed upon these circumstances of alienation and division. It was mainly at nights in their quarters and deep into the bushes, away from the control of the masters and their cohorts, that Africans experienced their way of being or humanized themselves through music, dancing and rituals.

In the full light of day, the missionaries with their religious mix of biblical religion, Catholicism, wielded religious power and authority with its emphasis on punishment, and Protestantism, with its concentration on justification by faith through grace, with little regard for the belief structures of the Africans or Indentured Indians. The undisguised ideology of the European churches was to bring the "one gospel" into different cultures and thereby to promote a monoculture or the denial of the right to be different.[29]

The biblical religion espoused by the European churches was nothing short of the imposition of a universal: the biblical story about one particular people, Israel, and of one faith expression, Judeo-Christianity centred on Jesus Christ as the saviour of the world. Biblical religion for the European churches began with Jesus Christ as the eternal Son of God and moved to the Incarnation, earthly life, death, resurrection and exaltation of Jesus Christ (Christology from above); or with the history of Jesus Christ as the eternal Son of God and then moved to the Incarnation (Christology from below). I have highlighted here the structure of belief of white European Christianity and that of the enslaved and formerly enslaved Africans. For white European Christianity, the belief structure moves from Supreme Being (God) to Jesus Christ to context. But for the enslaved and formerly enslaved Africans, the movement is from Supreme Being (God) to humanity to society. Whereas white European Christianity is struggling to build or win belief, enslaved Africans are struggling to survive from day to day and for authenticity. The one (white European Christianity) imposes the universal on the particular; for the other (Caribbean religions), the particular interprets the universal.

So, instead of Myalism, Pocomania, Shango, Voodoo, Islam, Hinduism, Rastafarianism being the faith expressions of Caribbean people, all of which are indigenous to Caribbean culture, Christianity is. Christianity, officially, is not indigenous to Caribbean way of being, structured as it is on the beliefs and faith practices of Catholicism, Methodism, Moravianism, Anglicanism, Seventh Day Adventism and many of the other Fundamentalist expressions of faith.

Structuring of Spirituality against Resistance

One of the consequences of this alienated existence and imposed way of being by those faith expressions implanted in the Caribbean is that spirituality is structured against resistance to oppressive social systems and practices. This point is evidenced by the structure of worship and understanding of salvation.

Over the past 15 years as a minister in the Methodist church, I have had numerous opportunities to conduct worship. And that is part of the problem. Worship is a command performance by the preacher, a sit-and-stand exercise routine. The preacher instructs and the congregation follows. The whole experience, as it stands, is individualistic though communal; an isolated experience, though largely social, largely non-imaginative though cerebral, very cerebral, and non-participatory though responsive. The members of the congregation are mainly passive consumers rather than active participants in constructing awareness of the sociality of existence. And this lack of social awareness is in large measure the problem.

Paradoxically, at play, in cricket (see below pp. 187–202), Caribbean people see the system as the enemy. But, at worship rituals, they see themselves as the enemy, in dire need of forgiveness from guilt and sin. It is still the same today. Today's worship is still structured to comfort the afflicted, not to afflict the comfortable.

Interested Folk Culture Worship
What will structure the worship experience for relating to the sociality of existence and thereby for resistance, is *interested folk culture worship*. However, there is the awareness that worship is transcultural,[30] which means that it is beyond specific ways of being of a particular people and place. In any culture anywhere, one should know that one is praying, baptizing and celebrating Divine memory. Nonetheless, worship is also contextual, counter-cultural and cross-cultural.[31] Contextually, worship re-expresses the way of being of a local or a particular culture. In its counter-cultural dimension, worship is intended to resist and transform foreign or non-particular influences and practices as well to expose dehumanizing and oppressive values that may be conditioning the way of being of a particular people and place so that worshippers are challenged to live differently. In its cross-cultural manifestation, worship acknowledges that there is something in all ways of being, in all communities that is appropriate to worship. This means that for worship to be truly counter-cultural or a radical space of resistance, it has to be contextual. Interested folk culture worship is both counter-cultural and contextual.

Interested folk culture worship is organized around particular social ills and issues, with the use of guitars, drums and calypso and reggae songs in the liturgy. So, instead of members turning up weekly to be led by the Holy Spirit's guidance through the preacher or liturgist, the worship experience for a month or quarter or for a particular week focuses on social themes such as unemployment, domestic abuse, HIV/AIDS, obesity, drug addiction, etc. Appropriate prayers, hymns or songs or choruses, Bible readings with proclamation and the sermon will also focus on the particular issue. All of this will be prepared by a worship team from the congregation, alternately comprised of youths, women, men, farmers, fishermen, etc. And in the worship experience itself, people from the community or congregation who are affected by the particular issue are given opportunities to "testify", exhort, pray and be prayed for and with. In so doing, the worship experience becomes real and a place of radical possibilities as awareness is raised and minds and wills are turned towards organizing for social transformation. In other words, a particular community of interest in the interest of the whole community undertakes worship together.

Effectively, interested folk culture worship fundamentally affects relationship and ministry in the local congregation. Traditionally, the basis of membership in the local congregation is geography, a community of believers gathered from the inhabitants of a particular area. In other words, the church is formed around where people live, despite the inherent understanding and practice that the church is formed around a spiritual experience or 'beliefs'. Even so, geography is constitutive of interests. There are social realities wherever people live and geography remains the determinative factor of relationship and ministry in the local congregation. Thus, one "believes" in order to belong.

What is being advanced here is the proposition that a community of interests should be the basis of membership, not geography, so that the local congregation is formed around *how* people live, as opposed where people live. In this way, worship grows out of the lived realities or social interests of the local congregation, which essentially means that the structures of spirituality are no longer isolated phenomena, unrelated to the sociality of existence. Now, one belongs in order to "believe". And in addition, unavoidably, the proclamation from the Bible and the weekly Bible study sessions are centred in the social realities that directly impact the daily life of congregants.

Salvation has generally not being taught as having any material implications. The understanding of salvation in the Caribbean was limited to liberation from sin and guilt. By pointing to this limitation, the benefits of grace are not eliminated – the assurance that the resources of divine mercy and forgiveness are always at hand, gifts ready to be bestowed on all who ask for them. Rather, it is to be acknowledged that salvation is also liberation from unjust social structures, alienation and despair, human indignity and oppression that destroy people's lives.

What our former colonial masters did to suit their own exploitative agenda and what many of the churches in the Caribbean still continue to do and thereby contribute to their own irrelevance is that they fail to respond and relate to people in the concrete realities of their lives. They divorce faith from the cultural, political and economic conditions of people's lives. Where people are related to in the sociality of their existence, then something is known of the form of alienation being experienced and the ways and manner of the oppression and discrimination being felt; and salvation of necessity is oriented towards being set free to live in communion with both God and neighbour, or to establishing justice and righteousness in the whole of the community.

Effectively, it is the understanding of salvation as redemption – liberation from the forces of the bondage of sin and death – and emancipation – liberation from structural and systemic bondage that keeps persons from being truly human – that orientates salvation towards resistance. For a biblical resistant hermeneutic, salvation is a quest for social justice.

Cultural Expressions as Hermeneutical Practices of Resistance

Moreover, with a biblical resistant hermeneutic that holds the particular ways of being of Caribbean peoples as the authentic ground of their experience of God, using those specific ways of being as a lens ought to condition the people's discourse about experiences of God. In Caribbean social history, the co-relationship between the history of two of the Caribbean's most loved and unifying cultural expressions, cricket and carnival, and the development of theological perspectives gives credence to the point.

To track the co-relationship an analysis of the socio-cultural meaning of cricket, both on and off the field of play, within the context of the social forces at work in the colonial (1492–1838), post-"emancipation" (1838–1960) and post-"independence" (1960s onwards) periods is undertaken. Correspondingly, the contextuality and historical development of theological perspectives relative to the social forces at work off the field of play and the style of play on the field as well how cricket is instructive for hermeneutical practices within the Caribbean context are accounted for. Cricket is used here as the cultural symbol of British imperialism in the

Caribbean and the impetus for Caribbean peoples' quest for self-identity and self-determination.

Colonial Era

Social Forces and Style of Play. Cricket's origin in the Caribbean was incidental.[32] Credit for its introduction is due to the English military, not the English Planters. Though its introduction was incidental and therefore not part of the civilizing project of the Planters, nonetheless its potential as a tool of domination was quickly spotted by the Planters and utilized as such. What the Planters brought was a culture of terror[33] – a terrified minority faced with an exceedingly large majority whom they did not see as human beings but as frightened chattel.

Cricket was played by the English military as a means of relaxation. From observing the military at "play", the frightened and enslaved Africans pounced upon the game, mastering its rudiments and understanding its principles and assumptions, as they judged that it embodied the potential opportunity for full expression and humanization for themselves, which the ruling elite deliberately denied them. What was fun for the English military was pregnant with socio-cultural and political meaning and significance for the enslaved Africans.[34] So, who plays and who does not play and from what club or country, who captains, who fields where and bats at what number, represents social roles and has social meaning and significance. Thus, social roles, relations and tensions get played out on the cricket field. In essence, cricket is a reflection of the society at play.

During the colonial period, the white European plantocracy was in full command of the political, economic and cultural reins of power, which was exercised to maintain social distance between the white minority and the black majority. In cricket, the social distance was demonstrated in the prejudicial and discriminatory selection policy.[35] The enslaved and formerly enslaved were routinely excluded from both playing in and leading club or national teams. This was not on the basis of either merit or ability but rather because of race and colour. In all spheres of West Indian life, whites were held as superior and blacks as inferior. So, if one had inferior skills but was white, one played and represented club and nation, but if one had superior ability to all comers but was black, one was marginalized. Marginalization for the blacks, however, was a site of resistance. Hilary Beckles, one the Caribbean's foremost historians, was obliged to conclude that the politics and history of the times "were driven by the same ambition:

how to keep the black man in his place and maintain white institutional hegemony".[36]

Cricket, therefore, was a highly contested cultural and politicized activity.[37] For the enslaved and formerly enslaved, cricket was a paradox: a game West Indians hate to love as it is a game of the colonizer that is a reminder of his imposed social, political, racial, cultural and personal inferiority.[38] On the field of play, English players took a no risk policy, improvizing nothing and daring less. Moreover, one abides by the rules, assumptions (the umpire's decision is final, spectators do not cross over the boundary) and the morality of the game.

As cricket was an import, it meant that the style of play would be of the English variety. In English culture, cricket was played and watched with inhibited restraint, with not too much faith in it with little if any emotion demonstrated in victory or defeat, with the polite clap and standing ovation to mark outstanding achievement or milestone.[39]

Contrary to the English style of play, the enslaved and formerly enslaved Africans played and watched with manifest passion and aggression. They crossed the boundary with impunity to celebrate success and register disapproval of the umpire's decision and tactics of players. The game was one of co-participation between players and spectators. With no hope of upward social mobility and an emphasis on things white, the best was to perform and out-perform the whites. Cricket provided a vent for frustration, so batsmen hit the ball hard, bowlers bowled fast and spectators crossed boundaries.

In the circumstances, cricket as culture was both mirror and arena. As mirror, cricket was a reflection of colonial racial domination by Whites over Blacks; and as arena, play was used as an outlet for anger and frustration against the oppressive social system and to register opposition. In short, what we have here is white European domination underpinned by an ideology of race and class demonstrated in a contested cultural performance.

Theological Perspectives. During the colonial era, the colonizers made every effort to ensure that slaves and their descendants were disunited and disorganized and could not remodel any of their former African customs and practices. Both self-determination and self-identification were consciously and systematically denied and stamped out during the era of establishing and maintaining slave plantation societies. Nevertheless, the colonizers could not destroy the consciousness of an African way of being, which was expressed in Africans' conception of life, death and supernatural powers. To survive, slaves and their descendants had to adopt the religious ways and beliefs of Christianity, the religion of the colonizers, even appearing to acculturate to European values and customs for purposes of personal advancement within the social system, yet without losing the quest for self-identity.

What emerged out of this manner of survival and quest to regain lost identity were the syncretic religions of Myalism, Pocomania, Shouters, Shakers, with their emphases on magicization, spirit-possession and biblical episodes of the Exodus and experience of the early church at Pentecost (Acts 2). Actually, the syncretic religions, despite their inclination to engage in ecstatic worship, which provided a temporary escape from the harsh realities of suffering and injustice, represented a means to humanize themselves, find meaning and resist hegemony.

In sum, the way of being, in this colonial period, shows the strife between the policy of white European Christianity to impose and deculturize, and the quest of the enslaved for authenticity, self-discovery, self-hood and self-realization, as the ground for their experience of God was unrelated to their socio-cultural circumstances.

Post-"emancipation" Era

Social Forces and Style of Play. On the back of wide-spread social unrest and agitation for better working conditions, increase in salaries and for political self-determination culminating in adult suffrage and the formation of the West Indian Federation, the 1960–66 years were characterized by rising nationalist consciousness and a sense of solidarity among West Indians. In cricket, the signal triumph of these struggles was the appointment of Frank Worrell, a black working class Barbadian, as the first non-white captain of the West Indies cricket team and a selection policy ostensibly based on merit and ability. Such marked changes in leadership and self-determination in cricket were not reflected in the political and economic areas. The black working class masses "exercised abstract political power in an economic vacuum, which produced a lack of confidence in social life and willingness to accommodate to the status quo".[40]

As Worrell set about engendering confidence in the players, he brought about a different style of play and created a new team ethic. Whereas in previous years it was each man for himself, and so there were brilliant individual players, now with Worrell, there was a team of brilliant cricketers cooperating to accomplish common goals.[41] In play, though there was still dash, panache, calypso-style batting, shots in and out of the book, it was all now done with the requisite self-discipline.

Consequently, with the quest for political self-determination and the direct challenge to race and class demonstrated in the fact that Trinidad, Barbados and Jamaica attained political "independence" during the period, the Worrell years as captain, 1960-66, were most expressive of social aspirations.

However, what Worrell built so assiduously was ruined during the 1968–77 years. By May 1962 the West Indian Federation had collapsed, which led to many West Indian islands seeking and receiving insular "independence". Insular "independence" is a seeking after the wind for it was nothing more and nothing less than "foreign economic control ruling, black political directorate reigning".[42] Besides, these years saw the emergence of the Black Power movement with its emphasis on black self-identity and social justice. In addition, post-political "independence" problems of unemployment and underdevelopment began to bite hard.

Going by the theory that style in cricket must be seen in relation to the social environment,[43] it is unsurprising that individualism, brilliant individual style of play, insularity and poor leadership returned to the fore in cricketing performances. This was the period that produced the individual geniuses, the incomparable Garfield Sobers, Afro-West Indian, and the great Rohan Kanhai, an Indo-West Indian. The one, Sobers, represented and maintaining the West Indian style of play characterized by dash, panache, disciplined and not so disciplined aggression; while the other, Kanhai, represented both the West Indian style of play and the quest for identity. Thus, whereas in the Worrell years, the one team represented the many different islands or the masses, in the Sobers and Kanhai years, it was the individuals, who represented the masses, the many different islands. Both Sobers and Kanhai were in effect "representatives" as well as "historic players".

Theological Perspectives. In these socio-political and economic circumstances, white European Christianity had the upper hand and made little attempt "to come to terms with the meaning of faith and challenges to faith in its context".[44] It did so with the explicit support of the ruling elite and in complicity with their socio-economic and political agenda of control and the maximization of profit. Disregarding the fact that the Africans and Indians did not represent one collective but different peoples from different cultural contexts with differing cultural traditions and customs, the foreign missionaries ploughed ahead with the proclamation of their "one universal gospel" derived from the biblical story of "one race", Israel, and of "one faith expression", Judeo-Christian. No attempt was made to use the cultural traditions and customs, in whatever form they survived the middle passage and their creolized forms created in the West Indies, as an epistemological lens into the biblical story. The intention was to fashion a Christian colonial man or woman, to Christianize was to civilize and to civilize was to Christianize. In this civilizing-Christianizing project, the masses complied as they tried to beat the oppressors or white Europeans at their own game, and thereby strove to imitate European life-styles and values.

What we have in these years, 1960–77, then, is the working out of the theory, in both cricket and theology, that theology, not theological perspectives, can represent a collective of people with their own particular histories and cultural identities. In cricket, it is possible for a team to be made up of players from different nationalities and/or ethnicities. The one team can represent these differences in the common goal of winning. Yet what was made possible in cricket ought to have proved impossible to do in theology. It proved possible, however, because theology is understood as that word spoken about God in a particular context, which is timeless, universal and unchanging[45] and as such can get interpreted in any context. However, as Watty points out "if theology is timeless, universal and unchanging, then there is no need to transport it from one country to another as peoples of all countries would have already had access to the one known truth about the One Eternal, unchanging and universal God".[46] Where theology is transported, it serves to distort and preclude contextual understanding.

Post-"independence" Era

Social Forces and Style of Play. During the 1977–80s years, worse than insular "independence" was to come in political and economic matters. The state and style of play did change in 1980s, 1990s and 2000s. With the onset of structural adjustment, globalization and the penetration of American cultural imperialism lengthening roots in Caribbean societies, they were discovering that the political and economic "independence" they struggled for and won, they never gained.

Moreover, with mass migration to greener pastures, in ways genuine and ingenious that baffles even the most astute of immigration authorities, and not for the first time in Caribbean history, wherever possible within the Caribbean itself but mostly to North America, Britain and Canada, "home" was experienced as a different reality. Those who migrated to North America and changed allegiance to the American flag were given the "national" designation "Resident Alien"; and those who migrated to Britain and Canada had their ethnicity affixed before their country of adoption. Notwithstanding, those who were born overseas found that they neither "belong" to the Caribbean nor their country of birth.

"Home", too, was a different reality for many cricketers. With internationalization, professionalization, commercialization and marketing of cricket, lucrative contracts with overseas teams, particularly in England and Australia, business enterprises and the West Indies cricket board itself became the order of the day. Cricket was now a commodity and no longer expressive of any particular cultural and social formations. Players now found themselves domiciled for some months of the calendar year in the country of the team to which they were contracted. Add to this overseas tour commitments and it adds up to the fact that West Indian players ceased to be the "home boy" of their village or club. In other words, the one representing the many theory no longer stands up and neither are there "historic" players any longer. For example, where is "home" for Clive Hubert Lloyd, black Guyanese born former captain of the West Indies cricket team, now of British citizenship, who has lived, and still lives, in England for these many years past.

At home itself, as it was abroad, the issue of identity was a live and real one. Caribbean societies are doubly diasporic in nature.[47] When the indigenous inhabitants, the Amerindians were exterminated by the marauding Europeans, Africans and Asians were brought into the Caribbean for purposes of plantation labour. And from the end of the Second World War to the present day, many Caribbean people migrated to Britain, North America and elsewhere. In each movement, identities had to be constructed. A debate has developed, therefore, as to whether there is a Caribbean identity or there is Caribbean and identity.[48]

What was significant, however, for the 1977–80s years was that West Indian societies were structurally adjusted at precisely the time when the West Indies cricket team was dominating world cricket. While the West Indies cricket team was dominant, West Indian societies were struggling to survive from day to day. The forces to overcome were no longer represented on the field of play but in the increasing economic globalization in the world with its networks of Corporations and markets. Cricket was now no longer tied to struggle and politics but to economics.

In consequence, while in the 1977–80s the style of play was still flamboyant, aggressive with controlled panache and flair, filled with improvization to release "limitations" imposed, daring and judicious, in the 1980s, 1990s and 2000s, it was markedly different. Now, in a globalized world with West Indian economies under pressure, the style of play was tentative, defensive, doubtful and strokeless, about graft and occupation of the crease without production and unentertaining, despite the presence of Brian Lara and Carl Hooper. As far back as 1963, C. L. R. James discerned that "in cricket, the West Indies have evolved a style of their own, even if in independence as a whole they have yet to do so".[49] In short, the West Indies cricket team, in these globalized times, is torn between "the ways of their raising and the influences of an imported culture".[50]

Essentially, the failure of West Indian societies to develop a style for independence has led to the undermining and consequent collapse of our own style in cricket. The failure on the field of play is reflective of the wider failure in Caribbean economies in sugar, bauxite, oil, and bananas and offshore banking. In short, we no longer have a product,[51] no style of our own. In West Indian societies, there is no style of our own on or off the field of play. In sum, the one reflects the other, and the other the one.[52]

Theological Perspectives. Earlier, it was observed that in the 1960–66 period, missionaries were unwilling to engage with existential issues and the cultural particularities of Africans and Indians as sites for theological reflection. The opposite was the case in the post-"independence" years of 1968–77 and 1977–80s. This period saw the emergence of the religio-political movements of Rastafarianism and the Revivalist cults of the Revival Zion, Streams of Power and Jordanites[53] as well as the formation of CADEC (Christian Action for Development in the Caribbean) and ARC (Action for the Renewal of the Churches) out of the Caribbean Conference of Churches. Rastafarianism is a rejection of White Christianity and ideology in favour of a religious ideology that grounds its experience of the Supreme Being in black identity and employs indigenous symbols for worship. Revivalism endeavours to connect with African roots and religious heritage. Through both CADEC and ARC, the Caribbean Conference of Churches promotes ecumenism, social development and social justice. All three religio-political organizations are engaged in the one struggle for self-discovery, empowerment, identity and the recovery and reassertion of African culture and heritage.

However, radical attempts by Rastafari and the Caribbean Conference of Churches to re-connect with African roots and religious heritage and the promotion "of social change in obedience to Jesus Christ and in solidarity with the poor"[54] have lost both teeth and momentum at the same time.

The American invasion of Grenada in 1983 and the subsequent demise of the Grenada revolution, unprecedented (American) cultural penetration and the flourishing of the Pentecostal/Fundamentalist sects are contributing factors. For example, Rastafarianism is now more style and fashion than lived reality; and the Caribbean Conference of Churches now focuses on HIV/AIDS and uprooted peoples of the Caribbean.

What is happening here is that the church and the neo-African religions are turning inward and thereby away from their socio-economic, political and cultural context of origin. Needless to say inward is the wrong direction to face. The day may be deferred but is unavoidable, when Caribbean peoples must reject the monotheism and monoculture of foreign and traditional churches or faith expressions and ground with the socio-religio-cultural traditions, practices and customs of their heritage. In such groundings is a turn towards Caribbean theological perspectives of peoplehood,[55] as connections and reconnections are made with all the cultures, religions and traditions that define us as Caribbean people. For purposes of authenticity of existence, that day cannot come too soon.

What the foregoing analysis has revealed is that cricket integrates, humanizes and equalizes.[56] In this regard, cricket is as cultural as it is theological. Culture is the wellspring of theology.

Cricket as Hermeneutical Practice of Resistance

Cricket is a game of order. The umpire is the ruler and his decisions are final. The field of play is a "sacred" space. To traverse that "sacred" space, the boundary line, is to trespass. And trespassers are persecuted.

Yet in West Indian cricket history that order has been challenged and that "sacred" space traversed when in the estimation of the cricketing public the rule of that order is unjust, a feat needs public acknowledgement or opposing tactics are judged to be unfair. For the West Indian cricketing public, the boundary is artificial. It is not unknown in West Indies cricket history for the cricketing public to cause disruption of play, on the field, directed against the rule of that order, corresponding to the upheaval and disruption of the social order in society. At such times, cricket is not only a mirror and arena but also social drama.[57]

In 1953, at the Bourda cricket ground in Guyana, the turmoil in the society spilled over into the field of play. The year 1953 saw the electoral victory of the People's Progressive Party in Guyana. Soon after, the British hounded that party from office suspended the constitution. It was a time of rising national consciousness. On the field of play, the West Indies cricket team was locked in battle with of all teams, England. In the match, England had the upper hand, having already scored 435 runs in their first innings and the West Indies had 139 for 7.[58] McWatt and Holt, two of the West Indian batsmen from Guyana, were staging a comeback when umpire Badge Menzies judged McWatt run out, a decision deemed dubious by the cricketing public. Bottles were thrown on the field and play was disrupted for some time. Of significance, is the fact that the cricketing public's open disapproval was directed at the umpire, Badge Menzies, not the English players.

In 1960, at the Queen's Park Oval in Trinidad, the struggle in the society against American imperialism was again played out on the cricket field. In 1960, Trinidad and Tobago was locked in battle with American imperialism to get back the Chaguramas military base. It was a time, too, of the quest to secure political self-determination from Britain. On the cricket field, the West Indies cricket team was again locked in battle against, of all teams, England. Again, England was in the ascendancy. The West Indies were in desperate straits with 98 for 8 when Ramadhin, in partnership with Singh, was staging a recovery, England having made 382. Trinidadian umpire Leekow gave Ramdhim, the West Indian batsman from Trinidad, run out in circumstances that seemed doubtful and West Indies were all out for 112. The cricketing public rioted. The protest, however, was directed at the perceived partiality of umpire Leekow, not the English players.

In 1968, at the Sabina Park cricket ground in Jamaica, the class conflicts and tensions in society spilled over once again on to the cricket field. In the 1960s, the social stratification that characterized Jamaican society manifested itself in unequal distribution of incomes and colour prejudice[59] and in who sat where in the cricket stadium. The elite and middle class, usually of the fairer hue, were seated in the covered and shaded stands, while the working class, usually the blacks were seated in semi-covered and shaded stands or stood in open areas. Such social stratification was on open display in Sabina Park that day. On the cricket field, the black West Indian cricket team was definitely losing to the white English team. England, having made 376 and the West Indies 143, asked the West Indies to follow on. At 204, in the second innings, the Jamaican umpire Sang Hue gave Butcher, a West Indian batsman from Guyana, caught out in what appeared to be an unfair decision. The cricketing public threw bottles from the semi-covered and shaded stands and open areas of the stadium and invaded the field of play. The police were called in to restore order. The entrance and involvement of the police made the drama real as "the actors lived their roles".[60] As in Guyana and Trinidad, the anger of the cricketing public was directed at the Jamaican umpire, Sang Hue, not the players.

The point of the above three examples is to show that resistance was against the system symbolized by the umpire. One should note here that resistance was generated by and centred in the socio-existential realities of the cricketing public – rising nationalist consciousness in Guyana, the struggle against American Imperialism in Trinidad and class conflicts and tensions, and black consciousness in Jamaica. The umpire perceived as the symbol of order and control, the chief upholder of the system, the guardian of the assumptions, rather than the players, was seen as the cause of the injustice and partiality. The umpire was the one to attack; his decisions were the ones to challenge and over-turn despite the boundary and the assumptions of the game. Now, this manner of resistance is instructive for Caribbean biblical hermeneutical practice. In the examples cited, culture is the "text". The Readers are the cricketing public who are literate and conscious of their socio-existential realities. Their "reading" of the "text" led them to resist the perceived unjust system. They were not just readers of the word but doers of the word. In short, where biblical hermeneutics is done using an "inside out" reading strategy, from the text to the context, especially without the socio-ideological agenda at work in the text identified, unjust and oppressive systems remain untouched, though perhaps exposed and criticized. But where biblical hermeneutics is done using the "outside in" approach, from context to text, where the socio-ideological agenda at work in the text is divined, then unjust and oppressive systems are exposed, challenged and resisted.

Accordingly, the "inside out" reading strategy is oriented towards redemption and the "outside in" approach to resistance and eventual liberation. In unjust and oppressive systems, it is human beings that are at stake, their humanity, their way of being, their self-realization. To engage in a reading of biblical texts that moves from the interpretation of the message of the biblical text to the context of reader, with the social realities of the reader remaining unaffected, is to fail to see the system as a cause of oppression and "downpression", and consequently readers seek liberation only from the personal bondage of sin and death. But to read text through the epistemological lens of contextual realities is to succeed in seeing the system as a cause of oppression or downpression. As a result, readers seek liberation from structural and systemic bondage that keeps them dehumanized and prevents them from realizing their full human potential.

It is not unreasonable to assume that many of the cricketing public in attendance at the cricket match are Bible reading, weekly Sunday worshippers in their chapel of membership. Yet, while in the cultural context of cricket they are inclined to understand the cultural meaning of a bad decision at a cricket match by the "system" (the umpire) and respond by resisting, they do not resist the "system" (oppressive social structures and practices) as a result of interpreting biblical texts. Even when the "umpire" in the wider society is identified, they are hesitant to "cross boundaries". This hesitancy is due to the way in which they are taught to understand and interpret biblical texts, despite the cultural-literacy consciousness demonstrated at a cricket match. Without a socio-structural analysis of biblical texts – what were the political, ideological, theological, economic circumstances that produced this text? Does the text take sides? Whose voice dominates or is silenced in the text? What religious perspective of God is expressed in the text? What is the reader's way of knowing into the text? – there is no socio-structural understanding of contextual realities, which will lead to a strategy to re-engage the sociality of existence. Despite this, the argument holds that the manner of resistance at the cricket match is instructive for biblical hermeneutics within the Caribbean context.

Moreover, what the disruption of play, the resistance to the system, in Guyana 1953, Trinidad 1960 and Jamaica 1968 has shown is that there is a relationship of social struggle for self-determination and self-identification between "play", resistance and subversion.[61]

The foregoing discussion is represented in Table 6.2.

Table 6.2: Cricket and theology in socio-historical praxis

Periods	Social forces	Style of Play/ way of being (Cricket)	In Theology	Style of Play/ way of being (Theology)
	System of oppression and negation White European domination	English: dull and regimented Africans: risky, exuberant, expressive, aggressive	Theology of imposition, Deculturization, Shango, Obeah, Voodoo, Pocomania, Jordanites, Shouters	Struggle between the policy of white European Christianity to impose and deculturalize and the quest of enslaved Africans for self-discovery, self-hood, self-realization and authenticity
	Ideology of race Deracination, Alienation	*1953: disruption of play, Bourda, Guyana*		

Post-"emanci-pation"	Rise in nationalist self-consciousness Sense of common history, culture and political identity Appointment of first Black cricket captain	Dash, panache, uninhibited, attacking with due respect for disciplined necessity, Team ethic *1960: disruption of play, Queen's Park Oval, Trinidad*	Theology of imitation	Non-creative, imitative, disconnect with existential realities, unreality and unrelatedness, distortion and prevention of contextual understanding of theology
Post-"indepen-dence"	Collapse of Federation, Cultural evaluation, Post-"independence" political problems, Beginning of IMF structural adjustment programme Structural adjustment, Under-development, Unemployment, Reign without rule Foreign control made more foreign, Globalization, 'home' as different reality, Dependent growth, Loss of particularities, Cultural penetration and imperialism	Individually brilliant players, loss of team ethic, cavalier, aggressive *1968: disruption of play, Sabina Park, Jamaica* Attractive, daring and judicious, attacking to release 'limitations' imposed Tentative, defensive, strokeless, unentertaining, occupation of the crease without production	Theology of development, Decolonization of theology, Black Power movement, Rastafarianism, Revivalism, Caribbean Conference of Churches, Pentecostalism, Fundamentalism My suggestions: Need to reconnect with socio-religio-cultural heritage, practices, customs and traditions and resistance Caribbean theological perspectives of peoplehood	Rejection of white European Christianity but not by the masses, struggle for self-identity, social justice and development, Reassertion of African culture and heritage, Commerciali-zation of religion, Electronic church

From Table 6.2, the following conclusions can be drawn:

- The colonial, post-"emancipation" and post-"independence" periods witnessed thoroughgoing struggle against and resistance to foreign forms, systems and ideology. A struggle that was not enjoined by the missionaries. Both the Africans, and their descendants, and the Europeans found themselves in foreign lands. The Africans came from freedom to captivity and the Europeans came to hold captives captive. In these circumstances, the missionary church was its opposite to its *raison d'être*.
- Nationalist consciousness and affirmation were lost in the neo-colonial global order.
- The more economic growth became dependent on foreign investment, the more denationalized the cultural systems became and the more inward/pastoral the church looked.
- Resistance is the authentic way of being for Caribbean peoples as they are likely to determine their own future and define who they are for themselves when resisting alienation and domination.
- When we consume or are consumed by the products and ways of being of others, we neither become ourselves nor resist foreign domination.

Carnival as hermeneutical practice of resistance

Besides cricket, carnival, another of the Caribbean's premier cultural expressions, also demonstrates the relationship of social struggle for self-determination and self-identification between "play", resistance and subversion. Carnival provides valuable insights into biblical hermeneutical practices within the Caribbean.

The French Planters introduced carnival in the Caribbean, at the end of the eighteenth-century.[62] The manner and content of the masquerade, however, were adopted and then changed by Blacks during the post-emancipation era to include African traditions and customs, and have continued to morph over the years.[63] In its original manifestation, carnival was a festival in which the French Planters mimicked the *negre jardin* or field labourer. The French Planters blackened their faces and wore the tattered clothes of enslaved African field workers.[64] But this was no mere mimicry or "play". In reality, it served as another form of dehumanizing the enslaved Africans.

Nonetheless, when the emancipated Africans in their canboulay adopted the festival or midnight procession in which there were singing and dancing, armed with sticks and torches, marching through the streets,[65] this, too, was no mere imitation of the French Planters but was symbolic and revolutionary in content and intent. Torches symbolized that a new day of freedom had dawned. A transculturation process was taking place as the emancipated Africans turned the *negre jardin,* a parody intended to dehumanize them, into a *canboulay,* a mask of a mask or a liberating practice,[66] a safe way of doing dangerous things. Here, the masquerade's political potential as "rituals of rebellion" was undisguised.[67] Even so, the fact that it also functioned as release from the stress and strain of oppressive and exploitative plantation life meant that it did nothing more than affirms the status quo.[68] In such circumstances, the masquerade was reduced to a state where it is "role serious, not real serious".[69]

Such differences in content and intent mean that carnival, then, as now, was a contested cultural performance.[70] On the one hand, there is ritualized role reversal, by both oppressor and oppressed, and on the other, "lampooning liberty"[71] by the oppressed. In this regard, the carnival masquerade seeks to strike a balance between consensus and conflict, control and spontaneity, compliance and subversion.[72] Where the balance is upset in favour of consensus and control, carnival is stylized. A stylized masquerade means that power is contested ritually and consequently entrenched. But where it leans towards conflict, spontaneity and subversion, carnival is "ritualized resistance";[73] a veritable symbol of freedom as there is a breaking through of the imposed patterns of society that creates a new understanding of self and society, albeit with gaiety.

It is these two traditions – *negre jardin* and *canboulay* – that are in flux in contemporary Caribbean carnival culture. While the concept of creating images of images remains – artists and their masquerades portraying social realities or continuing human experience – there are the absence of facemasks and the loss of irony and their concomitant critical, political and revolutionary edge and intent. Such absence and loss are due in no small measure to middle class participation, the institutionalizing of carnival administration and the branding of carnival with an emphasis on marketing and profit. Thus, the emphasis has shifted from mimicry and irony to an assertion of selfhood. Gone are the days when mas' was a political action and a revolutionary act. Now, the subverters are subverted.[74] For V. S. Naipaul "carnival is neither an illusion nor a direct reflection of social reality but a stylised rendering of concerns and values of society".[75] Emphasis is now on colour, such that carnival is a riot of colours, more stylized than political and revolutionary. It is play that has lost its link to subversion and resistance.

Accordingly, the carnival masquerade is reflective of a wider Caribbean struggle or dilemma: economic benefits versus the quest to reflect cultural history and reality.[76] In reality, the Caribbean dilemma is "how to eat and remain human"[77] as the economic seems inimical to the cultural and the cultural to the economic. Such tension between the cultural and economic is a tough struggle albeit but "text" nonetheless, a version of Caribbean reality. This is our epistemology, our way of knowing and reading into "text".

What is being acknowledged here is that carnival has the potential for resistance. Carnival, too, illustrates the "outside in" approach to the reading of "text", as indicated above. In carnival, masquerades display in costumes and masks. They dress as queens, kings and princesses of bands, which represent their "reading" or understanding of socio-political and economic realities. Such "reading" of social realities is in effect a direct challenge to structures, hierarchies and values, albeit symbolic and with gaiety. This demonstrates that oppressive systems need not always be challenged violently. "Play" or masquerading is also a revolutionary tool, a safe way of doing dangerous things. The prophets of Israel and Jesus have used prophecy and parables to say dangerous things safely. It is to the loss of the Caribbean peoples' liberation from oppressive and unjust systems in their societies that carnival is now more gaiety than a revolutionary a tool. In effect, carnival is a revolutionary tool and should be used as such.

Conclusion

The foregoing highlighted the critical importance of knowledge of place whether of biblical texts or one's context in resisting oppressive social systems and practices. Randall Bailey warned "unless one is aware of one's cultural biases and interests in reading the text and appropriating the tradition, one may be seduced into adopting another's culture, one which is diametrically opposed to one's health and well-being".[78] To avoid such seduction, it is important to understand that there is a socio-ideological agenda and social practices at work in the composition of biblical texts as well as in the context of the interpreter of biblical texts. One should then discern the cultural meaning of the socio-economic and historical realities of one's context in order to construct an alternative consciousness as well as democratizing the biblical hermeneutical process so that a real-life situation is engaged in analysing material realities. Finally it is crucial to judge those realities and organize for social transformation whilst ensuring that theology arises from praxis and is grounded in the lived realities of people. It is a biblical resistant hermeneutic that will put an end to the alluring ways of a foreign culture, establish knowledge of place and consequently bring about authenticity of existence.

Notes

1. Vaage ed., *Subversive Scripture*, p. 12.
2. Jose Miguez-Bonino "Marxist Critical Tools: Are They Helpful in Breaking the Stranglehold of Idealist Hermeneutics" in R. S. Sugirtharajah (ed.) *Voices From the Margins – Interpreting the Bible in the Third Word* (London: Orbis Books/ SPCK, 1995), p. 64.
3. David Robert Ord and Robert B. Coote, *Is the Bible True? Understanding the Bible Today* (London: SCM Press, 1994), p. 51.
4. Terrence Fretheim, *Creation, Fall and Flood* (Minneapolis, MN: Augsburg, 1969), p. 23.
5. Hans Walter Wolf and Walter Brueggemann, *The Vitality of Old Testament Traditions* (Atlanta, GA: John Knox Press, 1982), pp. 101–13.
6. Ord and Coote, *Is the Bible True?* pp. 72–73.
7. Hugo Assmann, *Theology for A Normal Church* (New York: Orbis Books, 1976), p. 68.
8. Ibid.
9. Ibid.
10. Mosala, *Biblical Hermeneutics*, p. 29.
11. Mosala, *Biblical Hermeneutics*, p. 28.
12. Lecture delivered by Dr Terrence Fretheim on "Is the Portrayal of God Reliable?" at the Vancouver School of Theology, Summer School Public Lecture Series, 6 July 1995.
13. Ibid.
14. Jennings, The Word in Context, p. 3.
15. Vaage, *Subversive Scriptures*, p. 14.
16. Antonio Gramsci, *Selection From Prison Notes* (London: Lawrence and Wishart, 1971), p. 6.
17. Gramsci, *Selection From Prison Notes*, p. 10: "the mode of being of the new/ organic intellectual can no longer consist in eloquence, which is an exterior and momentary mover of feelings and passions, but in active participation in practical life, as constructor, organiser, 'permanent persuader' and not just a simple orator; from technique-as-work one proceeds to technique-as-science and to the humanistic conception of history, without which one remains 'specialized' and does not become 'directive' (specialised and political)"; see also Anne Shawstack Sassoon, *Gramsci's Politics* (London: Croom Helm, 1980), p. 139.
18. bell hooks, *Teaching To Transgress, Education as the Practice of Freedom* (New York, London: Routledge, 1994), p. 3.
19. M. Williams and R. L. Buder, *Psychology For Language Teachers: A Social Constructivist Approach* (Cambridge: Cambridge University Press, 1997), p. 51.
20. Ibid., pp. 53–56.
21. Jim Wallis, *God's Politics* (Oxford: Lion, 2005), p. 241.

22. See 2006 Budget Statement entitled "Gearing Up For Growth" delivered Wednesday 30 November 2005 by Dr The Hon. L. Errol Cort, MP, Minister of Finance and The Economy, pp. 72–76.

23. Ibid.

24. G. Parrinder, *Religion in Africa* (New York: Praeger, 1969), p. 27.

25. Elizabeth Thomas-Hope "The Pattern of Caribbean Religions", pp. 9–5, Geoffrey Parrinder "The African Spiritual Universe", pp. 16–24 in Brian Gates (ed.) *Afro-Caribbean Religions* (London: Ward Lock Educational, 1980); see also George Mulrain "African Cosmology and Caribbean Christianity" in Burton Sankeralli (ed.) *At the Cross Roads – African Caribbean Religion and Christianity* (Trinidad and Tobago: Caribbean Conference of Churches, 1995), pp. 50–51.

26. Don Robotham "The Development of a Black Ethnicity in Jamaica" in Rupert Lewis and Patrick Bryan (eds) *Garvey: His Work and Impact* (Trenton, NJ: Africa World Press, Inc. 1994), pp. 26–28.

27. Mrs Flannigan, *Antigua and the Antiguans, Volume II* (London: Saunders & Otley, 1844), p. 53.

28. Ibid., p. 55–56

29. Harold Sitahal *"Dealing with Plurality in the Caribbean ... The C.C.C and Pluralism"* in Sankeralli *At the Crossroads*, p. 225.

30. James Scherer and Stephen Bevans, *New Directions in Mission and Evangelism* (Maryknoll, NY: Orbis Books, 1999), pp. 180–84; see also, Knolly Clarke "Liturgy and Culture in the Caribbean" in Idris Hamid, *Troubling of The Waters*, pp. 141–63.

31. Ibid.

32. Tim Hector "Will We Continue to be Annihilated and Humiliated" Fan The Flame *Outlet Newspaper* 1 December 2000.

33. Tim Hector "The OECS in Time, Space and Sports" Fan The Flame *Outlet Newspaper* 21 April 2000.

34. C. L. R. James, *Beyond A Boundary*, p. 66.

35. Maurice St Pierre, "West Indian Cricket Part 1, A socio-historical Appraisal" in Hilary McD. Beckles, *Liberation Cricket, West Indies Cricket Culture* (New York: Manchester University Press, 1995), pp. 120–23.

36. Hilary McD. Beckles, "The Political Ideology of West Indies Cricket Culture" in Beckles and Stoddart *Liberation Cricket*, p. 150.

37. Neil Lazarus, "Cricket and National Culture in the Writings of C. L. R. James" in Beckles and Stoddart *Liberation Cricket*, p. 390.

38. Burton, "Ideology and Popular Culture", p. 104; see also Patterson, "The Ritual of Cricket", p. 142 in Beckles and Stoddart Liberation Cricket.

39. James, *Beyond A Boundary*, pp. 212–22; see also Tim Hector "Crisis in Society and Cricket – Women to the Rescue" Fan The Flame *Outlet Newspaper* 25 June 1999, p. 3.

40. Tim Hector "Will We Continue to be Annihilated and Humiliated" Fan The Flame, *Outlet Newspaper* 1 December 2000.

41. Ibid.

42. Ibid., p. 4.

43. James, *Beyond A Boundary*, p. 219.

44. Kirton, *Current Trends in Caribbean Theology*, p. 99.

45. William Watty "Decolonisation of Theology" in Idris Hamid (ed.) *Troubling of the Waters*, p. 53.
46. Ibid., p. 52.
47. Patrick Taylor (ed.) *Nation Dance: Religion, Identity and Cultural Difference in the Caribbean* (Bloomington, IN: Indiana University Press, 2001), p. 10.
48. See Barry Chevannes "Jamaican Diasporic Identity – The Metaphor of Yaad" and Abrahim H. Khan "Identity, Personhood and Religion in Caribbean Context" in Patrick Taylor (ed.) *Nation Dance* (Bloomington, IN: Indiana University Press, 2001).
49. C. L. R. James "Cricket in West Indian Culture" *New Society* 36, 6 June 1963, p. 9.
50. Tim Hector "Lara in Cricket Time and Social Place" Fan The Flame, *Outlet Newspaper* 9 April 1999.
51. Dorbrene E. O'Marde "West Indies Cricket: Is the Music Loud Enough?" speech delivered at the Carifesta V11 Symposium on "Continuing to Define Ourselves in a Changing World" 23 August 2000 held in St Kitts/Nevis.
52. Hector, "Will We Continue" Fan The Flame, *Outlet Newspaper*, 1 December 2000.
53. Kortright Davis, *Emancipation Still Comin' – Explorations in Caribbean Emancipatory Theology* (Maryknoll, NY: Orbis Books, 1990), p. 52; see also Neil Parsanlal "In Search of a Black Theology for the Caribbean: Rastafarianism and Revivalism" *Caribbean Journal of Religious Studies* 17 (1) April, 1996, pp. 5–7.
54. *Called To Be, Report of Caribbean Consultation for Development, Trinidad, November 1971* (Barbados: CADEC, 1972), p. 23; see also pp. 24, 33–34.
55. Burton Sankeralli, *At The Crossroads*, p. 224.
56. Tim Hector *"From Vivi to Sir Vivian"*, Fan The Flame *Outlet Newspaper*, May 26, 2000.
57. Orlando Patterson *"The Ritual of Cricket"* in Beckles and Stoddart eds., *Liberation Cricket, West Indies Cricket Culture*, p. 141.
58. Maurice St Pierre "West Indies Cricket – Part 11, An Aspect of Creolisation" in Beckles and Stoddart (eds), *Liberation Cricket, West Indies Cricket Culture*, pp. 132–34 (for the scores that follow I rely on the work of Maurice St Pierre in this publication).
59. Patterson "The Ritual of Cricket" in Beckles and Stoddart (eds), *Liberation Cricket, West Indies Cricket Culture*, p. 146.
60. Ibid.
61. Richard D. E. Burton "Creolisation, Ideology and Popular Culture" in Beckles and Stoddart (eds), *Liberation Cricket, West Indies Cricket Culture,* pp. 92–93.
62. Thomas Bremer and Ulrich Fleischamann (eds), *Alternative Cultures in the Caribbean (*Frankfurt: Vervuert Verlag, 1993), p. 140.
63. Errol Hill "Traditional Figures in Carnival: Their Preservation, Development and Interpretation" *Caribbean Quarterly* 31 (2) June, 1985, p. 20.
64. Ruth Wust, "The Trinidad Carnival From Canboulay to Pretty Mass", unpublished MA Thesis, Berlin (1987).
65. Ibid.
66. Ruth Wust "The Trinidad Carnival: A Medium of Social Change" in Bremer and Fleischamann (eds), *Alternative Cultures*, p. 152.
67. Remco Van Capelleveen, "Peripheral Culture in the Metropolis: West Indians in New York City" in Bremer and Fleischamann (eds), *Alternative Cultures*, p. 140.

68. Abner Cohen, "A Polytechnic London Carnival as a Contested Cultural Performance" *Ethnic and Racial Studies* 5 (1) January 1982, pp. 23–41.
69. Barton, *Afro-Creole*, p. 245.
70. Cohen, *A Polytechnic London Carnival*, p. 37.
71. Victor Turner, "The Spirit of Celebration" in Frank Manning (ed.) *The Celebration of Society: Perspective on Contemporary Cultural Performance* (Bowling Green, OH: Bowling Green State University Popular Press, 1983), pp. 187–91.
72. Capelleveen, *Peripheral Culture*, p. 140.
73. Ibid., p. 141.
74. Barton, *Afro-Creole*, p. 278.
75. V. S. Naipaul, *The Middle Passage* (London: Deutsch, 1962), p. 90.
76. Dorbrene E. O'Marde, "Calypso in the 1990s" *Antigua Carnival Souvenir Magazine*, April1990, p. 40.
77. George Lamming, Opening address Rex Nettleford cultural conference, UWI Jamaica March 1996 *Caribbean Quarterly* 43 (1&2) March–June 1997, p. 6.
78. Randall C. Bailey "The Danger of Ignoring One's Own Cultural Biases in Interpreting The Text" in R. S. Sugirtharajah (ed.) *The Postcolonial Bible* (Sheffield: Sheffield Academic Press, 1998), p. 77.

Chapter 7

Conclusion

In the foregoing, it is argued that biblical texts come from a life world. In this life world, political, theological and socio-economic perspectives, practices and systems are inscribed and re-inscribed in the interpretation of experiences. In other words, biblical texts are not an exercise in dictation. Biblical texts are written from particular perspectives out of particular experiences.

From this argument, the following conclusions are drawn:

1. Interpreting biblical texts within the Caribbean context, beginning with the human condition or lived experiences, gives more agency to the material circumstances of the interpreter than the material circumstances out of which the biblical texts emerged and thereby lessens the effectiveness of biblical texts as tools of analysis for social change and justice.

2. Where biblical hermeneutics are done from within institutionalized systems and conventions, biblical texts are tamed.

3. Interpreting biblical texts from a social location of power and privilege, sterilizes biblical texts of their political, ideological, social and economic aspects and implications, and consequently,

4. Where biblical texts are sterilized of their political, economic, ideological and social interests and practices, the need to take sides in social struggle for social change and justice is greatly reduced, if not altogether eliminated.

5. Where biblical texts are approached out of a concrete commitment to and involvement in social struggle for social change and justice, this results in resistance to oppressive systems and practices occurs.

6. Where there is socialization of the means of power and governance in society, that is, participation and partnership in the social system, social relationships of equality and justice are formed.

7. Reconciling personal relationships in social systems of inequality and unequalness in power and status does not emancipate from systemic or structural injustices and inequalities.
8. Re-reading biblical texts from the particularities of the experiences of the interpreter facilitates the exposure of the ideology, biases, silences, vested interests and dominant voices within biblical texts.
9. A reading strategy that is (a) critically aware of the cultural meaning of contextual realities, (b) comes out of a concrete commitment to and involvement in the struggle for social change and justice; (c) seeks to establish the "place" of the biblical text (the social, ideological, economic, theological aspects that produced the text); and (d) "place" of the reader (the class, ideological commitment and stance as well as hermeneutical presuppositions) results in resistance rather than opposition, to oppressive systems and practices.

From the argument and findings in the above, it is acknowledged that biblical texts are written by those in *politics*. With this admission, what becomes critical for interpreting biblical texts as effective agents of social change and justice is to examine the *political* character of biblical texts as well as the *politicization* of the hermeneutical process. An explanation as to how I am using politics, political and politicization here is in order.

By *politics*, one means "administering the power and governance of the state"[1] or administering public policy within the total complex of human relations in society. The emphasis here is on administration, which makes it easy for this study to slip into the debate on Church and State relationship. While such a debate is not the principal focus of this study, the matter of faith and politics is intricately woven into the fabric of the argument that the Bible is a constructed text. Therefore, it is important to note that what is critical is for both faith and the administration of public policy to be held in tension, not polarized. The State is neither independent of God's rule nor exempt from morality. And neither is the Church to shy away from being exposed to ridicule and victimization from endeavouring to influence public policy and protect its image. Faith is not to hover over the complex of human relations in society or public policy. Concrete commitment and involvement are to be risked in the praxis of faith.

Furthermore, it cannot be overlooked that the Church exists in a socio-politico-economic context. The Church lives its life in society. It is an integral part of society (John 17:15–18). People must be related and responded to in the totality of the concrete realities of their lives. Thus, the social, cultural and economic conditions of people's lives cannot be divorced from matters of faith. The commerce between faith, practice and politics must seek to bring about a social process whose goal is human emancipation and development.

If politics is understood to encompass the total complex of the social, cultural, political and economic aspects of human relations in society, then, Philemon is a political biblical text. Whether we interpret the letter to Philemon as dealing primarily with the exercise of authority by Paul over Philemon or by Philemon over Onesimus, or reconciliation rather than social justice or vice versa, or running away as a means of subverting the social system and practices is immaterial. All these perspectives concern people involved in administering a public policy or reacting to the effects of such a policy. In the letter to Philemon, the key players are the master who is therefore also a manager of a household economy and thereby a member of the ruling elite that administers public policy. The slave is an exploited member of the dominated class and thereby one who counters oppressive public policy. Thus, all aspects of the social structure and system in Philemon have political dimensions.

By *political*, I intend "a particular view of social reality" or one's "conception of social organization".[2] In other words, with reference to the governance, power and socio-economic structure of society, one is concerned with such questions as how is power achieved and the society governed? Are they oppressive? Are they democratic? Do they favour the rich over the poor? Who are the dominant? Who are the dominated? Who controls the productive forces? Who owns what and how much and why? Whose ideas and beliefs dominate? How do the social forces contend?

The point is biblical text participates in this political process or gives a particular perspective on the social realities of its context. Despite the ambiguities of what Paul is asking Philemon to do, there is no denying that Paul is dealing with a social reality – the institution of slavery and the subversive nature of running away – that has implications for administering the social organization of the society.

By *politicization*, one means a process of educating or conscientizing people and organizing them to have a voice and a place in the political process.[3] As such, in order for people to critique, challenge, revolutionize, and participate in the decision-making process of society and become stakeholders in the social organization of their socio-geographic space, there needs be a politicization of the hermeneutical process. Not politicizing the interpretation of Philemon would imply not focusing on or analysing the governance, power relations and household economy of imperial Graeco-Rome. This would be to sterilize the letter by spiritualizing its social, ideological and economic aspects.

In effect, the resistant biblical hermeneutic within a Caribbean context concerns politicizing the hermeneutical process. One consequence of employing the tools of analysis utilized by this study is putting biblical texts to political use. What the biblical resistant hermeneutic within a Caribbean context does is to employ historical-materialist, postcolonial criticism to biblical studies and contextual bible study as tools of analysis to: (a) expose the social, ideological, economic, political and theological aspects of biblical texts; (b) unearth dominant and suppressed voices and interests buried within biblical texts, and reread texts from the socio-cultural experiences of the interpreter; (c) ensure that the hermeneutical process does not sanitize biblical texts of their political agency in its quest to draw lessons from particular contextual issues. Where biblical texts are not put to political use, they lose social relevance and agency as effective weapons in the struggle for social change and justice.

A critique of two examples from biblical hermeneutics within a Caribbean context demonstrates that the punches of biblical texts are pulled when the interpretive process is not politicized. In this regard, an analysis of 1 Cor. 14:34–36 is done, with the focus on the issue of women becoming clergy, in an article on "The word in context: the essential criterion for doing and reflecting authentic Caribbean theology"[4] by Stephen Jennings, a Baptist pastor and my fellow Seminarian; and also that of John Holder, a priest in the Anglican Diocese of Barbados, in an article on "Some Deuteronomic themes in a Caribbean context".[5]

For Jennings, the two critical factors in hermeneutics are how the Bible is understood and what he calls double contextualization.[6] Jennings defines the Bible as the "record and witness to the primordial revelation of God, particularly in the particularity of Yahweh, God of Israel, and Jesus of Nazareth".[7] Double contextualization refers to "interpreting and applying the Bible in its original context and interpreting and applying the Bible to our context".[8] For Jennings, the critical issue here is to ascertain what the text meant for the original audience, given the specific milieu of the time of writing.[9] Working from this understanding of the Bible and double contextualization, Jennings advances three exegetical questions for interpretation: to whom was the Apostle speaking? To what specific situation were the words addressed? What do the words or phrases mean? In sum, Jennings indicates that he is seeking to avoid confusion between the context and content of the text.[10]

Although Jennings attempts to put the text in its 'place', his interest in revelation assumes that the Bible is a socio-ideological production. The original message and audience that Jennings is trying to recover may yet be that of the legitimated and interested ruling, elitist and patriarchal class that composed biblical texts. That recovered message may not necessarily be God's, if the socio-ideological agenda at work in the text is not identified. It is not merely a question of identifying "to whom" and "to what specific situation words were addressed". One must also identify the ideology at work in that address which shaped and influenced the specific situation. If Jennings had identified the socio-ideological agenda at work in the text, he would have seen that the issue of women becoming clergy is an indication of power in ecclesiastical structures and systems. In other words, it is the ruling ecclesiastical authorities who decided who functioned as clergy in the church. Thus, was he to employ this level of analysis, Jennings would recognize that an ideology of male patriarchy and marginalization is at work and consequently the text serves or challenges class or gender interests.

For Jennings to have identified the socio-ideological interest at work in the text, he needed to have pushed the text back to its socio-historic origins. To do so is not to compare "how similar and/or different are the first century ecclesiastical situation to or from current realities"[11] as Jennings does. On the contrary, it would require one to see that the ecclesiastical situation as conditioned by the metropolitan context of Corinth and the wider imperial Graeco-Roman society and state is the context out of which the text emerged. The metropolitan context of Corinth, according to Richard Horsley, was a mixture of uprooted individuals who were not under the influence of their traditional social connections and commitment yet not outside the command and control of the imperial order and power relations of the provincial elite on the network of patron-client relations and family structure.[12] The imperial Graeco-Roman state and society were characterized by a patriarchal-hierarchical social structure in which women were marginalized and thereby excluded from leadership and participation in the decision-making processes of the society and where Christians were in subjection to the patriarchical societal order. Within this social matrix, it is the conflict between equality and hierarchy within imperial Graeco-Roman society that is reflected within the ecclesiastical situation.

Within the text or in the letter of 1 Corinthians itself, this conflict is demonstrable. At 1 Cor. 11:2–16, women are allowed to speak or prophesy when the community of faith gathers. But 1 Cor. 14:34–36 rescinds that right. Is there a contradiction here? Is 1 Cor. 14:34–36 a late addition to the text? that is, is it an attempt to bring women into line with the ideology of a patriarchical-hierarchical society?[13] Was Paul addressing only married women?[14] Or were early church tendencies influencing the social praxis of the church in Paul's name? Was the church at Corinth an alternative community of resistance to the Roman imperial order?[15] For De La Torre, the possibility exists that the text was neither about the injustices of the conflict between the role of women in the church and the ideology of a patriarchical-hierarchical society nor instructions for the community of faith to follow. Instead, it aimed to "illustrate the consequences of being a woman within patriarchal society".[16] The consequence of submission, subordination and exclusion of women by patriarchy is to overlook the socio-ideological agenda at work in 1 Cor. 14:34–36.

The difficulty with Jennings' interpretive approach is that he gets locked into an exegetical strategy that begins with the text as the word of God; and not in this case with the marginalization of women in the church or society by patriarchy. To begin exegesis with the biblical text is simply to recover that broad universal message of the text and apply it to a particular context. The danger with this approach is that if the interest or voice embedded in the biblical text is not identified, then one may well be identifying with an interest or voice which acts against one's own interest. The universal is not in the particular but the particular is in the universal. Where the interest or voice of the biblical text is not identified, Jennings may yet fall into the confusion between context and content of text that he is trying to avoid and the double contextualization approach may yet be double the trouble.

What is critical, therefore, is the social reality with which one begins the exegetical process, whether that of the reader's or the biblical text. In other words, whether one begins "from the outside in" or "from the inside out" is the critical issue. On the one hand, the "outside in" approach puts the reader in his/her "place" as he/she reads into the biblical text from out of his/her social reality, out of one's class and ideological position and commitment, that is, with cultural-literacy consciousness. Outlook conditions interpretation as the "outside in" approach gives the reader an "elsewhere" from which to stand and "read". On the other hand, the "inside out" approach "places" the reader to search for the socio-historical, economic and political factors that produced the text. Such a search helps the reader to identify the socio-ideological and theological agenda at work in the text or what the text is doing and consequently what the reader needs to do.

Inevitably, Jennings' exegesis does not result in resistance for four reasons. First, he does not come to the biblical text through the epistemological lens of the cultural meaning of the marginalization of women in the Caribbean context. Second, Jennings also fails to come to the text out of a praxis of resistance or with any mention of a concrete commitment or involvement against patriarchy; if he did, and he may have, he did not see it as a critical part of the interpretive process. Third, though attempts were made to come to grips with the context of the biblical text, this was not to give agency to the ideology, socio-economic and theological interests and agendas that produced the text. And fourth, there is no clear ideological stance, commitment or strategy arising from exegeting the text by which to re-engage the sociality of existence, in this case the marginalization of women in the Caribbean context.

Holder follows the hermeneutical path he identifies as cut by Hamid and Watty in the 1970s and taken as the model by other Caribbean hermeneutes throughout the 1980s and 1990s. That path he identifies as to take "seriously the experiences of Caribbean peoples and relate these experiences to theological insights of the biblical tradition".[17] He divines the hermeneutical assumption behind this reading strategy thus: "the Bible as the word of the Lord can speak to and illuminate the experiences of Caribbean peoples".[18] To demonstrate this reading strategy, He uses what he calls Deuteronomic themes of "Land, Identity and Leadership" and relates these to Caribbean experiences. First, Holder discerns that there is a *nahalah* or inheritance challenge of Deuteronomy, which gives the right of land ownership.[19] Next, he makes the hermeneutical leap to the Caribbean experience wherein the plantation economy of colonial times bequeathed a system that deprived Caribbean peoples of land ownership. Holder charges that it is the responsibility of Caribbean governments to ensure that Caribbean peoples experience "their *berakah* or blessings through their relationship with their nahalah".[20]

With regard to identity, He sees cultural imperialism as a social reality preventing Caribbean peoples' self-identity from having "the space to grow and firmly establish itself".[21] This condition, he confesses, led him to Deuteronomy "to find some theological insights about identity that can address Caribbean condition".[22] He points out that cultural imperialism threatens the identity of those to whom Deuteronomy is addressed. Holder does not say from whom the threat comes and why. Next, he posits that Deuteronomy deals with this cultural penetration by taking the addressees back into their past and infers that Caribbean people can only understand where they are when they understand from whence they came.[23]

In both examples, the exegetical starting point for Holder is the Bible as the word of God followed by attempts to contextualize the (original) message(s) mined. Essentially the reading strategy is one of contextualization, of recovering the message of the Bible for contemporary Caribbean social realities.

Now, it is not that Holder does not show cultural-literacy consciousness. He does. But having begun the exegetical process from the "inside out", with what the text meant originally or with the Bible as the word of God, he becomes bogged down with concerns or issues that do not permit him to divine the socio-ideological issues of the text. The "inside out" approach does not allow the interests and experiences of the reader to shape or condition what is read. Cognizance that the biblical text is already an interpretation, a version of reality that takes sides, is also critical even if the exegetical starting point is the biblical text. The ideology of that version of biblical texts always needs identifying. Holder is also trying to make the universal fit the particular.

Admittedly, land and identity are relevant and critical issues in the Caribbean. However, when they are interpreted out of a different social reality, the issues that can arise may remain relevant and critical but not embraced by Caribbean people, as causal particularities are not dealt with. In other words, here, with Holder's reading strategy, we may have answers from the Bible to questions that are not being asked by Caribbean people. It is when biblical interpretation is centred in the realities of people's lives that interpretation is about cause. In short, where exegesis is focused on the "inside out" approach, that is, from the social reality of the text without its socio-ideological agenda identified, it turns the Bible into a weapon of criticism; but where it employs a reading strategy that is centred on the "outside in" approach, that is, from the social reality of the reader, the Bible functions as a weapon of struggle.

In effect, Holder's exegesis of some Deuteronomic themes does not lead to resistance on account of four factors. First, Holder's way of knowing into Deuteronomy came less from the cultural meaning of land and identity in Holder's Caribbean context and more from understanding the contextual origins and purpose of Deuteronomy. Even though he identifies colonial plantation economic practices as they pertained to land ownership and cultural imperialism as impacting negatively on Caribbean peoples' self-identity, it is the context and purpose of Deuteronomy that is unpacked, not the causal particularities of the problem of land and identity in a Caribbean context. Unpacking the cause of the problem of land and identity would mean that it is the contextual realities of Caribbean peoples that provide the epistemological lens by which to approach a "reading" of Deuteronomy. Such contextual realities as may arise from the analysis of the cause of the problem of land and identity would form not only the basis for how to "read" Deuteronomy but also for action.

Second, Holder does not refer to any concrete commitment or involvement against cultural imperialism or land ownership issues for which he struggled; if he did, he did not use it as part of the interpretive process. If so, such praxis of resistance would yield a different approach to Deuteronomy and a different outcome from his exegetical efforts.

Third, the agency that is given to Deuteronomy concerns "knowledge of the context, date and purpose of Deuteronomy",[24] not the socio-ideological interests and agenda that are at work in Deuteronomy. To have identified the socio-ideological interests and agenda of Deuteronomy, wherever this exegetical activity might have fallen in the process, would be to avoid identifying ideas and interests that may be inimical to the problem of land and identity in the Caribbean. Caribbean hermeneutes cannot afford to approach biblical texts as if they were not written from a specific perspective and out of particular contextual realities, which need to be identified before whilst applying biblical texts to contextual realities.

Fourth, there is no strategy for re-engaging with the sociality of existence or, in Holder's case, for struggling against cultural imperialism and the legacies of the colonial plantation economy.

What this study shows is that where one has, first, analysed the cultural meaning of social realities; second, engaged in a praxis of resistance against that which may be oppressive in those social realities; third, given agency to the materiality of biblical texts and the context of the interpreter wherein the socio-ideological agenda and social practices that produced the text are identified; and fourth, implemented a strategy for re-engaging the social realities, then resistance occurs.

In sum, this work has not claimed that biblical texts are direct consequences of political, economic and social circumstances. Rather it has taken seriously the view that religious perspectives that find expression in biblical texts convey the ideology and political and socio-economic relations and circumstances of a particular society.

The way forward is to use aspects of the socio-cultural history of the Caribbean as epistemological lens for biblical hermeneutics employing the biblical resistant hermeneutic reading strategy developed by this work. For example, Black Power, the Middle Passage, Anansi as folk-hero and community could be used as epistemological lens. Black Power is defined as a defiance and protest movement against socio-economic conditions of oppression, domination and discrimination.[25] It functions to promote economic and political independence and the evolution of a native philosophy and culture.[26] Admittedly, in the Caribbean context, the term black power is complicated by such factors as the varieties of racial types and mixtures and the process of class formation. However, the reality of the struggle against socio-economic conditions of oppression, domination and discrimination that it represents and addresses will not frustrate its use as an epistemological lens by which to read biblical texts.

Disintegration is one of the problems in the Caribbean. Colonialism has saddled Caribbean societies with the legacy of fragmentation of our societies into social classes, Island States, different languages and religious denominations and movements. In the biblical story, it is to be noted how Israel moved from an extended family to a tribal league to a monarchical state to priestly aristocracy and then to a church. As such, community is an expressed interest in the Bible. Its story is about a particular community of people. Thus, community as lens may yield fruitful biblical hermeneutical insights into Caribbean integration.

The Middle Passage was the crossing of the Atlantic from Africa to the Caribbean and the Americas of approximately 9–15 million Africans who were captured, enchained and forced to leave their homeland.[27] Olaudah Equiano, a former slave who paid for his freedom and became an Abolitionist, described the transatlantic crossing as a "wretched situation … aggravated by the galling of the chains, now insupportable, and the filth of the necessary tubs into which the children fell and almost suffocated. The shrieks of the women and the groans of the dying rendered the whole scene of horror almost inconceivable".[28] In these anguished and hopeless circumstances, Equiano and his fellow Africans considered death as a friend.[29] As such, biblical texts such as the Psalms and Job and biblical motif of the crucifixion of Jesus can be re-read with the lament of pain, despair, injustice and death as epistemological lens.

The point is not that the socio-cultural aspects of Caribbean history should help us reach conclusions about the biblical text and afterwards we find religious justification for them. Rather, it is that the socio-cultural concerns should condition or give shape to the biblical interpretive process. An integral dimension of this interpretive process is its interaction with the socio-ideological interests and social practices that are expressed in biblical texts. The intention to re-engage with the sociality of existence with the expressed aim of bringing about a just social order must always govern these two dimensions. Failure to employ this interpretive process means that biblical hermeneutics within a Caribbean context will continue to engage with biblical texts for personal spiritual development and not societal transformation.

Notes

1. Leonardo Boff, OFM, *Faith On the Edge, Religion and Marginalized Existence* (San Francisco, CA: Harper & Row Publishers, 1989), p. 39.
2. Ibid., p. 38.
3. Ibid., p. 40.
4. Stephen Jennings "The Word in Context: The Essential Criterion For Doing and Reflecting Authentic Caribbean Theology" *Caribbean Journal of Religious Studies* 8 (2) April 1988.
5. John Holder "Is This The Word of The Lord? In Search of Biblical Theology and Hermeneutics, The Eastern Caribbean" in Hemchand Gossai and Nathaniel Samuel Murrell (eds), *Religion, Culture and Tradition in the Caribbean* (New York: St Martin's Press, 2000).
6. Jennings, *The Word in Context*, pp. 3–4.
7. Ibid., p. 3.
8. Ibid., p. 4.
9. Ibid., p. 4.
10. Ibid., p. 8.
11. Ibid., p. 4.
12. Richard A. Horsley "Submerged Biblical Histories and Imperial Biblical Studies" in R. S. Sugirtharajah (ed.) *The Postcolonial Bible* (Sheffield: Sheffield Academic Press, 1998), p. 169.
13. Miguel A. De La Torre, *Reading The Bible From the Margins* (Maryknoll, NY: Orbis Books, 2003), p. 170.
14. Elizabeth Shussler Fiorenza *In Memory of Her: A Feminist Theological Reconstruction of Christian Origins* (New York: Crossroad, 1983), pp. 230–33.
15. Horsley, *Submerged Biblical Histories*, pp. 170–71.
16. De La Torre, *Reading the Bible*, p. 170
17. John Holder, *Is This The Word of The Lord*, pp. 135–36.
18. Ibid. p. 136.
19. Ibid.
20. Ibid.
21. Ibid.
22. Ibid.
23. Ibid.
24. John Holder, "Some Deuteronomic Themes in a Caribbean Context" *Caribbean Journal of Religious Studies* 14 (1993): 6.
25. Hamid, *Troubling of the Waters*, pp. 106–17
26. Ibid., p. 122.
27. Eric Williams, *Capitalism and Slavery* (London: Andre Deutsch, 1964), pp. 3–35.
28. Olaudah Equiano, *Equiano's Travels* (London: Heinemann, 1967), p. 29.
29. Henry Louis Gates Jr. and William L. Andrews, *Pioneers of the Black Atlantic, Five Slave Narratives from the Enlightenment 1772–1815* (Washington, DC: Counterpoint: 1998), p. 218.

BIBLIOGRAPHY

Caribbean Social History

Baptist Missionary Society (BMS) Periodical Account V (1813).

Barrett, Leonard E. *Soul Force* (New York: Anchor Press, 1974).

Barton, Richard D. E. *Afro-Creole, Power, Opposition and Play in the Caribbean* (Ithaca and London: Cornell University Press, 1997).

Beckford, Robert, *Dread and Pentecostal A Political Theology for the Black Church in Britain* (London: SPCK, 2000).

Beckles, Hilary *Black Rebellion in Barbados, The Struggle Against Slavery 1627–1838* (Bridgetown: Caribbean Research and Publications Inc., 1987).

Beckles, Hilary and Shepherd, Verene, *Caribbean Freedom: Society and Economy From Emancipation to the Present* (Bridgetown: Caribbean Research and Publication, Inc., 1989).

Beckles, Hilary and Stoddart, Brian (eds), *Liberation Cricket, West Indies Cricket Culture* (Manchester and New York: Manchester University Press, 1995).

Beckwith, Martha *Jamaica Anansi Stories* (New York: American Folklore Society, 1924).

Birbalsingh F. and Shiwcharan, C. (eds), *Indo-West Indian Cricketers* (London: Hansib Publishing Ltd., 1988).

Bisnauth, Dale, *History of Religions in the Caribbean* (Jamaica: Kingston Publishers, 1989).

Brathwaite, Edward Kamau, *Wars of Respect, Nanny and Sam Sharpe*, Agency for Public Information, Kingston, Jamaica, 1977.

Bremer, Thomas and Fleischamann, Ulrich (eds), *Alternative Cultures in the Caribbean* (Frankfurt: Vervuert Verlag, 1993).

Caldecott, Alfred, *The Church in the West Indies: West Indian Studies No. 14* (London: Frank Cass & Co. Ltd., first published 1898, Reprinted 1970).

Campbell, Horace *Rasta and Resistance From Marcus Garvey to Walter Rodney* (London: Hansib Publishing Limited, 1985).

Coleridge, William *Charges Delivered to the Clergy of the Diocese of Barbados and the Leeward Islands*, (London: J. G. & F. Rivington, 1835).

Davis, Charles T. and Henry, Louis-Gates, *The Slave's Narrative* (Oxford: Oxford University Press, 1985).

Dookan, Isaac, *A Pre-Emancipation History of the Caribbean* (London: Collins, 1974).

Mrs Flannigan, *Antigua and the Antiguans*, Volume II (London: Saunders & Otley, 1844).

Gates, Brian (ed), *Afro-Caribbean Religion* (London: Ward Lock Education, 1980).

Genovese, Eugene D., *Roll Jordan Roll – The World the Slaves Made* (New York: Vintage Books, 1974).

Goveia, Elsa, *Slavery in the British Leeward Islands at the end of the Eighteenth Century* (New Haven, CT and London: Yale University Press, 1965).

Grimshaw, Anna, *The C. L. R. James Reader* (Oxford UK and Cambridge, MA: Blackwell, 1992).

La Trobe, Benjamin, A *Succinct View of the Missions Established Among the Heathens by the Church of the Brethren or Unitas Fratum, In a Letter to a Friend* (London: M. Lewis, 1771) Letter dated 26 November 1770.

Hall, Catherine, *Civilising Subjects* (Cambridge: Polity Press, 2002).

Hall, R., "Acts Passed in the Island of Barbados 1643-1672, No. 42" in Hilary Beckles (ed.) *Black Rebellion in Barbados – The Struggle Against Slavery 1627–1838* (Bridgetown: Caribbean Research and Publication, Inc. 1987).

Harris, Raymund, *Scriptural Researches on the Licitness of the Slave Trade* (London: 1788).

Hart, Richard, *Slaves Who Abolished Slavery* (Barbados, Jamaica, Trinidad and Tobago: University Press of the West Indies, 1985, 2002).

Higman, B. W., *Writing West Indian Histories* (London: Macmillan, 1999).

Hill, Robert A. (ed.), *The Marcus Garvey and UNIA Papers* (Berkeley, CA: University of California Press, 1983–1985).

Hinton, J. H., *Memoir of William Knibb, Missionary in Jamaica* (London: 1897).

Hutton, J. E., *A History of Moravian Missions* (London: Moravian Publications Office, 1922).

Jacques-Garvey, Amy (ed.), *Philosophy and Opinions of Marcus Garvey Vols. 1 & 11* (Dover, MA: The Majority Press, 1986).

Jacques-Garvey, Amy and Essien-Udom, E. U., *More Philosophy and Opinions of Marcus Garvey* (London: Frank Cass, 1987).

Jakobsoson, S., *Am I Not a Man and a Brother? British Missions and the Abolition of The Slave Trade and Slavery in West Africa and the West Indies 1786–1838* (Uppsala, 1972).

James, Cyril L. R., *Beyond a Boundary* (London: Stanley Paul, 1969).

———, *The Black Jacobins* (London: Penguin Books, 1980 3rd edition).

Lampe, Armando, *Christianity in the Caribbean – Essays on Church History* (Barbados: University of the West Indies Press, 2001).

Lewis, Rupert and Patrick Bryan (eds), *Garvey: His Work and Impact* (Trenton, NJ: Africa World Press, Inc., 1994).

Manning, Frank (ed.) *The Celebration of Society: Perspective on Contemporary Cultural Performance* (Bowling Green, OH: Bowling Green State University Popular Press, 1983).

Martin, Tony (ed.), *The Poetic Works of Marcus Garvey* (Dover, MA: The Majority Press, 1983).

Meeks, Brian *Narratives of Resistance – Jamaica, Trinidad, the Caribbean* (Jamaica: The University Press of the West Indies, 2000).

Osborne, Francis J. SJ, "Coastlands and Islands, First Thoughts on Caribbean Church History", in Inez Nibb-Sibley, *The Baptists in Jamaica* (Kingston: Jamaica Baptist Union, 1965).

Naipaul, V. S. *The Middle Passage* (London: Deutsch, 1962).

Negro World Newspaper 14:6, 24 March 1923.

Pares, Richard, *Planters and Merchants* (Cambridge, UK, published for the economic history review at the University Press, 1960).

Patterson, Orlando, *Slavery and Social Death* (Cambridge, MA: Harvard University Press, 1982).

Rogozinski, Jan, *A Brief History of the Caribbean: From Arrawaks and Caribs to the Present* (New York: Lengrun, 1992).

Robotham, Don, "The Development of a Black Ethnicity in Jamaica", in Rupert Lewis and Patrick Bryan, *Garvey: His Work and Impact* (Trenton, NJ: Africa World Press, Inc., 1994).

Sherlock, Philip, *Shout for Freedom: A Tribute to Sam Sharpe* (London: Macmillan, 1976).

Sunshine, Catherine A., *The Caribbean: Survival, Struggle and Sovereign* (Washington, DC: EPICA, 1985).

Thomas, Clive, *The Poor and Powerless* (New York: Monthly Review Press, 1984).

Taylor, Patrick (ed.), *Nation Dance: Religion, Identity and Cultural Difference in the Caribbean* (Bloomington, IN: Indiana University Press, 2001).

Turner, M., *Slaves and Missionaries – The Disintegration of the Jamaican Slave Society 1787–1834* (Urbana, IL: University of Illinois Press, 1982).

Walcott, Derek, *What the Twilight Says – Essays* (London: Faber & Faber, 1998).

Williams, Eric, *Capitalism and Slavery* (London: Andre Deutsch, 1964).

Theological Perspectives within a Caribbean Context

Boothe, Hyacinth, "A Theological Journey For An Emancipatory Theology", *Caribbean Journal of Religious Studies* 17 (1), 15–21, April 1996.

Boodoo, Gerald M., "Gospel and Culture in a Forced Theological Context", *Caribbean Journal of Religious Studies* 17 (2), September 1996.

Caribbean Conference of Churches (CCC) *Called To Be* document (n.d.).

Ching, Theresa L, "Latin American Theological Method and its Relevance to Caribbean Theology", *Caribbean Journal of Religious Studies* 12 (1), April 1991.

Davis, Edmund, "'Contextualisation as a Dynamic Process of Theological Education",*Caribbean Journal of Religious Studies* 2 (2), September 1979.

Davis, Kortright, *Emancipation Still Comin'*, (New York: Orbis Books, 1990).

———— (ed.), *Moving Into Freedom*, (Bridgetown, Barbados: The Caribbean Conference of Churches, 1977).

————, "Sunshine Christopher's' Bearers of Christ in the Caribbean", *The Journal of Religious Thought* 49 (2), 7–24, Winter Spring 1992–1993.

Erskine, Noel Leo, *Decolonising Theology, A Caribbean Perspective* (Maryknoll, NY: Orbis Books, 1981).

Goodridge, Sehon S., *Facing the Challenge of Emancipation: A Study of the William Hart Coleridge First Bishop of Barbados, 1824–1842* (Barbados: Cedar Press, 1981).

Gordon, Ernle, "Emancipatory Theology (A Theological Journey) Gospel & Culture", *Caribbean Journal of Religious Studies* 17 (1), 22–37, April 1996.

Gregory, Howard (ed.), *Caribbean Theology: Preparing for the Challenges Ahead* (Jamaica: Kingston Publishers, 1995).

Hamid, Idris (ed.), *Out of the Depths* (Trinidad: St Andrew's Press, 1977).

——— (ed.), *In Search of New Perspectives* (Barbados: CADEC, 1971).

——— (ed.), *Troubling of the Waters* (Trinidad: Rahaman Press, 1973).

Jagessar, Michael N., *Full Life For All: The Work and Theology of Philip A. Potter – A Historical Survey and Systematic Analysis of Major Themes* (Zoetermeer: Uitgeverij Boekencentrum, 1997).

——— "Unending the Bible: The Book of Revelation Through the Optics of Anansi and Rastafari"; unpublished paper presented at the Black Theology Annual Conference on Reading and Re-reading the Bible, 27 July 2006 Queens College, Birmingham.

Jennings, Stephen, "Caribbean Theology or Theologies", *Caribbean Journal of Religious Studies* 8 (2), 1–9, September 1987.

———, "The Word in Context: The Essential Criterion For Doing Theology and Reflecting Authentic Caribbean Theology", *Caribbean Journal of Religious Studies* 9 (1), 3–20, April 1988.

Kirton, Allan, *Peace: A Challenge to the Caribbean* (Barbados: CADEC, 1982).

———, *Peace, Human Rights and Development* (Barbados: CADEC, 1982).

Kirton, Allan and Watty, William, *Consultation for Ministry in a New Decade* (Barbados: CADEC, 1985).

———, "Current Trends in Caribbean Theology and the Role of the Church", *Caribbean Quarterly*, 37 (1), 1991.

Father Lett, Leslie, Speech Delivered to Caribbean Studies Association, St. Kitts/Nevis, 2 June 1984.

———, *Third World Theology, The Struggle for the Kingdom* (Cambridge: Jubilee Research Centre, 1986).

Mitchell, David I. (ed.), *With Eyes Wide Open* (Jamaica: Kingston Publishers, 1973).

——— (ed.), *With Eyes Wide Open – A Collection of Papers by Caribbean Scholars on Caribbean Christian Concern* (Barbados: CADEC, 1973).

Murrell, Samuel, "Wrestling With The Bible In The Caribbean Basin: A Case Study On Grenada in Light of Romans 13:1–7", *Caribbean Journal of Religious Studies* 8 (1), 12–23, April 1987.

Parsanal, Neil, "In Search of a Black Theology For The Caribbean: Rastafarianism and Revivalism", in *Caribbean Journal of Religious Studies* 17 (1), April 1996.

Potter, Philip, *Life in All Its Fullness* (Geneva: World Council of Churches, 1981).

Russell, Horace O., "The Emergence of the 'Christian Black' the Making of a Stereotype", *Caribbean Journal of Religious Studies* 2 (1), April 1979.

Sankeralli, Burton (ed.), *At the Cross Roads – African Caribbean Religion and Christianity* (Trinidad and Tobago: Caribbean Conference of Churches, 1995).

Smith, Ashley, "The Christian Minister As Political Activist" *Caribbean Journal of Religious Studies* 2 (1), April 1979.

———, "Theological Education in the Caribbean – A Critique and some Proposals", *Caribbean Journal of Religious Studies* 11 (1), April 1990.

———, "Sin and Salvation a Contemporary View From a Corner of the 'South'", *Caribbean Journal of Religious Studies* 17 (2), September 1996.

Watty, William, *From Shore to Shore – Soundings in Caribbean Theology* (Barbados: Cedar Press, 1981).

Weir, Emmette J., "Towards a Caribbean Liberation Theology" *Caribbean Journal of Religious Studies* 12 (1), 46–48, April 1991.

Williams, Lewin, "What, Why and Wherefore of Caribbean Theology", *Caribbean Journal of Religious Studies* 12 (1), 29–40, April 1991.

———, "Caribbean Theology and Ministerial Formation", *Caribbean Journal of Religious Studies* 18 (1), April 1997.

Biblical Hermeneutics within a Caribbean Context

Aymer, Albert, "Mark's Understanding of Discipleship as a Paradigm for Christian Life and Witness in the Caribbean Today", *Caribbean Journal of Religious Studies* 12 (2), September 1991.

CADEC, *Called To Be, Report of Caribbean Consultation for Development, Trinidad, November 1971* (Barbados: CADEC, 1972).

Coleridge, William, *Charges Delivered to the Clergy of the Diocese of Barbados and the Leeward Islands* (London: J. G. & F. Rivington, 1835).

Gossai, Hemchand and Murrell, Nathaniel S., *Religion, Culture and Tradition in the Caribbean* (New York: St Martin's Press, 2000).

Gayle, Clement H., "The Crisis of the Pulpit", *Caribbean Journal of Religious Studies* 12 (2), September 1991.

Gayle, Clement H. and Watty William W., *Caribbean Pulpit* (Barbados: Cedar Press, 1983).

General Baptist Repository, vol. 1, Supplement 1802.

Jagessar, Michael N. *Full Life for All – The work and theology of Philip Potter: A Historical Survey and Systematic Analysis of Major Themes* (Zoetermeer: Uitgeverij Boekencentrum, 1997).

Jagessar, Michael and Anthony Reddie, *Postcolonial Black British Theology – New Textures and Themes* (Peterborough: Epworth, 2007).

Kirton, Allan and Watty, William (eds), *Consultation for Ministry in a New Decade* (Barbados: CADEC, 1985).

Mulrain, George M., "Is There a Calypso Exegesis?", in R. S. Sugirtharajah (ed.), *Voices From the Margins – Interpreting the Bible in the Third World* (Maryknoll, NY: Orbis Books, 1995).

———, "Hermeneutics within the Caribbean Context", in R. S. Sugirtharajah (ed.), *Vernacular Hermeneutics* (Sheffield: Sheffield Academic Press, 1999).

Nathan, Ronald, "The Spirituality of Marcus", *Black Theology in Britain* 3 (1999): 45.

Nicholas, Joseph E., "West Indies Cricket and Biblical Faith", *Caribbean Journal of Religious Studies* 13 (2), September 1992– April 1993.

——— "Feminine Presentation of God in the Bible" *Caribbean Journal of Religious Studies*, 16 (1), April 1995.

Persaud, Winston, "Hermeneutics of the Bible and Cricket as text: Reading as an Exile", in Fernando F. Segovia (ed.) *Interpreting Beyond Borders* (Sheffield: Sheffield Academic Press, 2000).

Potter, Philip, *Life in All in its Fullness* (Geneva: World Council of Churches, 1981).

Rahim, Jennifer, "Patterns of Psalmology, in Lovelace's *The Wine of Astonishment*" *Caribbean Journal of Religious Studies* 16 (2), 3–17, September 1995.

Wynter, Doreen, "Vashti's Voice", *Caribbean Journal of Religious Studies* 17 (2), September 1996.

Swanson, Theodore N., "Clouds Like A Man's Hand – Emerging issues in Biblical Interpretation", *Caribbean Journal of Religious Studies* 2 (1), April 1979.

Biblical Hermeneutics and Theology

Amirtham, Samuel (ed.), *A Vision For Man, Essays on Faith, Theology and Society in Honour of Joshua Russell Chandran* (Madras: Christian Literature Society, 1978).

Assmann, Hugo, *Theology for A Normal Church* (New York: Orbis Books, 1976).

Boff, Leonardo OFM, *Faith On the Edge – Religion and Marginalized Existence* (San Francisco, CA: Harper & Row Publishers, 1989).

Boone, Kathleen C., *The Bible Tells Them So – The Discourse of Protestant Fundamentalism* (London: SCM Press, 1990).

Camps, Arnulf, "The Bible and the Discovery of the World: Mission, Colonization and Foreign Development", in S. Freyne, *The Bible As Cultural Heritage, ("Concilium")* (London: SCM Press, 1995/1).

Cone, James H. and Wilmore, Gayraud S., *Black Theology – A Documentary History Volume Two: 1980–1992* (Maryknoll, NY: Orbis Books, 2003).

Coote, Robert B. and Mary P. Coote, *Power, Politics and the Making of the Bible* (Minneapolis, MN: Fortress Press, 1990).

Coote, Robert B. David Robert Ord, *Is the Bible True? Understanding the Bible Today* (London: SCM Press, 1994).

Croatto, J. Severino, *Biblical Hermeneutics: Towards a Theory of Reading as the Production of Meaning* (New York: Orbis, 1987).

De La Torre, Miguel A., *Reading the Bible From the Margins* (Maryknoll, NY: Orbis Books, 2003).

Equiano, Olaudah, *The Interesting Narrative and Other Writings* (New York: Penguin Books, 1995).

Felder, Cain Hope (ed.), *Stony the Road We Trod: African American Biblical Interpretation* (Minneapolis, MN: Fortress Press, 1991).

Fretheim, Terrence, *Creation, Fall and Flood* (Minneapolis, MN: Augsburg, 1969).

Genovese, Eugene D., *Roll Jordan Roll, The World the Slaves Made* (New York: Vintage Books, 1976).

Gilmore, Gayraud S. *Black Religion and Black Radicalism* 3rd. edn (Maryknoll, NY: Orbis Books, 1998).

Gottwald, Norman K. and Horsley, Richard A. (ed.), *The Bible and Liberation – Political and Social Hermeneutics* (Maryknoll, NY: Orbis Books, 1993 revised edn).

Hopkins, Bishop John Henry *The Bible View of Slavery: A Letter From the Bishop of Vermont, New England to the Bishop of Pennsylvania* (London: Saunders, Ottley & Co., 1863).

————, *Scriptural, Ecclesiastical and Historical View of Slavery: From the Days of Patriarch Abraham to the Nineteenth Century* (New York: Pooley & Co., 1864).

Horsley, Richard A., *Jesus and the Spiral of Violence – Popular Jewish Resistance in Roman Palestine* (Minneapolis, MN: Fortress Press, 1933).

Jagessar, Michael and Reddie, Anthony, *Postcolonial Black British Theology – New Textures and Themes* (Peterborough: Epworth, 2007).

Kwok Pui Lan, "The Bible in the Non-Biblical World", *Semeia* 59, 2000.

Liburd, Ron, " 'Like ... a House Upon the Sand?' African American Biblical Hermeneutics in Perspective", *Journal of the Interdenominational Theological Centre* xxii (1), 71–91, Fall 1994.

Merton, Thomas *Faith and Violence* (Notre Dame, IN: University of Notre Dame Press, 1968).

Mosala, Itumeleng S., *Biblical Hermeneutics and Biblical Theology in Southern Africa* (Grand Rapids, MI: Eerdmans, 1989).

————, 'The Implication of the Text of Esther For African Women's Struggle For Liberation in South Africa', *Semeia* 59, 2000.

Ord, David Robert and Robert B. Coote, *Is the Bible True? Understanding the Bible Today* (London: SCM Press, 1994).

Parrinder, G., *Religion in Africa* (New York: Praeger, 1969).

Placher, William C., *Narratives of A Vulnerable God* (Philadelphia, PA: Westminster John Knox Press, 1994).

Prior, Michael, *The Bible and Colonialism, A Moral Critique* (Sheffield: Sheffield Academic Press, 1977).

Rawick, George P., *From Sundown to Sunup, The Making of the Black Community* (Westport, CN: Greenwood Publishing Company, 1972).

Roberts, J. Deotis, *A Black Political Theology* (Louville, KY: Westminster John Knox Press, 1974, reprinted 2005).

Rowland, Christopher and Corner, Mark, *Liberating Exegesis: The Challenge of Liberation to Biblical Studies* (London: SPCK, 1991).

Scherer, James and Bevans, Stephen, *New Directions in Mission and Evangelism* (Maryknoll, NY: Orbis Books, 1999).

Schottroff, Willy and Wolfgang Stegemann, *God of the Lowly: Socio-historical Interpretations of the Bible* (Maryknoll, NY: Orbis Books, 1984).

Segovia, Fernando, *Decolonizing Biblical Studies, A View From the Margins* (Maryknoll, NY: Orbis Books, 2000).

————, *Interpreting Beyond Borders* (Sheffield: Sheffield Academic Press, 2000).

Segovia, Fernando F. and Tolbert, Mary Ann, *Reading From This Place vol. 1 – Social Location and Biblical Interpretation in the United States* (Minneapolis, MN: Fortress Press, 1995).

————, *Teaching the Bible – The Discourses and Politics of Biblical Pedagogy* (Maryknoll, NY: Orbis Books, 1998).

Segundo, Juan Luis, *Liberation of Theology* (New York: Orbis Books, 1976).

Shorter, Aylward, *Towards a Theology of Inculturation* (New York: Orbis, 1988).

Shussler Fiorenza, Elizabeth, *In Memory of Her: A Feminist Theological Reconstruction of Christian Origins* (New York: Crossroad, 1983).

Spencer Miller, Althea; O'Brien, Kathleen and Dube, Musa W. (eds), *Feminist New Testament Studies – Global and Future Perspectives* (New York: Palgrave Macmillan, 2005).

Sugirtharajah, R. S. (ed.), *Voices From the Margins – Interpreting the Bible in the Third World* (Maryknoll, NY: Orbis Books, 1995).

———— (ed.), *Voices From the Margins – Interpreting the Bible in the Third World*, revised and expanded third edition (Maryknoll, NY: Orbis Books, 2006).

———— (ed.), *The Postcolonial Bible* (Sheffield: Sheffield Academic Press, 1998).

———— (ed.), *Asian Biblical Hermeneutics and Postcolonialism* (Maryknoll, NY: Orbis Books, 1998).

———— (ed.), *Vernacular Hermeneutics* (Sheffield: Sheffield Academic Press, 1999).

————, *The Bible and the Third World – Precolonial, Colonial and Postcolonial Encounters* (Cambridge: Cambridge University Press, 2001).

————, *Postcolonial Criticism and Biblical Interpretation* (Oxford: Oxford University Press, 2002).

————, *Postcolonial Reconfigurations: An Alternative Way of Reading the Bible and Doing Theology* (London: SCM Press, 2003).

————, *The Postcolonial Biblical Reader* (Boston, MA, Oxford, Victoria: Blackwell Publishing, 2006).

Thompson, Barry P. (ed.), *Scripture: Method and Meaning, Essays Presented to Anthony Tyrell Hanson on his 70th-Birthday* (Hull: Hull University Press, 1987).

Ukpong, Justin, "Developments in Biblical Interpretation: Historical and Hermeneutical Directions", *Journal of Theology For Southern Africa* 108, November 2000.

Vaage, Leif E. (ed.), *Subversive Scriptures – Revolutionary Readings of the Christian Bible in Latin America* (Pennsylvania, PA: Trinity Press International, 1997).

Weems, Renita, "The Hebrew Women Are Not Like The Egyptian Women – The Ideology of Race, Gender and Sexual Reproduction in Exodus", *Semeia* 59, 25–34, 1992.

Wallis, Jim, *God's Politics* (Oxford: Lion, 2005).

West, Gerald O., *Biblical Hermeneutics of Liberation – Modes of Reading the Bible in Southern African Context* (Pietermaritzberg: Cluster Publications; Maryknoll, NY: Orbis Books, 1991).

————, *Contextual Bible Study* (Pietermaritzburg: Cluster Publications, 1993).

————, *The Academy of the Poor – Towards A Dialogical Reading of the Bible* (Sheffield: Sheffield Academic Press, 1999).

Wicker, Kathleen O'Brien, Spencer Miller, Althea and Dube, Musa W. (eds), *Feminist New Testament Studies, Global and Future Perspectives* (New York: Palgrave Macmillan, 2005).

Wimbush, Vincent L., "Biblical Historical Study as Liberation: Toward an Afro-Christian Hermeneutic", *Journal of Religious Thought* 42 (2), 9–21 (1985–1986).

————, "Historical/Cultural Criticism as Liberation: A Proposal For An African American Biblical Hermeneutic", *Semeia* 59, 2000.

Wolf, Hans Walter and Brueggemann, Walter, *The Vitality of Old Testament Traditions* (Atlanta, GA: John Knox Press, 1982).

Interpretation of Philemon

Barton, S. C., "Paul and Philemon: A Correspondence Continued", *Theology* 90, 98–99, 1987.

Bieberstein, Sabine, "Disrupting the Normal Reality of Slavery: A Feminist Reading of the Letter of Philemon", *Journal For the Study of the New Testament* 79, 105–16, 2000.

Birney, James G., *Sinfulness of Slaveholding in all Circumstances: Tested by Reason and Scripture* (Detroit, MI: Charles Wilcox, 1846).

Blassingame, John W. (ed.), *Frederick Douglass Papers, Series on: Speeches, Debates, Interviews, Vol. 3 1855–63* (New Haven, CT: Yale University Press, 1985).

Equiano, Olaudah, *The Interesting Narrative and Other Writings* (London: Penguin Books, 1995).

Felder, Cain Hope, "The Letter to Philemon", in *The New Interpreter's Bible* (Nashville, TN: Abingdon Press, 2000).

Fitzmyer, Joseph A., SJ, *The Letter to Philemon: A New Translation with Introduction and Commentary* (New York, London: The Anchor Bible, Doubleday, 2000).

Harris, Raymund, *Scriptural Researches on the Licitness of the Slave Trade* (London: 1788).

Hopkins, Bishop John Henry, *Scriptural, Ecclesiastical and Historical View of Slavery: From the Days of Patriarch Abraham to the Nineteenth Century* (New York: Pooley & Co., 1864).

Lightfoot, J. B. *Saint Paul's Epistles to the Colossians and to Philemon* (London: Macmillan & Co. Ltd., 1912).

Martin, Ralph P., *Interpretation – A Bible Commentary for Teaching and Preaching – Ephesians, Colossians and Philemon* (Atlanta, GA: John Knox Press, 1991).

Nordling, John G., "Onesimus Fugitivus: A Defence of the Runaway Slave Hypothesis in Philemon", *Journal For the Study of the New Testament* 41, 79–119, 1991.

Osiek, Carolyn, *Philippians and Philemon* (Nashville, TN: Abingdon Press, 2000).

Petersen, Norman R., *Rediscovering Paul, Philemon and the Sociology of Paul's Narrative World* (Philadelphia, PA: Fortress Press, 1985).

Preiss, Theo, *Life in Christ and Social Ethics in the Epistle to Philemon; Studies in Biblical Theology No. 13, Life in Christ* (London: SCM Press, 1952).

Schussler Fiorenza, Elizabeth, *Searching the Scriptures – A Feminist Commentary* (London: SCM Press Ltd., 1995).

Weems, Renita J., "Reading Her Way Through the Struggle: African America Women and the Bible", in Gottwald, Norman K. and Horsley, Richard A. (eds), *The Bible and Liberation – Political and Social Hermeneutics* (Maryknoll, NY: Orbis Books, 1993 revised edn).

Wheaton, N. S., *Discourse on St Paul's Epistle to Philemon* (Hartford, CT: Press of Case, Tiffany and Company, 1851).

Westerman, William, L., *The Slave Systems of Greek and Roman Antiquity* (Philadelphia, PA: The American Philosophical Society, 1955).

Young, Rev. David, *Slavery Forbidden by the Word of God* (Aberdeen: G. & R. King, 1847).

First Century Social History and Theology

Beker, J. Christian, *Paul's Apocalyptic Gospel – The Coming Triumph of God* (Philadelphia, PA: Fortress Press, 1982).

Carcopino, Jerome, *Daily Life in Ancient Rome – The People and the City at the Height of the Empire* (London: Penguin Books, 1991 3rd edition).

Cadoux, C. J., *The Early Church and the World* (Edinburgh: T. & T. Clark, 1st edn, 1925, Reprinted 1955).

Combes, L. A. H., "The Metaphor of Slavery in the Writings of the Early Church", *Journal For the Study of the New Testament, Supplement Series* 156 (Sheffield: Sheffield Academic Press, 1998).

Crossan, John Dominic and Reed, Jonathan L. *In Search of Paul – How Jesus' Apostle Opposed Rome's Empire with God's Kingdom* (London: SPCK, 2004).

Davis, David Brian, *The Problem of Slavery in Western Culture* (New York, Oxford: Oxford University Press, 1966).

de Ste Croix, G. E. M., *The Class Struggle in The Ancient Greek World* (Ithaca, NY: Cornell University Press, 1980).

Esler, Philip F., *The First Christian in their Social World – Scientific Approaches to New Testament Interpretation* (London and New York: Routledge, 1994).

Crossan, John Dominic, *The Birth of Christianity* (Edinburgh: T. & T. Clark, 1998).

Freyne, Sean, *Galilee: From Alexander to Hadrian* (Edinburgh: T. & T. Clarke, 1980).

Finley, M. I., *Ancient Slavery and Modern Ideology* (London: Chatto & Windus, 1980).

———, *Slavery in Classical Antiquity – Views and Controversies* (Cambridge: Heffer, 1968).

Hengel, Martin, *Judaism and Hellenism* (London: SCM Press, 1974).

Horsley, Richard A., *Sociology and the Jesus Movement* (New York: Continuum 1989).

———, (ed.), *Paul and Empire: Religion and Power in Roman Imperial society* (Harrisburg, PA: Trinity Press International, 1997).

———, (ed.), *Paul and Politics – Ekklesia, Israel, Imperium, Interpretation* (Harrisburg, PA: Trinity Press International, 2000).

Kautsky, John H., *The Politics of Aristocratic Empires* (New Brunswick, NJ, London: Transaction Publishers, 1997, rev. edn).

Kyrtatas, Dimitris J., *The Social Structure of Early Christian Communities* (London, New York: Verso, 1987).

Osiek, Carolyn, RSCJ, *What Are They Saying About the Social Setting of the New Testament* (New York/Mahwah, NJ: Paulist Press, 1992).

Patterson, Orlando, *Slavery and Social Death* (Cambridge, MA: Harvard University Press, 1982).

———, *Freedom Vol. 1 Freedom in the Making of Western Culture* (London: I. B. Tauris & Co. Ltd., 1991).

Samply, J. Paul, *Walking Between the Times – Paul's Moral Reasoning* (Minneapolis, MN: Fortress Press, 1991).

Tidball, Derek, The Social Context of the New Testament (Exeter: The Paternoster Press, 1983).

Troeltsh, Ernst, *The Social Teaching of the Christian Churches*, trans. Olive Wyon (London and New York: 1931).

Westermann, William L., *The Slave Systems of Greek and Roman Antiquity* (Philadelphia, PA: The American Philosophical Society, 1955).

Sociology and Religion

Ashcroft, Bill, Gareth Griffiths, Helen Tiffin, *The Postcolonial Studies Reader* (New York: Routledge, 1995).

Davis, Angela, *Women, Race and Class* (Reading: Cox & Wyman Ltd., 1981).

Douglass, Frederick, *Narrative of the Life of Frederick Douglass* (Boston, MA: Bedford/ St Martin's, 1993).
Duncombe, Stephen, *Cultural Resistance Reader* (London, New York: Verso, 2002).
Equiano, Olaudah, *Equiano's Travels* (London: Heinemann, 1967).
Ferguson, Russell, Givens, Martha, Minh-Ha, Trin T. and West, Cornel, *Out There: Marginalisation and Contemporary Culture* (New York: The MIT Press, 1990).
Freire, Paulo *Pedagogy of the Oppressed* (Middlesex: Penguin Books, 1972).
Gates Jr, Henry Louis. and William L. Andrews, *Pioneers of the Black Atlantic, Five Slave Narratives from the Enlightenment 1772–1815* (Washington, DC: Counterpoint: 1998).
Gramsci, Antonio, *Selection From Prison Notes* (London: Lawrence and Wishart, 1971).
hooks, bell, *Teaching To Transgress, Education as the Practice of Freedom* (New York, London: Routledge, 1994).
John Mc.Leod, *Beginning – Postcolonialism* (Manchester: Manchester University Press, 2000).
Mullard, Chris, *Race, Power and Resistance* (London, Boston, MA, Melbourne: Routledge & Kegan Paul, 1985).
Parrinder, G., *Religion in Africa* (New York: Praeger, 1969).
Weber, Max, *The Theory of Social and Economic Organisation* (London: Free Press, 1964).
Williams, M. and Buder, R. L., *Psychology For Language Teachers: A Social Constructivist Approach* (Cambridge: Cambridge University Press, 1997).

Journals

Asia Journal of Theology
R. S. Sugirtharajah, "From Orientalist to Post-Colonial: Notes on Reading Practices", 10 (1), 1996.
Black Theology in Britain
Alexander, Valentina, "Onesimus's Letter to Philemon" 4 (May), 2000.
Caribbean Journal of Religious Studies
Nicholas, Joseph, "West Indies Cricket and Biblical Faith" 13 (2), September 1992– April 1993.
Holder, John, "Some Deuteronomic Themes in a Caribbean Context" 14 (2), 12–16, 1993.
Jennings, Stephen, "The Word in Context: The Essential Criterion For Doing and Reflecting Authentic Caribbean Theology" 8 (2), 1–12, April 1988.
Parsanlal, Neil, "In Search of a Black Theology for the Caribbean: Rastafarianism and Revivalism" 17 (1), April, 1996.
Caribbean Quarterly
Gonsalves, Ralph E., "Our Caribbean Civilisation: Retrospect and Prospect", 44, (3 & 4), 131–50, September–December, 1998.
Hill, Errol, "Traditional Figures in Carnival: Their Preservation, Development and Interpretation" 31 (2), 14–34, June, 1985.
Kirton, Allan, "Current Trends in Caribbean Theology and the Role of the Church", 37 (1), 98–107, 1991.

Lamming, George, Opening address Rex Nettleford cultural conference, U.W.I. Jamaica March 1996, 43 (1&2), March–June 1997.

Roper, Garnet, "The Impact of Evangelical and Pentecostal Religion", 37 (1), 35–44, March 1991.

Concilium

Dictionary of American Biography (London: Oxford University Press, 1929, Vol. 2).

Ecumenical Review

Raiser, Konrad, "Celebrating an Ecumenical Pilgrimage: and Address to Honour Philip Potter on the Occasion of his 80th Birthday", October 2001.

Ethnic and Racial Studies

Cohen, Abner, "A Polytechnic London Carnival as a Contested Cultural Performance", 5 (1), 23–41, January 1982.

General Baptist Repository

Interpretation

Brueggemann, Walter, "That The World May be Redescribed", 56 (4), 359–67, October 2002.

Dunham, Robert E., "Between Text and Sermon: Philemon 1-25" 52 (2), April 1998.

Jamaica Journal

Reckford, Mary, "The Slave Rebellion of 1831", June 1969: 26–28.

Journal of Biblical Literature

Porter, Frank C., "The Place of Apocalyptic Conceptions in the Thought of Paul" 41 (1/2), 183–204, 1992.

Feeley-Harnik, Gillian, "Is Historical Anthropology Possible? The Case of the Runaway Slave" in Gene M. Tucker and Douglas A. Knight (eds), *Humanizing America's Iconic Book*, Society of Biblical Literature Centennial Addresses, 1980.

Frilingos, Chris, "For My Child Onesimus: Paul and Domestic Power in Philemon" 19 (1), 91–104, Spring 2000.

Gottwald, Norman K., "Social Classes as an Analytical and Hermeneutical Category in Biblical Studies" 112 (1), 3–22, Spring 1993.

Glancy, Jennifer A., "Slaves and Slavery in the Matthean Parables" 119 (1), 67–90, Spring 2000.

Journal of Caribbean History

Hall, Douglas, "Incalculability as a Feature of Sugar Production During the Eighteenth Century" 35 (1), 2001.

Journal of the Interdenominational Theological Centre

Journal For the Study of the New Testament

de Vos, Craig S., "Once a Slave, Always a Slave? Slavery, Manumission and Relational Patterns in Paul's Letter to Philemon", 23 (82), 89–105, 2001.

Biebersstein, Sabine, "Disrupting the Normal Reality of Slavery: A Feminist Reading of the Letter to Philemon" 23 (79), 105–16, September 2000.

Nordling, John D., "Onesimus Fugitivus: A Defence of the Runaway Slave Hypothesis in Philemon" 41 (1991), 97–119, February 1991.

Theissen, Gerdhard, "The Social Structure of Pauline Communities: Some Critical Remarks on J.J. Meggit – Paul, Poverty, Survival" 84 (2001), 65–84, 2001.

Journal For the Study of the New Testament, Supplement Series

Journal of Theology For Southern Africa

Bosch, David, "Paul on Human Hopes" 67, 3–16, June 1989.

————, "Mission and the Alternative Community: How My Mind Changed" 41 (December), 6, 1982.

————, "The Churches as the Alternative Community" 13 (December), 1975.

New Society

James, C. L. R., "Cricket in West Indian Culture" 36, 6 June 1963.

New Testament Studies

Barclay, John M. G., "Paul, Philemon and the Dilemma of Christian Slave-ownership" 37 (2), 161–86, April 1991.

Rapske, B. M., "The Prisoner Paul in the Eyes of Onesimus" 37 (2), 187–203, April 1991.

Novum Testamentum

Deming, Will, "A Diatribe Pattern in 1 Corinthians 7:21–22: A New Perspective on Paul's Direction to Slaves" 37 (Fasc. 2), 130–37, April 1995.

Religion and American Culture

Harrill, J. Albert, "The Use of the New Testament in the American Slave Controversy: A Case History in the Hermeneutical Tension Between Biblical Criticism and Christian Moral Debate" 10 (2), 149–86, Summer 2000.

Religion in Life

Knox, John, "Paul and the 'Liberals'" 49, Winter 1980.

Religion and Theology

Taylor, N. H., "Onesimus – A Case Study of Slave Conversion in Early Christianity" 3 (3), 259–81, 1996.

Semeia

Callahan, Allan, "The Slavery of New Testament Studies" 83/84, 1998, Slavery in Text and Interpretation.

Callender, Jr., Dexter E., "Servants of God(s) and Servants as Kings in Israel and the Ancient Near East" 83/84, 1998, Slavery in Text and Interpretation.

Horsley, Richard A., "The Slave Systems of Classical Antiquity and their Reluctant Recognition by Modern Scholars" 83/84, 1998, Slavery in Text and Interpretation.

———— "Paul and Slavery: A Critical Alternative to Recent Readings" 83/84, 1998, Slavery in Text and Interpretation.

Milne, Pamela J., "What shall we do with Judith: A Feminist Reassessment of a Biblical Heroine" 62, 37–58, 1993.

Patterson, Orlando, "Paul, Slavery and Freedom: Personal and Social-historical Reflections", 83/84, 1998, Slavery in Text and Interpretation.

Wimbush, Vincent L., "Reading Texts Through Worlds, Worlds Through Texts" 62, 129–40, 1993.

Social and Economic Studies

Gray, Obika "Discovering the Social Power of the Poor" 43 (3), 169–89, 1994.

Social Text

Certeau, M., "On The Oppositional Practices of Every Day Life" 3, 3–43, 1980.

Studies in Black Theology

Preiss, Theo, "Life in Christ and Social Ethics in the Epistle to Philemon" 13, Life in Christ (London: SCM Press, 1952).

Theology

The Journal of Religious Thought

Davis, Kortright "'Sunshine Christopher's bearers of Christ in the Caribbean" 49 (2), 7–24, Winter Spring 1992–1993.

Articles

2006 Budget Statement entitled "Gearing Up For Growth" delivered Wednesday 30 November 2005 by Dr The Hon. L. Errol Cort, MP, Minister of Finance and The Economy.

Gottwald, Norman K., "Socio-historical Precision in the Biblical Grounding of Liberation Theologies", address to the Catholic Biblical Association of America at its annual meeting, San Francisco, August 1985.

Jagessar, Michael, Unpublished Master's Thesis entitled "A Theological Evaluation of Wilson Harris' Understanding of Community as reflected in the 'Guiana Quartet', An Interdisciplinary Study of Theology and Caribbean Literature" (Jamaica: University of the West Indies, 1992).

La Trobe, Benjamin, *A Succinct View of the Missions Established Among the Heathens by the Church of the Brethren or Unitas Fratum, In a Letter to a Friend* (London: M. Lewis, 1771) Letter dated 26 November 1770.

O'Marde, Dorbrene E., "Calypso in the 1990s", *Antigua Carnival Souvenir Magazine*, April 1990.

———, "West Indies Cricket: Is the Music Loud Enough?" speech delivered at the Carifesta V11 Symposium on "Continuing to Define Ourselves in a Changing World" 23 August 2000 held in St Kitts/Nevis.

Lecture delivered by Dr Terrence Fretheim on "Is the Portrayal of God Reliable?" at the Vancouver School of Theology, Summer School Public Lecture Series, 6 July1995.

Hall, Stuart, "Encoding and decoding in the Television Discourse", Paper presented to the Council of European Colloquy on "Training in the Critical Reading of Television Language", University of Leicester, September 1973.

Ruth Wust, "The Trinidad Carnival From Canboulay to Pretty Mass", unpublished MA Thesis, Berlin (1987).

Newspapers

Negro World Newspaper
Outlet Newspaper Fan The Flame by Tim Hector:
17 April 1998
24 April 1998
9 April 1999
25 June 1999
21 April 2000
1 December 2000
19 January 2001
9 March 2001

INDEX

justice 2, 14, 31, 38, 48, 50, 51, 57,
59, 72, 78, 92, 95, 96, 97, 100,
101, 125, 126, 136, 138, 150,
152, 153, 164, 166, 170, 175,
177, 179, 187, 191, 194, 199, 209
order 6, 33, 48, 50, 57, 78, 102,
116, 119, 129, 132, 147, 154,
160, 165, 180, 195, 216
realities 1, 4, 8, 10, 11, 15, 20, 27,
51, 55, 68, 73, 94, 129, 158, 170,
186, 197, 201, 202, 209, 213,
215,
Society 1, 3, 4, 10, 14, 24, 25, 28, 30, 31,
35, 36, 37, 40, 41, 47, 50, 59, 67, 70,
71, 72, 74, 75, 85, 89, 90, 91, 92, 93,
94, 95, 97, 99, 102, 116, 117, 118,
120, 121, 125,130, 131, 132, 150, 154,
158, 163, 166, 174, 184, 188, 195,
196, 198, 201, 207, 208, 209, 211,
212,
plantation 27, 29
slave 122,
South Africa
Apartheid 11, 94, 146
Spencer Miller, Althea 52, 57, 80, 156,
167
Spiritual resistance *see* resistance
Spirituality 2, 4, 6, 9, 15, 144, 170, 180,
184–85, 186
Sugirtharajah R. S. 5, 10, 21 133, 136,
Supremacy 7
white 44
Supreme Being 181, 184, 194 *see* also
God

T
Tainos 9
Taylor, Buchell51 51, 133
Taylor, N. H 120, 124, 135, 137
Text *see* Biblical
Theology 9, 15, 38, 56, 92, 96, 118, 156,
157, 170, 175, 176, 179, 192, 195,
198, 199, 202
Black 59

interpretation 4
liberation 50
pastoral 95
see also biblical interpretation
Thessalonians 27, 34, 93
Timothy 27, 34, 93
Titus 27, 93, 109, 113
Trinidad and Tobago 36, 196,

U
Universal Negro Catechism 39
Universal Negro Improvement
Association 40

V
Values 4, 76, 78, 85, 112, 127, 136, 185,
192, 201
British 35, 47
European 190
foreign 19, 45, 74, 166
religious 176
Voodoo 183, 184, 198

W
Walcott, Derek 55, 81
Weems, Renita J. 131
West Indies 7, 21, 24, 54, 146, 148, 190,
192, 193, 195, 196,
United Theological College of the
7, 52
see also resistance
Wheaton, N. S. 108, 109, 111, 113, 114,
115, 116,
Whites 22, 28, 35, 44, 109, 188, 189, see
also British
Williams, Eric 36, 150
Worship 1, 6, 15, 18, 27, 67, 94, 144,
154, 157, 170, 180, 182, 185, 186,
190, 194, 198
West, Gerald O. 10, 11

Y
Yahweh 171, 173, 210
Young, David 113